Conversations with May Sarton

Literary Conversations Series
Peggy Whitman Prenshaw
General Editor

Conversations
with May Sarton

Edited by Earl G. Ingersoll

University Press of Mississippi
Jackson and London

Copyright © 1991 by the University Press of Mississippi

94 93 92 91   4 3 2 1

The paper in this book meets the guidelines for permanence and durability of the Committee on Production Guidelines for Book Longevity of the Council on Library Resources.

Library of Congress Cataloging-in-Publication Data

Sarton, May, 1912–
    Conversations with May Sarton / edited by Earl G. Ingersoll.
        p.   cm.—(Literary conversations series)
    Includes index.
    ISBN 0-87805-532-0 (alk. paper). — ISBN 0-87805-533-9 (pbk.)
    1. Sarton, May, 1912–   —Interviews. 2. Authors, American—20th century—Interviews. I. Ingersoll, Earl G., 1938–   . II. Title.
III. Series.
PS3537.A832Z464   1991
811'.52—dc20   91-27647
                                                             CIP

British Library Cataloging-in-Publication data available

Books by May Sarton

Encounter in April. Boston: Houghton Mifflin, 1937.
The Single Hound. Boston: Houghton Mifflin, 1938; Toronto: Thomas Allen, 1938; London: Cresset Press, 1938; Toronto: George J. McLeod, 1948.
Inner Landscape. Boston: Houghton Mifflin, 1939; London: Cresset Press, 1939.
The Bridge of Years. New York: Doubleday, 1946; New York: Norton, 1971.
The Lion and the Rose. New York: Rinehart, 1948; Toronto: Clarke, Irwin, 1948.
Shadow of a Man. New York: Rinehart, 1950; Toronto: Clarke, Irwin, 1950; Toronto: Ambassador Books, 1952; London: Cresset Press, 1952.
The Leaves of the Trees. Mount Vernon, Iowa: Cornell College Chapbooks, 1950.
A Shower of Summer Days. New York: Rinehart, 1952; Toronto: Clarke, Irwin, 1952; London: Hutchinson & Hutchinson, 1954; New York: Norton, 1970.
The Land of Silence. New York: Rinehart, 1953; Toronto: Clarke, Irwin, 1953.
Faithful Are the Wounds. New York: Rinehart, 1955; Toronto: Clarke, Irwin, 1955; London: Gollancz, 1955; New York: Norton, 1972.
The Birth of a Grandfather. New York: Rinehart, 1957; Toronto: Clarke, Irwin, 1957; London: Gollancz, 1958.
The Fur Person. New York: Rinehart, 1957; Toronto: Clarke, Irwin, 1957; London: Muller, 1957; New York: Norton, 1968; New York: New American Library, 1973.
In Time Like Air. New York: Rinehart, 1958; Toronto: Clarke, Irwin, 1958.
I Knew a Phoenix. New York: Holt, Rinehart & Winston, 1959; Toronto: Clarke, Irwin, 1959; London: Peter Owen, 1963; New York: Norton, 1969.
Cloud, Stone, Sun, Vine. New York: Norton, 1961; Toronto: George J. McLeod, 1961.
The Small Room. New York: Norton, 1961; Toronto: George J. McLeod, 1962; London: Gollancz, 1962; New York: Norton, 1976.
Joanna and Ulysses. New York: Norton, 1963; Toronto: George J. McLeod, 1963; London: John Murray, 1963; Glasgow: Blackie & Sons, 1967.
Mrs. Stevens Hears the Mermaids Singing. New York: Norton, 1965; Toronto: George J. McLeod, 1966; London: Peter Owen, 1966.
Miss Pickthorn and Mr. Hare. New York: Norton, 1966; Toronto: George J. McLeod, 1966; London: Dent, 1968.
A Private Mythology. New York: Norton, 1966; Toronto: George J. McLeod, 1966; New York: Norton, 1967.
Plant Dreaming Deep. New York: Norton, 1967; Toronto: George J. McLeod, 1967.
As Does New Hampshire. Peterborough, New Hampshire: Richard R. Smith, 1967.

The Poet and the Donkey. New York: Norton, 1969; Toronto: George J. McLeod, 1969.

Kinds of Love. New York: Norton, 1970; Toronto: George J. McLeod, 1970.

A Grain of Mustard. New York: Norton, 1971.

A Durable Fire. New York: Norton, 1972; Toronto: George J. McLeod, 1972.

As We Are Now. New York: Norton, 1973; Toronto: George J. McLeod, 1973; London: Women's Press, 1983.

Journal of a Solitude. New York: Norton, 1973; Toronto: George J. McLeod, 1973; London: Women's Press, 1985.

Collected Poems. New York: Norton, 1974; Toronto: George J. McLeod, 1974.

Punch's Secret. New York: Harper & Row, 1974; Toronto: Fitzhenry & Whiteside, 1974.

Crucial Conversations. New York: Norton, 1975; Toronto: George J. McLeod, 1975; London: Gollancz, 1976.

A World of Light. New York: Norton, 1976.

A Walk Through the Woods. New York: Harper & Row, 1976; Toronto: Fitzhenry & Whiteside, 1976.

The House by the Sea. New York: Norton, 1977; Toronto: George J. McLeod, 1977.

Selected Poems. New York: Norton, 1978; Toronto: George J. McLeod, 1978.

A Reckoning. New York: Norton, 1978; Toronto: George J. McLeod, 1978; London: Gollancz, 1980; London: Women's Press, 1984.

Halfway to Silence. New York: Norton, 1980; Toronto: George J. McLeod, 1980.

Recovering: A Journal. New York: Norton, 1980; Toronto: George J. McLeod, 1980.

Writings on Writing. Orono, Maine: Puckerbrush Press, 1980.

Anger. New York: Norton, 1982.

A Winter Garland. Concord, New Hampshire: W. B. Ewert, 1982.

Letters from Maine. New York and London: Norton, 1984.

The Magnificent Spinster. New York: Norton, 1985; London: Women's Press, 1986.

The Phoenix Again: New Poems. Concord, New Hampshire: W. B. Ewert, 1987.

The Silence Now: New and Uncollected Earlier Poems. New York and London: Norton, 1988.

After the Stroke: A Journal. New York: Norton, 1988; London: Women's Press, 1988.

The Education of Harriet Hatfield. New York: Norton, 1989; London: Women's Press, 1990.

Contents

Introduction

When the author Hilary Stevens awakens in the opening lines of May Sarton's novel *Mrs. Stevens Hears the Mermaids Singing,* the first sensation that she feels is "dread." It is the day "those interviewers" are due to arrive. As her day unfolds, however, Mrs. Stevens overcomes that dread to respond to the questions of her young interviewers perceptively, extensively, and graciously. As the novel's largest segment, this fictionalized interview offers a paradigm of the literary interview as a contemporary genre.

As the following conversations indicate, May Sarton has frequently been interviewed, largely because her interviewers know they will find her an honest and enthusiastic subject. Like Mrs. Stevens, Sarton typically "prepares" for her interviewers' questions by reviewing her life and work beforehand, reflecting upon areas which might be explored in the interview, and facing with openness and honesty an encounter which other writers have often viewed as an invasion of their privacy or a potential trap in which they will be encouraged to make statements that they will later regret. Like the fictionalized interview with Mrs. Stevens, May Sarton's literary conversations are successful because she has approached them as collaborative efforts to gain insight. She has answered questions about her childhood, her relationships with other women as well as with men, her aspirations as a writer, her sense of an audience, and more than anything else her own feelings, without the guardedness often evident in other literary conversations. Overall, the interviews in *Conversations with May Sarton* divide themselves roughly into two groups: those from the 1970s, driven by the energy of Sarton's having broken through to a larger audience, and those from the 1980s, representing the views of an older writer and woman confronting the challenges of sickness and age.

Paula G. Putney's begins the collection with the earliest, fully literary interview. (It might be useful at the outset to distinguish the

"literary interview," in which the questioner approaches the conversation as a serious effort to increase understanding of the writer's
work and views on the profession, from the "celebrity interview"
which focuses almost entirely upon the writer's personality.) As
a participant in the sessions devoted to Sarton at the Modern Language Association conventions in the mid-seventies, Putney testifies
to the directing of academic attention to Sarton's work. Putney
chooses as her focus *Mrs. Stevens Hears the Mermaids Singing*
(1965) and a woman's battle to become a writer. Sarton speaks
eloquently of her efforts to avoid being marginalized as a "woman
writer"; she recalls disdainfully the traditional term "Poet-ess!" and
adds, "I'd rather be called a donkey!" She speaks of the need for
androgyny in the writer and discusses the relationships in *Mrs.
Stevens,* underlining what becomes increasingly evident: that novel
was the major turning point in her career.

The *Publishers Weekly* interview, conducted by Barbara Bannon,
points up another aspect of Sarton's struggle to gain a reputation
among readers outside the academic world. Bannon's interview
came about as a result of the reissue in 1974 of *Mrs. Stevens Hears
the Mermaids Singing,* with an introduction by Carolyn G. Heilbrun.
As Bannon indicates, Sarton's has been "one of the most interesting
and long-overdue literary recognitions." Sarton herself shares some
of her own sense of being reborn in the early years of the Women's
Movement, reminding her audience, however, that her novel of
"coming out" predates the resurgence of modern feminism in the
seventies. She asserts: "For many years I felt I was under a gravestone. I wanted to push it up and shout, 'Here I am.' " Among these
early interviews, the Bannon selection announces several recurrent
themes. Sarton describes, as she will in later conversations, her
painful experience as a young woman in the theater which she chose
as an alternative to Vassar: "I think it would have been very bad for
me to have gone to college. I would have become a political blue
stocking." She also announces here the recurrent themes of her
passionate admiration for older women and the primacy of solitude
in her daily life.

Dolores Shelley personalizes her conversation with Sarton by
beginning with the questions central to this collection: "Why has she
received so little critical attention? And why has it come so late in her

career?" Sarton explores answers to those questions by starting with her insistence upon staking her reputation as a writer on her poetry. She writes lyrical poetry, and unfortunately the lyrical poetry Sarton admired in her mentors, especially Louise Bogan, seemed to go out of fashion just as she was mastering that form. Her poetry, she adds ironically, provides little opportunity for the "intellectual analysis" central to most serious criticism. Furthermore, she has worked in more than one genre—the novel as well as poetry, and by the time of this interview the journal too. Finally, Sarton suspects, her reputation has been limited by her sexual preference: "I'm bisexual and, of course, men don't particularly like this." She proceeds to offer the first extensive discussion of her homosexuality, stressing that she did not "come out" for a long time because she did not want her writing to be pigeonholed as "lesbian" when she has wanted to write for an audience which transcended the boundaries of nationality, class, age, and gender.

In a number of ways, Jane S. Bakerman's "Work Is My Rest" is a prototype of almost a dozen interviews with Sarton which have been conducted in the past decade and a half. Like Putney's conversation, it offers a thorough-going and sensitive exploration of Sarton's life and work by an academic who has contributed to the scholarship on Sarton. However, by the time Bakerman interviewed her, Sarton had moved to Wild Knoll, her "house by the sea." Thus, Bakerman couches her questions about Sarton's life and work in the context of the writer's home and workplace. Although Sarton had spoken of her "coming out" novel *Mrs. Stevens Hears the Mermaids Singing* with Putney, she speaks with Bakerman for the first time about the autobiographical aspects which impinge on her poetry, the literary achievement by which she aspires to be remembered. Sarton opens her ongoing discussion of the importance to her writing of a figure she calls a "Muse," a passionately admired, usually older woman who energizes the writing of poems—and only poems, not novels, memoirs, or journals. In her conversation with Bakerman, Sarton also continues to define the nature of her relationship to the Women's Movement, stressing that she is a feminist but not an "aggressive feminist." She adds, *"I like men"* [her emphasis].

Many of these concerns are further elaborated in the Karla Hammond interviews, conducted on the same occasion but divided for publication. With Hammond, she speaks of early influences—her parents, her teacher Anne Thorp at the Shady Hill School, the actress Eva Le Gallienne who was instrumental in directing her energies into the theater—and the reading which she did as a young writer. (We need to recall that Sarton was only seventeen when she published in *Poetry* magazine.) Most importantly, however, she speaks with Hammond about her "coming out" and elaborates on the crucial importance to her poetry of a series of muses around whose beings her poems have taken shape, "crystallized," to use her term.

Sarton's conversation with Robin Kaplan and Shelley Neiderbach rounds out this group which I call the seventies interviews. Like the Paula Putney and the two Hammond interviews, the Kaplan and Neiderbach interview is reprinted from what continues to be the most important academic/critical work on the writer, *May Sarton: Woman and Poet* (1982), edited by Constance Hunting. In this interview Sarton offers the most extensive discussion of the importance to her of "muses" for her poetry. She also provides the first full elaboration of her concerns with lesbianism, especially her fear of its becoming a "fashion" and her anxiety about being marginalized as a "lesbian writer." She indicates her pleasure in beginning to be acknowledged; and yet even the special sessions at the Modern Language Association conventions and the purchase of her papers by the New York Public Library have not diminished her sense of struggling with the "literary establishment." "I'm nowhere," she tells Kaplan and Neiderbach, "I've never won a prize, I'm not in the anthologies. I'm not even in the *Norton Anthology,* my own publisher's, which is used widely in the United States for teaching." In this way we see Sarton in the seventies acknowledging the bounty of a larger audience produced by the growth of the Women's Movement, her concern with preserving her access to all readers, and overriding both these concerns the frustration that she had not gained the full recognition of the literary/academic establishment upon whose judgment literary "immortality" has traditionally rested.

Nancy Corson Carter's interview from 1982 continues several of Sarton's concerns from the seventies. We find, for example, her continuing frustration with what she sees as the "literary establishment." She tells Carter: "I can't imagine another writer who appeals to so many people in such depth—people write to me and say,

'You've saved me from suicide; you've changed my life; when I was mortally ill you brought me back; this is the year that Sarton saw me through'—but whom the literary establishment regards as having no value." She continues: "I don't know any other writer like me at all. There are writers who've been discovered after they die, but they did not have the enormous audience that I already have." It is this awareness of a large readership for whom she has served as a role model which increasingly becomes an alternative to the literary "immortality" which she senses she may miss in the twenty-first century.

Because she has become increasingly aware of her leadership position as a role model for women, the Sarton of the eighties is frequently more assertive and even combative. She tells Carter with some relish of her earlier conflict with Norton, her publisher, following their failure to advertise *Mrs. Stevens*. Her response was to take out a full-page advertisement in the *New York Times* to draw attention to her book. Once again we find the awareness of her faithful readers. She indicates that when her collection of poems *Halfway to Silence* appeared in 1980, it sold 5,000 copies in the first month, without reviews and advertising. A sense of success on her own terms is clear in her gratitude and pride in having garnered a loyal following in the seventies; she tells Carter: "Wherever I go now I have big audiences, often standing room only. Just think of being seventy and having it all happen!"

Another index of Sarton's having achieved recognition is the appearance of the interview conducted by Karen Saum in the *Paris Review,* collected in *Writers at Work, Seventh Series,* edited by George Plimpton. As many would agree, the *Paris Review* has set the standard for the literary interview as a contemporary genre. The inclusion of the Sarton interview in *Writers at Work* clearly indicates that she is beginning to receive the long-overdue attention which her work has deserved for decades. The Saum interview is among the most comprehensive, ranging through comments upon her major publications and her most extensive remarks about writers like Paul Valéry and François Mauriac who have influenced her style as well as writers like Virginia Woolf, Elizabeth Bowen, and Edna St. Vincent Millay who were role models. She returns once more to the topic of muses for her poetry, but the Sarton of this interview and of the eighties interviews in general has moved beyond the need to talk extensively about her "coming out" and focuses her interviewer's attention on the reputation which she will leave behind. She tells Saum: "But as for the vision in the whole of my work, I would like to feel that my work is universal and human on the deepest level. I think of myself as a maker of bridges—between the heterosexual and the homosexual world, between the old and the young."

Sarton's concern with posterity is evident also in her long conversation with Kay Bonetti. She focuses upon her poetry because she believes that it will outlast her writing in other genres, especially her journals. About her journals she has developed some ambivalence. She is appreciative of their having brought so many readers, yet as she tells Bonetti, "I do underrate my journals," one suspects because in her hierarchy of forms poetry is always first. It has "something given in it which is very precious." Unlike the novels and journals, poems cannot be "willed," and therefore they are "rarer." Perhaps Sarton is engaged here in responding to the Virginia Woolf who once teased her with the notion that writing poetry is easy, while writing novels is hard work.

The Bonetti conversation also returns to the now older Sarton's growing awareness of her aloneness, her being an "outsider," as Carolyn Heilbrun called her. In speaking with Bonetti, Sarton offers an extensive commentary on her statement: "I don't belong to any society." She stresses her Belgian birth and her kinship to her scholarly father who was also a "loner." Unlike other young women of her class, she never "came out" socially, and her decision to go into the theater rather than to attend Vassar cut her off from the society of college friends. At the very least, becoming an actress was certainly unexpected of a young woman of her class in the thirties. It was not until she moved to Nelson, New Hampshire, in her fifties that she developed anything approaching "roots," and one senses envy in her comments upon the rootedness of Southern writers like Eudora Welty and Flannery O'Connor. She recalls again how her "coming out" in *Mrs. Stevens* had its costs and yet she has felt that "the lesbians don't back me because I don't want to be known as a lesbian writer." She speaks of a love affair with a man whom she might have married, were he not already married, and of her desire to have children. She continues: "But, I shudder when I hear so

much hatred of men. And granted that there are a lot of male
chauvinists and granted that we have to fight for equal rights and all
the rest of it, but there's a danger in the extreme militants, I think, of
dividing the world into two, and we've got to live together." Much of
Sarton's sense of aloneness, then, results from her fierce resolution to
preserve the integrity of her own values at all costs.

The conversation with Bill Heyen and Mary Elsie Robertson has a
special place in this collection. Their interview is the last before the
stroke which has faced Sarton with her most severe challenge. The
last interviews, like her most recent work, are shaped by the obsta-
cles of pain and fatigue which have made her last years both a trial
and a triumph. As she tells Michael Finley, "I try to live as if every
day might be my last and yet, is eternal." She has not so much
resigned herself to old age as lovingly embraced it: "The truth is, I
love being older, and I always knew I would. I dislike being sick—
that's the nuisance, right there—but I would never want to go back.
You pay a high price for emotional involvement, the love affairs
and so on. I'm rather glad to be out of that."

That theme of aging recurs in most of the late interviews, several of
which—the Bonetti, Goldman, Wheelock, McNally, Robitaille—
appear in print for the first time. As these interviews demonstrate,
Sarton has become a spokesperson for those in their "upward
years." Two of the conversations, in fact, focus upon Sarton's insights
into the experience of the older creative individual. In the interview
from Connie Goldman's series "I'm Too Busy to Talk Right Now:
Conversations with Creative People Over Seventy," Sarton dismisses
concern with what age has done to her: "Old age can be very
beautiful, but it depends on what has gone on inside the face. In
other words, wrinkles are of no importance at all, compared to the
quality of life lived, which is what you see in the face." What has
mattered, she indicates, is the lack of energy to work: "not a line of
poetry ran through my head. I thought, I'm finished. I was terrified."
She sums up her gracious acceptance of her life in this way: "when
I get very upset and badgered by various things, I think, Well, how
would you change it? Would you like this to be different, or that? and
I realize that I'm living the life I've chosen and I love my life."

In the other interview focusing upon old age, the transcript of a
film in his series "Writing in the Upward Years," Stephen Robitaille

asks Sarton about her recent writing activity, and she describes the difficulty she has had with the fibrillating heart condition following her stroke in 1986. Lacking the energy for poetry and the novel, she has returned to the journal, since she can write as little as a paragraph a day and still feel she is writing. She tells Robitaille that she has taken her motto from her friend Karen Saum's organization H.O.M.E.—"Expect a miracle." Her "miracle" would be feeling well again. At the same time, Sarton has chosen as her emblem the phoenix, which she borrowed from D. H. Lawrence. Overall, one finds in these recent interviews persistent expressions of her indomitable spirit, the passion and energy which have driven her life through eight decades.

As with the other books in the Literary Conversations series, the interviews are reprinted here uncut. Transcriptions of audiotape texts have been lightly edited to enhance intelligibility. As a result, repetition is inevitable and has been preserved. It marks her characteristic method of responding to what are understandably similar questions, since more recent interviewers are frequently not aware of earlier responses. And Sarton herself often redirects a question toward characteristic responses. Despite their similarities and repetitions, each of these interviews is a unique contribution to a more complete understanding of what Sarton has revealed about her aims and methods as a writer and her sense of identity as a woman. As she herself acknowledges in the more recent conversations, her reputation as a significant twentieth-century American writer has grown measurably in the past decade. This collection adds to that long overdue recognition.

Many individuals have contributed to the completion of this volume. I wish to thank Bob Gilliam in Drake Memorial Library for his assistance in locating journals and providing copies of the interviews. I owe a debt of gratitude to the students of the Ronald E. McNair Program who assisted with the research for this project—John Stevenson, Caren Mulford, and especially Elizabeth Meyer for her transcribing/editing of the Bonetti tape. I am also grateful to May Sarton, who responded so enthusiastically to my proposal for this collection, and to the interviewers, editors, and publishers who gave their permission to print or reprint their material. Few writers, one suspects, have as many loving friends as May, willing to support book projects such as this one.

This book is for Erma Doop Cosgrove and Patricia Cosgrove, who read May's work before I did, and for Rose Neth Ingersoll and Mary Cosgrove Ingersoll, whose loving support made its completion possible.

EGI
March 1991

Chronology

1912   Eleanore Marie Sarton is born in Wondelgem, Belgium, on 3 May, daughter of Mabel Elwes Sarton and George Sarton.

1914–18 With the outbreak of World War I, the Sartons became refugees, first in England and in 1916 in the United States. The Sartons lived in New York and Washington before settling in Cambridge, Massachusetts. There George Sarton began his *Introduction to the History of Science* under the auspices of the Carnegie Institute, teaching one course at Harvard in exchange for user privileges at the Widener Library.

1917–26 MS attends the Shady Hill School in Cambridge.

1924   MS becomes a naturalized citizen.

1926–29 MS attends the High and Latin School in Cambridge, from which she was graduated in 1929.

1929–36 MS is an apprentice in the Civic Repertory Theatre, directed by Eva Le Gallienne, in New York and a member of First Studio and Director of the Apprentice Group of the Civic Repertory Theatre.

1933–36 MS founds and directs the Apprentice Theatre for one year 1933–34 at the New School for Social Research in New York City. The company put on ten modern European plays never seen in the United States. The next year 1934–35 they became the Associated Actors Theatre and produced five plays at the Wadsworth Atheneum, Hartford, Connecticut. The company failed in 1936 after a brief season at the Charles Street Theatre in Boston.

1937   *Encounter in April,* MS's first volume of poetry, appears.

1937–40 MS teaches at the Stuart School in Boston.

1938   *The Single Hound,* novel, appears.

1939   *Inner Landscape,* poetry, appears.

1944–45 MS works in the Office of War Information, writing scripts for documentary films.

1946   *The Bridge of Years,* novel, appears. MS serves as Poet-in-Residence during the summer at Southern Illinois University at Carbondale.

1947   MS is awarded the Golden Rose of the New England Poetry Society.

1948   *The Lion and the Rose,* poetry, appears.

1950   *The Leaves of the Tree,* poetry, and *Shadow of a Man,* novel, appear.

1950–53 MS teaches composition at Harvard.

1951–52 MS lectures at the Breadloaf Writers' Conference.

1952   *A Shower of Summer Days,* novel, appears.

1953   *The Land of Silence,* poetry, appears. MS is named a Lucy Martin Donnelly Fellow at Bryn Mawr College and receives the Reynolds Poetry Award.

1953–54 MS lectures at the Boulder Writers' Conference.

1955   *Faithful Are the Wounds,* novel, appears. MS receives a Guggenheim Fellowship in Poetry, Honorary Phi Beta Kappa at Radcliffe, and the Tidewater Prize.

1957   *The Birth of a Grandfather*, novel, and *The Fur Person*, novel, appear.

1958   *In Time Like Air*, poetry, appears. MS is a candidate for the National Book Award and is made a Fellow of the American Academy of Arts and Sciences and named an Honorary Doctor of Letters by Russell Sage. MS moves to Nelson, New Hampshire.

1959   *I Knew a Phoenix*, memoir, appears.

1959–60 MS is named a Phi Beta Kappa Visiting Scholar.

1959–64 MS serves as Lecturer in Creative Writing at Wellesley College.

1960–61 MS serves as Danforth Visiting Lecturer in the College Arts Program.

1961   *Cloud, Stone, Sun, Vine*, poetry, and *The Small Room*, novel, appear.

1963   *Joanna and Ulysses*, novel, appears.

1965   *Mrs. Stevens Hears the Mermaids Singing*, novel, appears. MS is writer-in-residence at Lindenwood College.

1966   *A Private Mythology*, poetry, and *Miss Pickthorn and Mr. Hare*, novel, appear.

1967   *As Does New Hampshire*, poetry, and *Plant Dreaming Deep*, journal, appear. MS receives a National Foundation of the Arts and Humanities Grant.

1968   MS serves as writer-in-residence at Lindenwood College.

1969   *The Poet and the Donkey*, novel, appears.

1970   *Kinds of Love,* novel, appears.

1971   *A Grain of Mustard,* poetry, appears. MS is made an
        Honorary Doctor of Letters by New England College.

1972   *A Durable Fire,* poetry, appears. MS is writer-in-residence
        at Agnes Scott College.

1973   *As We Are Now,* novel, and *Journal of a Solitude,* journal,
        appear. MS moves to York, Maine.

1974   *Collected Poems, 1930–1973,* poetry, and *Punch's
        Secret,* children's book, appear.

1975   *Crucial Conversations,* novel, appears. MS receives the
        Alexandrine Award from the College of St. Catherine and
        is awarded an honorary doctorate from Clark University.

1976   *A World of Light,* memoir, and *A Walk through the
        Woods,* children's book, appear. MS is awarded honorary
        doctorates from Bates College, Colby College, and the
        University of New Hampshire.

1977   *The House by the Sea,* journal, appears.

1978   *Selected Poems,* poetry, and *A Reckoning,* novel, appear.

1980   *Halfway to Silence,* poetry, and *Recovering,* journal,
        appear.

1981   *Writings on Writing,* essays, appears. MS receives honor-
        ary doctorate from the University of Maine.

1982   *Anger,* novel, appears. MS is writer-in-residence at Colby
        College.

1983   MS receives honorary doctorate from Bowdoin College.

1984   *Letters from Maine,* poetry, and *At Seventy,* journal,
          appear.

1985   *The Magnificent Spinster,* novel, appears. MS receives
          honorary doctorate from Bucknell University.

1986   *Letters to May,* letters from her mother, edited by MS,
          appears. MS receives the Maryann Hartman Award from
          the University of Maine.

1987   *The Phoenix Again,* poetry, appears.

1988   *The Silence Now,* poetry, *After the Stroke* journal, and
          Honey in the Hive, portrait of Judith Matlack, appear.

1989   *The Education of Harriet Hatfield,* novel, appears.

Conversations with May Sarton

Sister of the Mirage and Echo: An Interview with May Sarton

Paula G. Putney/1972

From *May Sarton: Woman and Poet*, ed. Constance Hunting (Orono, Maine: National Poetry Foundation, 1982), 213–25. Paula G. Putney's interview first appeared in *Contemporara*, 2.3 (1972): 1–6. Reprinted by permission of Constance Hunting and the National Poetry Foundation.

Out of this interview with May Sarton one theme in particular seems to emerge: the battle which a woman must endure to succeed as a professional writer, which does not appear to be so thoroughly exacting for a man. Sarton confronts this special problem from many angles in the novel, *Mrs. Stevens Hears the Mermaids Singing*, and eventually comes to this summary:

> ". . . the crucial question seems to me to be this: what is the *source* of creativity in the woman who wants to be an artist? After all, admit it, a woman is meant to create children, not works of art. . . . A man with a talent does what is expected of him, makes his way, constructs, is an engineer, a composer, a builder of bridges. It's the natural order of things that he construct objects outside himself and his family. The woman who does so is aberrant. . . . Maybe it's this: the woman who needs to create works of art is born with a kind of psychic tension in her which drives her unmercifully to find a way to balance, to make herself whole. Every human being has this need: in the artist it is mandatory. Unable to fulfill it, he goes mad. But when the artist is a woman she fulfills it at the expense of herself as a woman."

Q. Let's begin with structure. Structure provides discipline, but it also creates conflict, because it can be confining. Everything you write reflects your awareness of structure. But there is also a constant awareness of freedom. How do you manage to keep discipline and freedom balanced?

3

A. Your question goes right to the center of the problem. I found myself saying the other day in a moment of self-congratulation, which I don't often indulge in, that if I have any genius I believe that it is this—that I'm at the same time a tremendously emotional, aware, perhaps over-sensitive, even neurotic person *and* I am a highly disciplined person. In the combination of these two I see myself as stemming from two people who gave me very different things. My father, of course, who produced an incredible amount of work (people think it was a whole research institute, you know), did so because he was so highly disciplined and because he appreciated the value of routine. My mother, ultra-sensitive, was committed to life itself.

Q. You say that "routine, discipline, shape, form are ways to freedom from time." I got to thinking about that and realized that it had never occurred to me before that I am a prisoner in time. But we all are in the sense that we have just one lifetime . . . there isn't any other.

A. Exactly. And routine is the one way in which one learns not to waste time. When it comes to a work of art, the matter of form is complex. In poetry I know that I can't write in form unless the intensity is very great. In other words, I have to be inspired to use form. But when I am, then I can put a poem through sixty drafts to get that final crystalline thing that I want. I think of it when I'm teaching. The poem works like an aeroplane—it *flies* because of all the tension, the mechanical tensions within it. Every screw has to be screwed in exactly right, every single thing has to be balanced exactly right. And a poem is only as strong as its weakest word. It will not fly, doesn't soar in the mind unless it has form. The terrible thing about free verse is that it's all over the place. You could go on revising forever. The boundary focuses. Just as in a painting, the frame, just as in the theatre, the proscenium arch. About this I'm old-fashioned because at present the arena theatre is the fashionable thing. But I love the proscenium arch, for ballet especially. Because a dynamic symmetry with what is going on inside that to me has a far greater potency than what you get in the arena theatre, which gives you greater intimacy. It's a little bit like free verse, which gives the illusion of spontaneity, the sense of a person talking. It's more personal in some ways—free verse—but what I want in a poem, in the best of my poems, is something solid as a rock and also transparent. Of course, this is the other thing—music is thrown out of poetry now because of a wish for spontaneity, for the spoken voice and for the tone of voice. As you know, I write free verse too. Certain things work better in free verse. As far as the novels go, the form is terribly important too. Partly, it encloses and helps you stick with the relevant. Otherwise in a novel as rich in characters as *Kinds of Love,* there are thousands of possible threads that could have been explored further. The seasons, the formal aspects of the book, even the journal which I needed as a change of key, hold it together.

Structure is very important to me in life and in art. I think what form does at its best, if you're dealing with a really good work of art, is to set the work in the eternal present in a way that non-form can't. Just as in the Catholic mass—I'm not a Catholic—the structure of the mass gives the true believer the sense that he is in the eternal present, the present when Christ said, "This is my body." And this is what structure is really all about.

Q. You often speak of "webs, fabric, tapestries," using them as metaphors for human relationships. But there is never a suggestion of being 'trapped' by relationships, only enriched and challenged. For instance, we see Mrs. Stevens 'caught' in an interview, but there is never any sense of limitation about this. How do you account for this quality?

A. Well, she is trapped in a way—all her love affairs are disastrous. But perhaps she's not trapped because she's able to turn them into poetry. There's the answer. This is a thing that we could talk about indefinitely because I'm not sure where I stand. I used to agree with Edmund Wilson in that piece on the wound and the bow—the artist is the wounded person who also has the bow, the tremendously strong bow. Just before you came in I lay down for half an hour and thought, Why do I write novels and why do I write poems? and that maybe you were going to ask me this question. The novels deal with growth and relationship. Because poetry is an essence, it can very rarely deal with growth. Growth and relationships interest me enormously. I think that what I have to say about relationships, what my values are, if you will, is that it doesn't matter what the relationship is, whether it's a child with a grandfather, a woman with a woman lover, a marriage in its 75th year, a teacher with a student; what matters is the *quality* of the relationship. It's one of the things that concerned E. M. Forster, it's what Virginia Woolf was interested in— the quality of relationships. And I think we all are terribly aware of what poor quality many of our relationships have, because of the pressure of time, because of the violence in us—and it is the novelist's job to examine this violence. Edward Cavan, the hero of *Faithful Are the Wounds,* is violent, a violence which ends in suicide. Mar is violent in relation to Mrs. Stevens. *She* is, rather, in her way.

Q. The importance of human relationships is one of the recurring themes in everything you write. Can you explain your focus on this?

A. Where do *you* see it?

Q. I see it everywhere, but in *Kinds of Love* in almost every relationship Christina has . . . with Cornelius, or with Ellen, with Kathy, Jane Tuttle, with the old lover, Eben, the quality comes through as being extremely important. I feel it in *Mrs. Stevens* and in *Plant Dreaming Deep* because there is the same attention paid to the quality of relationships. For instance, the moment Hilary Stevens, at 15, recognizes love for what it is, and accepts the fact that we're born knowing how to love, her vision is enlarged. Now we all know this. But we spend most of our time running in the opposite direction.

A. Because of a fear of feeling, which I see as a real fact. Now why is that?

Q. It's a fear of exposure to some degree . . . ?

A. Perhaps because feeling is pain. There is as much pain as joy in any valid relationship because any relationship of any value is so demanding, and we rarely come up to what it can be, that we are always having a sense of failure, I think. This is true in the simplest of relationships. By simple, I mean what looks like an ordinary friend, and suddenly you find that he or she calls up some night when you're in a bad mood and you're angry and you tear the fabric of the friendship without meaning to do it, without wanting to do it. This happens to us all, now and then. And what we're really doing all the time, essentially is reweaving, trying to harmonize and bring together and deal with all these things. And form is one of the ways that helps us. Like the formal dinner at home, when people take trouble to set the table nicely, and immediately something happens to the family within the structure.

Q. Another persistent theme in your work is failure, but failure with a difference. There is some overriding strength which transforms failure into something else. How do you feel about failure?

A. I think we learn probably more from failure than from success and it's also much more of a challenge. I've found this out in my own times of trouble, but let's take just the writer for a moment. Bad reviews have been agonizing for me. Seeing my work publicly attacked makes me absolutely ill. But it also makes me grit my teeth and say, "God damn it, I'm going to do something better." Failure always has the seeds, I think, of self-awareness in it and of growth, whereas success in a funny way is depressing and flat. Or let's take marriages. You see an absolutely serene, apparently perfect marriage. I never envy this very much. I mean, I feel that these people have stopped growing at some point.

In spite of the relaxed atmosphere, there is an intensity about May Sarton, an awareness of her commitment to life and to art which becomes a presence in the room. One senses strength, a willingness to take risks, a courage of self-trust which is rare. I know at once that this woman has given up a great deal, that she knows what she is about, and that she is not afraid of her feelings. I know, too, that it would be impossible for May Sarton to turn away from a commitment, even if it is repaid with betrayal. One evening she told me that her first psycho-therapist had died of a coronary just as they were "getting down to the nub of things." The person she shared a house with "had come in as though to announce the death of a cat"— instead this terrible news. The next day she wrote a poem to Dr. Hall of which the refrain is, "Now the long lucid listening is done." It's a fine poem, yet it was two years before she learned what the poem had meant to his family. So May Sarton also knows about patience. And regardless of the cost, people and love are her central values. These are the ways to growth, to change, to understanding.

Q. I am fascinated by the "angel-demon" images which you often use. I find them everywhere . . . in the poems, the novels, the non-fiction. What do you attempt to suggest by these?

A. I think it's said in a poem in *A Durable Fire*—I took the epigraph from Baudelaire's *"Ange plein de gaité connaissez vous l'angoisse?"* In a way the angel and the demon are the same thing.

We all have both and both have value. *Plant Dreaming Deep* has given too gentle an image of me. And I think this is partly why it's reached a great many people who might have been frightened by the reality. Though if people read it carefully, they'd see the anguish.

I'd like to say something here about the machine. I once read a typescript after an interview and I was depressed because it seemed as though I had no sense of humor. I realized that in a typescript the laughter is never noted. You have to get it in or you lose the person. I mean I sometimes say things that sound terribly sententious, but I'm *laughing,* and if the laughter is taken out. . . .

May Sarton has an infectious humor which is inherent in everything she speaks about. Her anecdotes are so vivid that the listener sees, hears the absurdity or charm in many of her most serious-sounding remarks. The tension is frequently altered by this fundamental genuine humor.

Q. I hear in your writing a rare synthesis of life and art, of the real and the imagined. Yet the two will never be the same. Can you describe something of how this synthesis takes place?

A. I think it's that by making a work of art one is always refining, as if it were gold, getting down to the essence; you go through an awful lot of rocks and stuff to get these little bits of gold which are finally the poem. And there has to be an enormous amount of raw material. In other words, for me, at least, and for my art, I know that it's necessary to live hard. I'm not going to just sit in a room and talk about how pure my soul is. The essence is arrived at through a lot of raw material which you're struggling with, which you *have* to have. It's almost like roughage in digestion; you can't just live on oysters and champagne, you need the roughage, you need the trouble, you need the desperation because all of these things increase the intensity. And this I do think, whatever the eventual value of my work (and nobody can know that), I've gone on growing, and this is what gives me hope. I haven't stopped, you see. And the price of keeping on is keeping on *feeling* at a point of great intensity, and this is very expensive in anger, in behavior that stems from unresolved conflicts.

Q. One of the things I see in an overall view of your writing is a

deep intellectual approach to feeling which has matured in a remarkable way. I mean, the *intellectual* quality is there. But the *feeling* has
taken over almost as if a battle between the two has been resolved.
It's more than just a fine balance.

A. You mean that feeling has taken over the intellectual qualities?
I would not agree with that, although I think I know what you mean.
And I'm very glad, if so. I think there's more *flow*. I think that I'm less
tense, I have more confidence. I know much more about myself.

Q. I occasionally encounter the idea that it is easy for a woman to
be a writer because writing is something women can do 'acceptably.'
I happen to disagree with this point of view. What is your reaction?

A. Well, it's complex. I think that women have enormous gifts as
writers and of course, we've got some great writers to prove this.
They have a real gift because of their capacity for understanding
relationships, for thinking about feeling, which very often men just
don't want to do, and therefore, in some ways, women writers
are less sentimental than men. It's very hard to be a woman *anything,* I mean a professional woman. It's very hard and of course
there's tremendous resentment on the part of men. There's no doubt
about this deep-seated or below the conscious level in men; although
they don't mean to feel this way, they enormously resent the woman
who can create because she can create children and they can't, and it
isn't fair that she can also create poetry or paintings or sculpture or
music or whatever it may be, or that she can be a brilliant lawyer.
It somehow outrages them at a below-conscious level. And so the
woman writer who really produces gets slapped in the face. It's there
in the words, "lady-novelist" and "poet-ess"! Neither of these
would be said by a woman about a woman writer, but only by a man
about a woman writer. "Poet-ess!" I mean really! I'd rather be called
a donkey!

Q. In what ways do you feel that being a woman has made it
more difficult for you to achieve success?

A. Well, in my case I haven't faced the ultimate difficulty which
faces the woman who wants to be a complete woman, have a family
and also be an artist.

*Sarton is the only child of genius parents: her father Belgian and a
brilliant historian of science; her mother British, a painter and de-*

signer. Within a 'good' marriage May feels that her mother paid too high a price. So she has avoided marriage partly because of what her parents' marriage cost:

I not exactly chose, I don't think anybody goes around saying, "I'm not going to marry because I'm a great poet." You'd be a pretty arrogant human being if you did this. But the facts emerge from what we have to look at: Elizabeth Bishop never married, Virginia Woolf married but had no children; Elizabeth Bowen married but had no children. It looks as if the woman who is going to give the major part of her creative energy to an art is going to have a very hard time if she tries also to bring up a family. I don't mean to say it can't be done. I'm saying that I took the easier path. I've had many relationships, I've been in love many times, but I have not taken on the structure of a family.

Q. Has anybody ever tried to destroy you because you are a woman?

A. Whether it was because I'm a woman I don't know. I think people have *tried* to destroy me because they resent the—'glamour' is the only word that I can think of—that comes from quite a considerable achievement you accomplished when still young. What destroys are people who try to become you and can't and then turn against you. Actually, it was a psychiatrist, whom I went to for advice about destructive admirers, who had watched me working and she suggested, "Well, the trouble is that people want to become you and when they can't, they want to kill you."

Q. Men and women see themselves in given roles so that a departure from these roles represents impotency or loss for them. It's as though we are defined in terms of our maleness or femaleness rather than by our humanity. How do you feel about this in terms of your experience?

A. I'd like to think of my work as wholly human. I have a feeling that everybody who is interesting at all is somewhere in the middle of the spectrum, at one end of which would be the absolutely masculine man and at the other, the absolutely feminine woman. And in the middle is almost everybody concerned with the arts. I'm not talking in terms of sex now. There is a great deal of feminine feeling in any good masculine novelist. Obviously, he wouldn't be able to write about women if he didn't have it. And the same thing is true to some extent about any woman who writes about men. She's able to identify with, to some extent be a man when she's writing a love scene between a man and a woman. Of course, I'm both a novelist and a poet. There have been quite a few woman poets who wrote some novels. Elinor Wylie comes to mind, but her novels were not major compared to her poetry. The point is that when the evaluation is there, now that she's been dead a long time, what we read is the poems and we don't go back very much to the novels—they had a brilliant sparkle, but not the deep fire. I don't know any other woman who is equally a poet and a novelist. Among the men there is Penn Warren, and Randall Jarrell, though I think he was not a very important novelist.

Mrs. Stevens Hears the Mermaids Singing, *a novel which is highly autobiographical, extremely important, as well as brilliantly conceived, is the tortured account, tracking if you will, of the forces, the passions, the conflicts of 'artistic schizophrenia'—the terrifying duality with which every artist must contend if he is "to solve the equation through art." We observe Hilary Stevens from the 'virginal' state of feeling that she is two persons, through the degrees of 'consummation' requisite for becoming an important writer. I think it hardly an accident that with Mrs. Stevens May Sarton explores the quandaries inherent in being a woman and a writer, which she says is itself a contradiction in terms. " 'The women who have tried to be men have always lacked something: we have to rest on Sappho, Jane Austen, Colette . . ., we have to be ourselves.' " Later she queries, ". . . why is it women writers cannot deal with sex and get away with it? . . . Colette, of course, but she is untranslatable into English. How to do it in our obtuse language? The language of sex is masculine. Women would have to invent a new language. . . ." Throughout this novel we witness the reality of personal anguish exacted of the woman artist in our culture.*

Q. I am fascinated by some insights which you have given me. One is the notion that "people make their deaths as they make their lives," as I believe Christina comments in *Kinds of Love.*
A. Yes, I really got this from Rainer Maria Rilke. It is one of his

seminal ideas and I witnessed it when my mother was dying of cancer. It does not work if a person loses his mind, obviously. And people who have a stroke . . . it doesn't work. But people who have to handle a terminal disease and know it, I think they really do "make their deaths." I've seen several people grow old and die in very wonderful ways in which the death was really almost like an essence of what they were as human beings, much like Jane Tuttle in that same novel. Though she's quite different, part of her was my very dear old friend, the Belgian poet Jean Dominique, a woman who wrote under that pseudonym. She became so angelic as she failed, she taught me how to die. She taught me how to accept dependence. It's fascinating to think about characters in novels . . . how much goes into them. All novels are dug out of the self. The novelist is each of his characters *plus*. I mean the character is there, but the novelist is always there too. By the time you're twenty, you've known so many people: old grandparents, aunts, some of it should have come into your orbit if you were willing to look at it. I store experience the way a squirrel stores nuts for the winter, although everyone has to bury something, because you can't live with everlasting guilt, and we're all guilty.

Q. Another idea is that "nothing dies, everything is transformed." How does this happen?

A. I think I would have said, "Nothing is wasted, everything can be used." Even agony can be transformed into a work of art, like Mozart's "Requiem," when he knew he was dying. Agony is the great mover. What made you ask that? What piece of work of mine?

Q. I think it was *Kinds of Love*. Perhaps it is related to the idea that if we take Christina and Cornelius as the pivotal examples in that novel, they're really in the process of growing and changing, distilling, redefining things. The implication is that this is never going to end.

A. This is the great thing about growing older that I wish could be talked about more in works of art. I have it much in my mind to write more about old age. I think we're throwing away a whole period of life in America because we don't know how to handle it. We don't know how to handle it in other people and we don't know how to handle it in ourselves. And this is partly what I mean about making your death. I feel that I'm making my death now. I'm at a time in my life when I must learn what to let go and what to keep. Robert Frost has a poem that begins, "I could give all to Time except—except/ What I myself have held." And it ends, "And what I would not part with I have kept." I think often of this. When one is young, one devours everything, every relationship. You fall in love fifty times a day, almost greedily. And you almost have to, you need to. It's what makes you what you are finally. As one becomes older one becomes much more selective as to what is important and what is not. And this takes toughness, of course. You have to be able to say, "Now," and you have to be able to ask, "Is this really worth it?"

Q. From *Plant Dreaming Deep* I came to feel that you are in many ways "married to life."

A. Yes, I guess I am. I would like to believe that. Of course, life is tough and harsh and demanding and outrageous and beautiful and marvelous. It's everything. When I think of just a single day, I have so many thoughts, so many things take place that I never have time to examine and use. I think it's this—the danger is to get crowded and silted up. And this is why my life is quite a good one. It's those hours when I can think over what's been happening to me—I mean simply a lunch engagement or going out for a walk, when I can sort it out and say, "What really was this?" or, "Why was the light so beauti-ful?" "What is the quality of this light?" in February or March— it's always different. There are two things that happen when I'm alone that I never have when I am with people, even people I love very much, in my house. One of them is that I'm aware of the light in a way that I never am unless I'm alone, and the second is the flowers. The flowers become presences in a curious way. They're silent. And I always enjoy them. But I never really *look* at them unless I am alone.

Q. What would you say is the book you value most?

A. I think I value *Mrs. Stevens* because it was the hardest to write. It took the most honesty, for one thing. And then maybe *Faithful Are the Wounds,* which I think is a powerful book. (When I say praising things about my work I'm not comparing it to other people's—it's within my work that I think it's powerful and did something that maybe was fairly original. I don't know.) Books are like children, just like your children. You can't have favorites. You may say, "Johnny is awfully queer, but I really love him." I feel this about my books.

They're my blood and my bones. They go out in the world and get knocked.

Q. You've remarked that you feel your writing is becoming more autobiographical.

A. Yes. But *Kinds of Love* wasn't autobiographical at all—less so than any other novel. It takes a kind of arrogance to write autobiography and I didn't really think that anything I had to say about myself was that valuable until after *Plant Dreaming Deep,* when I realized that it was, because that book reached so many people . . . people outside the literary corridors. Of course, I'd love to have a few critics too. But what I really want is to reach people. That book did so. I have more confidence now. Before, I would have felt this to be ostentatious—who cares what I do from day to day? But now I realize it has value, partly because it has a great deal to say about living alone and many people do.

Q. There is another dimension about *Plant Dreaming Deep,* and perhaps living alone accounts for this quality. You make every one of those real people come alive as though they're characters in a novel.

A. The marvelous thing about Nelson, which I speak of in a poem, "Gestalt At Sixty" in *As Does New Hampshire,* was that everything that came to me there (and that comes to me) was distilled. I saw those people very well in the sense that we saw each other now and then and they were always there. But it was not cluttered like social life, you see. And so each meeting was important and vivid and could have its depth. This is what Nelson did for me.

May Sarton is more than acquainted with the perils of being a woman artist. She has endured fierce competition with men and is well aware of the influence which male critics can invoke. But she has not chosen to be abstract, nor has she remained silent. Instead, she has insisted on daring to speak for herself. In Mrs. Stevens Hears the Mermaids Singing *the aging Hilary startles her interviewers when she says:*

"Oh, we are all monsters, if it comes to *that,* we women who have chosen to be something more and something less than women! . . . one is nourishing a talent, expensive, demanding baby! Human? What does human mean? Having time and the wish to care intensely about

someone else? This is what women will do, willy-nilly, and what then?
. . . [It is] Love as the waker of the dead, love as conflict, love as the
mirage. Not love as peace or fulfillment!"

*No one can read even a few of the volumes of May Sarton's work
without being aware of her enormous vitality, of her humanity, of her
dedication to growth and change. She teaches us many things.
Seldom does a novelist or poet draw us so magically into the web of
human relationships which we can neither leave nor escape. One
does not sense about May Sarton any feeling that she can now rest
on her past achievements, that she has done enough. "Gestalt at
Sixty" is a remarkable statement for any artist, but it is clearly May
Sarton's invocation to "the Muse whom above all things she has
desired to know. Sister of the mirage and echo!"*

May Sarton
Barbara Bannon/1974

From *Publishers Weekly*, 24 June 1974, 14–15. Published by permission of *Publishers Weekly*.

One of the most interesting and long-overdue literary recognitions is that now coming to May Sarton, poet, novelist and memoirist, a woman in her sixties who has been writing since she was 19, and who has published 27 books in all.

This spring, Norton, her publisher for many years, has just brought out her *Collected Poems 1930–1973* and reissued her ninth novel, *Mrs. Stevens Hears the Mermaids Singing.* Published originally in the early 1960s, this novel has now come to be acknowledged as not only a beautifully written study of love in many aspects, but as an important and very early feminine consciousness book.

In her critical introduction to the new edition of *Mrs. Stevens* Carolyn Heilbrun writes of Sarton: "Agonizing, in letters and conversation, over life's injustices, she has never ceased to examine with artistry her demons of anger and despair, and her consolations of solitude and love. . . . Success that comes late has its special flavor particularly to a writer still productive, still capable of poetry and amazement."

Recently, *PW* talked with May Sarton about her work and her philosophy of life. Referring to the recognition she is only now receiving, she says, quite frankly, "For many years I felt I was under a gravestone. I wanted to push it up and shout, 'Here I am.' It is very hard to really *know* your work is good, but I have always had some proof of it in the very strong, moving letters I have received from my readers. This kind of support is very important to a writer who does not make money. You cannot live on no recognition. You must have some."

May Sarton is the daughter of the noted Harvard historian, George Sarton, and Mabel Elwes Sarton, a painter. She was 17, still in high school but entered at Vassar, when she went to the theater for the

16

first time to see Eva Le Gallienne in Ibsen. "I had never seen
anything like this," she says. "I fell completely in love with the
theater."

Persuading her scholarly parents, however reluctantly, to let her
forget college, she joined the Le Gallienne Civic Repertory Company, graduating from apprentice roles as the Wolf and an Indian in
Peter Pan to that of Tinker Bell opposite Le Gallienne's Peter Pan.
She became in time head of Le Gallienne's drama school and after
the sad financial failure of the Le Gallienne operation, she carried on
in the theater for as long as she could as founder and director of the
Apprentice Theater of the New School for Social Research.

"At that time all my energy was going into the theater," she says,
"and the theater is like an angel with its feet tied to a bag of gold. It
was only when the theater failed me [in the Depression years] that
my first book of poetry came out. If you can pattern a writer's life,
however, I think it would have been very bad for me to have gone to
college. I would have become a political blue stocking."

One of the themes that has always absorbed May Sarton is age
and growing older. "The most fatal thing in American life is the
arbitrary retirement age," she believes. "The greatest thing in my life
has been the older people who gave me encouragement and friendship when I was young. One of them was Virginia Woolf, whom I
met through Elizabeth Bowen.

"I am terribly upset at the way we treat old people today. You
make your old age by how you have lived your life. You must
prepare for old age. There are people who are nothing when they
are old because they have never been anything at any age. You stay
alive by living."

Solitude is another theme that recurs often in May Sarton's writings, most notably in her very personal *Journal of a Solitude*. "I have
always been a very private person," she says. "I left home when I
was 17. I have no family left and this is important because it freed
me. I did not have to stay in one place, as I would have done if I had
had a close family there. I could not have written as I have when my
mother and father were alive."

Interestingly, however, solitude has never meant loneliness to May
Sarton. Nor has a lack of family kept her from being aware of her
family background. The house in York, Maine, in which she lives

contains much of the lovely old Belgian furniture she inherited. "At one time," she says, "I became aware of the fact that I had all of this family furniture stored away in the cellar, and I thought, My God, my roots are dying in that cellar. So I did something about it.

"I try to live as if every moment of my life, every day, might be my last, and yet, also, as if every moment of life is eternal. You can only do this well in solitude. The older you get, the more you want to do away with whatever wastes time." The happy solitude in which one can simply work at peace, enjoy a home, a garden, a dog, and have friends, but not on an appointment schedule basis—these are now for May Sarton the most satisfying elements in her life.

"What makes a person want to write both poetry and the novel?" May Sarton asks herself on occasion. She has a rather good answer. "Poetry is one person's immediate feelings. It does not deal with growth and change. There are things one cannot say in poetry. Poetry does not answer to command. I have found the novel something to write when I cannot write poetry. The novel does what poetry can never do. It *must* deal with growth and change."

The most damaging element in American life, as Sarton sees it, is "the emphasis on sex rather than love. The deepest experiences in my life have had to do with other people I love. I believe love, not sex, is the 'way out' of feeling."

Work Is My Rest: A Conversation with May Sarton

Jane S. Bakerman/1976

From *Moving Out* 7.2 (1979), 8–12. Reprinted by permission of Jane S. Bakerman.

It's easy to talk with May Sarton. She's warm and outgoing, friendly and clear about what she wants to say. Above all, she's thoughtful; this quality is even apparent in her comments about her social life.

> One reason I try to see people only one at a time is because I will not tolerate anything but conversation in depth. I'm too old, and I think that if you're going to give time and yourself, which you want to give to anybody who comes to your house, you have to see them alone. The most I ever have is two people at once (except, of course, for families with children) . . . but I try not to entertain in the usual sense. Because I want to learn from the people who come here, and the minute there's small talk, something is gone!

One has the feeling that little "is gone" from Sarton's grasp of the complexity of life; indeed it is clear in almost every sentence that the idea of "leading one's real life" so vividly explored in all her work is the key to her own life. Sarton's "real life" centers chiefly in her work, her friends, and in her home.

She is not only one of the United States's best loved but also one of America's most productive writers, known as a poet, a novelist, and a diarist. She sees herself primarily as a poet, and her twelve books of poetry to date include *Encounter in April, The Lion and the Rose, In Time Like Air, A Grain of Mustard Seed,* and *Collected Poems* (1930–1973), as just a sample listing. Widely known for her novels, she has produced fifteen of them, including *Faithful Are the Wounds, The Small Room, Mrs. Stevens Hears the Mermaids Singing, Kinds of Love,* and *As We Are Now.* Sarton's readers are especially devoted to her "journals" and her reputation as a diarist is secure. Among those works are *I Knew a Phoenix, Plant Dreaming Deep, Journal of a Solitude,* and *A World of Light.*

It was largely through the journals that readers came to feel "at home" in the charming old house the author renovated in Nelson, New Hampshire, a feeling strengthened when the town's background was painted very effectively in the novel, *Kinds of Love*. In fact, they felt so "at home" that they really couldn't believe, at first, that she planned to leave that locale. Now, however, she is living near York, Maine, in a large, comfortable house, Wild Knoll, which faces the sea. Inside, one finds all the familiar furniture, pictures, flowers, plants, and books readers learned about in the Nelson journals; outside, though, the landscape is quite different.

Beyond the cultivated yard and gardens, lies a great meadow, cleft by a narrow, mown path, leading to the edge of a steep cliff. Only at the very end of the path, at the head of the cliff itself, can one see the shore, with the waves dashing against sharp rocks. The contrast is fascinating. From the house, even from Sarton's third-floor study, the view reflects peace and tranquillity; beyond the serenity lie power and danger. The whole setting is a good metaphor, and clearly, Sarton loves the place.

The contrast between the serene house and gardens and the wild sea really is a symbol for Sarton's life, for the life of the female artist is not an easy one, and much of the value and attraction of her work lies in her ability to write about and evaluate the tensions inherent in being a productive author. These themes are also apparent, of course, in her conversation.

Sarton's practical streak is very evident when she talks about her daily pattern pointing out that the presence of a workable time schedule is essential to her productivity. For her, routine is

> the balance wheel to a temperament. I mean, in other words, it's what keeps me steady. When I wake up and feel terribly tired, I sometimes think, Why don't I take the day off. But taking the day off is not a rest, compared to working. Work is my rest! It's the routine that's my rest. I get back to myself and I try not to hurry things.
>
> I realize that it's really true. I've said it somewhere in *Plant Dreaming Deep*—form is freedom. It's true of democracy itself; it's true of education. A messy class, where nobody pays attention, isn't a free class: it's a mess!

When her day is free from interruptions, the schedule is both pragmatic and gratifying.

I'm a morning person. Now that I'm in my sixties, I can't work in the afternoon at all, except if there were some extremity, where I had to get something finished. So whatever I do, I do now before eleven in the morning, and that means I have to get up very early. I've been getting up at five. It takes me two hours to do the flowers, do the bed, get my breakfast, water the plants. But I'm at my desk by seven. Then I work, and I'm ashamed to say, really not very long, about two hours a day on creative work.

I go and get the mail about eleven, walk the dog, have my lunch, rest, and then I have a wholly different day, which is the garden. In the summer, I try to garden two or three hours a day, when I don't have a guest.

I'm compulsive about the news; I look at three different news shows: local Boston, and Cronkite and Chancellor. While I'm getting my dinner, having a drink and eating my dinner, I do that.

And then I go to bed very early, by nine, and read. I read until about ten, but rarely *later* than that because I get very tired now. And it's been quite a full day, at that, because two or three hours of gardening is very stiff, physical work.

The "free" hours are also important for her writing, however:

Don't forget that one is carrying the book around like a baby. It's in the back of my mind. And this is why I think space around working is the key. It isn't the number of work hours. Those periods which look like empty time are when you're creating the best, I think. It's when you're doing nothing, seemingly, that you're creating. And the whole problem for most people is that they're so few times in their day when they're doing nothing.

The need for those incubation periods in the time space around working causes one difficulty for Sarton. She values and cherishes people, but their presence does pose a threat, not only to her actual working time, but also to her thinking time.

The trouble with the summers when I see so many people is that instead of thinking about my book when I go to bed or when I'm gardening or when I'm just sitting, I'm thinking about the people I've seen. That's *very* enriching for me, and I enjoy doing that, but it isn't as good for the creative part of me. And in the winter, that's what's good. When the balance is working, my life here is perfect!

In the same fashion, the influx of mail from her readers both nurtures and frets May Sarton. She has, after all, a huge readership, and

> what touches me very much, of all ages. Since the *Journal of a Solitude,* which brought the young (that and *As We Are Now,* curiously enough, since it deals with the old)—those two books brought me the young. I had thought, I had feared, that my audience was middle-aged, and it's simply not true. And, of course, I'm also writing books for children from the ages of four to six. So now I have *fans* who write me who are eight years old, and this is very satisfactory. It's a gamut: from 8 to 80!

These letters account for much of the desk time she puts in:

> About two hours a day on creative work, and then the rest is answering mail, which is my nightmare. Because it never gets any better. You see, if I go away for a week, I pay for it with months of being behind because I haven't answered. I answer about fifty letters a week, and that means if I take a week off, fifty are accumulated and fifty more are coming!

And yet, Sarton does answer each letter; the readers and other friends are important to her.

In addition to routine and thinking space, the writer, in Sarton's view, also needs to work daily and not simply wait for moments when she is seized with inspiration. Working without that excitement may not be easy, and it may not be great fun, but it's important:

> I think you have to *be* writing and be in the groove. It's getting in the groove—it's like a jazz player who has to *get* in the groove, who has to play some before he performs. Or it's like a ballet dancer, who has to practice on the day that he's going to perform, so that he'll be limber. It's that limbering up of all the muscles, the psychic muscles, if you will. Yes, I think writing every day is very important.

The intensity which the author employs during the creative writing sessions varies, as one might expect, with the inspiration of the moment and with the type of work in hand. That intensity is fairly strong, for example, when she is working on a children's story; they take only a few days because they are created in the same way she forms a poem.

It's quick all the way. I mean that I do it in about two days, but there are a hundred drafts. With a poem, it would be eleven or twelve hours at a stretch because when I'm really inspired, then I can really work. That's because your critical self is at white heat when your emotional self is at white heat—if you are a poet! And I think that is what makes a poet: the combination of the two.

You have to continually criticize your own impulse, if you will, and *fashion* it. It's like hammering out at white heat a piece of metal, and revision is that hammering out. It's far from dull! For, in that state of high excitement, when you're writing a poem, your critical self is just as wide awake as your emotional self.

True revision, which comes from *inside,* and which is your struggle with the material to make your personal truth known through it is vitalizing. And I can't do it if I'm not inspired. My critical self isn't that wide awake except when I'm really seized—there's no other word—by a poem—and it's been a long time since that's really happened—because there's no "Muse" at the moment.

Sarton perceives the "Muse" as a factor in her life, often a beloved person, which generates inspiration and idea and produces a special kind of excitement and energy to drive the two together. When the Muse is present, she usually works in highly disciplined, traditional poetic forms; otherwise, she uses free verse, which she finds enjoyable but not quite so fulfilling.

Not unexpectedly, the pace for a novel is much slower, though there are some exceptions:

I wrote *As We Are Now* in three months. But you see, that was like a poem, in that I was driven by passionate impulses. There were many things involved. It wasn't only the women in the nursing home [the book is set in a terrible home for the aged and ill], but things that were happening to me which I completely translated and nobody would ever know that they were there. Nevertheless, that was what gave the motor power to that book.

Generally, a novel takes from one to three years, and though that range is fairly great, Sarton tries to balance her work so that she can produce a book a year.

The long incubation period for the "Nelson Novel," *Kinds of Love* (three years) came in part because "I wanted a sort of rich tapestry of the village," and that desire was realized. Originally, however, the book was planned as an historical novel, and Sarton studied town and country histories as preparation.

> I did a *lot* of reading and then learned, by writing a hundred pages, that I'm not an historical novelist. I was stopped every minute by things I didn't know. What did they have for breakfast? What kind of shoes did they wear? There are so many questions, and I don't have an historical imagination—that's quite plain, and I learned it that way!
>
> Still, I think the research enriched the book because there were things I wouldn't otherwise have known that were sort of buried there.

Developing now is yet another novel, and this one, too, might "turn into a big novel," though after *Kinds of Love,* she swore "that I would never write another book that long again, and I haven't since!" Still, practically, the effort might be worthwhile, not only to protect the spirit of the book as she is beginning to perceive it, but also because, "It's easier to sell a long novel, frankly. And I'd like to have one best seller before I die . . ."

The actual writing of this new novel began in January of 1977, and as she "carries it around" with her, Sarton is working through a very basic problem. When she solves that, she feels confident, fictional inspiration will come:

> Now I'm stuck on the name of what will be the chief character. I have lists and lists of names. But once I get the name right, once that jells, the whole thing is going to explode, I know that!

To get a novel well in hand, Sarton begins by making a card index, but then she doesn't use it much, as a rule. "It's to help in the actual creation," and in a sense serves in place of an outline. For *Kinds of Love,* her good friend Elinor Blair, who also did the photographs in *Plant Dreaming Deep,* made a card index of all the characters,

> which was an enormous help. With such a large scale thing, you could very easily call someone's mother, for instance, Jenny, early in the book, and then suddenly on page 400, it's Mary, and you've forgotten. That card index made it possible for us to go over the whole manuscript very fast.

Some revision of a novel goes on from page to page during the writing, and for the final revision, Sarton will use notes made to herself in the original draft. These call attention to pages which need special attention:

> I'm apt to get the whole thing down and then go back because, I think, you really don't know the proportions (though you can predict the length) until you've *got* the whole thing down. My revising of a novel is mostly cutting, which you can do much better looking at the work as a whole.

Reworking of style is also very important, the "cutting out the awful; I enjoy that!" In this process, too, friends help.

> Everything I do is read by two or three people before it is ever typed, when it's in rough. Carol [Carolyn Heilbrun] is reading a journal now as well as another friend who is a copy editor. They note, partly, the little, stylistic things. In this journal, I, myself, noticed this, but certainly they will, too. "What a relief" keeps coming back all the time—"What a relief it's stopped raining"; "What a relief the sun is out . . ." Some of those will disappear!

Actually, then, Sarton tends to have several works in process at the same time. No wonder she needs "space" around the actual writing hours! At the time of this interview, the new journal was nearly finished, a novel was in its early stages, a children's book was forming, and she hoped to achieve it within the next few months. Poems are always hovering, currently, mostly free verse.

The new journal is a "journal of happiness," she says, and "therefore may be very dull for the reader. I don't know; we'll have to find out!" The title is *The House by the Sea,* and it centers on her life at Wild Knoll. May Sarton's doubts about the book's reception will probably be proved unfounded, particularly if it continues her pattern of incorporating tiny, informal essays in the work.

> Quite a large part of my journals is really short, very short, informal essays of two or three paragraphs. That's just what they are. They give you a chance to examine experience and to relate it to universal experience. It is this reflection which *makes* a journal; it's not just telling what happened today. That sounds obvious, but so often people who keep a journal don't realize this.
>
> And it's in the reflection that you get the originality of the mind of the person who is writing and also you get something that has universal bits, somehow. I find it a fascinating form in some ways.

Though this "journal of happiness" was kept for three years, Sarton considers two years the optimum time to cover; she gets "tired of it" and wants "to get back to imaginary people. They are never imaginary to me, but more real than real people." For, in dealing with imaginary people, she can come closer to "the whole truth."

> The difficulty in a journal is that the most interesting things I have to say would hurt people, and so I can't say them. I can't say them because I just don't want to hurt people; it isn't worth it to me. I don't have exaggerated ideas about my own importance, that it's important that I say some devastating thing about somebody when it just isn't.
>
> So very often I find myself stopped in trying to come to grips with something that has happened, in trying to find out why it happened and what was involved. In doing that, you're bound to be critical, not only of yourself (as I often am in my journals) but also of other people. I prefer to be critical of myself and let the other people not be attacked.

Neither *The House by the Sea, Plant Dreaming Deep,* nor *Journal of a Solitude* just happened to come about because the author had formed the diary habit.

> I've never kept one except for publication. I would never go through the hard work of keeping a journal if it weren't for publication. I think that people who keep journals not for publication are terribly narcissistic. It's very fashionable now; people are keeping journals more and more. But I very much doubt whether they really are honest with themselves. I think often, it's just a reflective mirror in which you see yourself in the best possible light.

For the serious diarist, the form can be good therapy and can serve "to make people look at themselves," but

> I don't believe that keeping a journal *changes* you very much. Funnily enough, I think that my novels *have* changed me. Except for *Journal of a Solitude,* perhaps, I've come to understand things on deeper levels through my novels rather than through my journals.

Variety of form, then, seems to be essential for Sarton as a person. Certainly, it is important for her as a writer.

At different periods you need different things. And at different
periods you certainly write different things. In fact, I would think that
writers are only interesting if they do that.

If one goes on, like some of the gothic novelists, just writing the
same book, it never grows; it's just the same old thing in a different
castle.

But I think of Virginia Woolf; every book was a new challenge. She
didn't even know technically how she was going to do it. That's the
only way I can imagine writing—at all—anything!

It's interesting and evidence of courage to hear such comments
from a woman who says she's "buttressed against defeat" because
she's had so much of it.

I really think, in a way, that success in any normal sense of the word
would frighten me to death because I then might become absolutely
arrogant and frightful. I've had to fight so hard to believe in myself that
I suppose a great success might make me into a monster!

Yet at the very next moment, she banishes the monster idea by
noting that some very good things have happened lately, like the
honorary doctorates recently from Bates and Colby Colleges (in
Maine), from the University of New Hampshire and Clare University
as well as from the Thomas Starr King School for Religious Leadership in Berkeley, California, which bring Sarton's total to seven.

Sarton uses the same duality of vision in surveying the feminist
movement. She does not pretend that change will be easy.

It's enormously complex! And I still believe that for a woman it's
very, very hard, still, to be a first-class artist and be married. Now, it's
going to change; men are already showing that they can be partners in
a new sense and not expect quite so much. And yet, I find that even
my very liberated young women friends who are married suddenly
realize that *they* are doing the laundry, *they* are doing the cooking.
Nobody's had a fight about this; it isn't even that they mind, but it's
just so *expected*.

Still, there is an "enormous change already." As an example, she
notes that when *Mrs. Stevens Hears the Mermaids Singing* came out,
she lost two jobs as a result. "And now, I think I'd be much safer.
Certainly, wherever I go, I can talk very openly about myself" and
about lesbianism if the subject arises. The author stresses, however,

that she speaks for herself and from her own ideals, rather than as a spokesperson for any movement.

I don't see myself, really, as a very aggressive feminist. But I certainly am grateful to the feminist movement for what it has done for me. I'm quite sure that my work has come up and been read in a new way because of the movement.

And I'm grateful because they have helped us to feel that we are sisters and can help each other. This attitude is quite new! When I was young, women writers were rivals and were really rather mean to each other. Therefore, you got it in the neck from everybody: the men because they didn't want women to be creative, the women because they were jealous. So I think that something very good is happening now, but I'm not an active Women's Libber, except through my work, perhaps. Even then, I think not really.

I like men. I think the greatest danger, you see, is that there's a lot of emphasis on lesbianism. I mean I think this has been exploited and badly used as a part of Women's Lib, and it shouldn't be.

But though I would say that I'm not an ardent Women's Libber, I hope that there are things in my books that can help women to understand themselves.

For the woman artist, one crucial decision may always remain, even after all the changes have been made.

There are severe choices that have to be made in life. You have to have a true vocation to be a writer, and I did have it. From the time I was twelve years old, I was dedicated to writing; it was a true vocation. If you have that, I think you should think twice about marriage. I think that because I would take marriage very seriously and would feel that I had to give a great part of myself to do it. Then, perhaps, I wouldn't have been able to do what I've been able to do.

It's not that I'm against marriage. It's that I'm for the creative part of me which wouldn't be completely free if I were married. I think it's that.

Late in the interview, I asked Sarton if there were anything she would like to say that I hadn't asked her to discuss.

I would like to say that I think one is primarily a poet and secondarily anything else. I don't think about how people are going to remember me—just as myself, that I kept on growing—as a pilgrim soul.

Keats says, you know, that life is a vale of soul-making, and I *believe* this absolutely.

The evidence of her belief in Keats's concept is in her work, and the evidence of the effectiveness of her work itself probably lies most firmly in her sense that readers are hearing her correctly. The sense that the readers are there and that they understand is good:

> It isn't praise so much as feeling that your work is getting through, that it's landed—that it isn't somewhere up in the air, trying to land, that gives you peace.

Form is freedom; work is rest; communication yields peace. Each of these ideas is simple to state; each is hard to achieve. Together, they contribute to soul-making. The effort is enormous; the result, as May Sarton *has* achieved it, is impressive!

To Be Reborn: An Interview with May Sarton

Karla Hammond/1977

From *May Sarton: Woman and Poet*, ed. Constance Hunting (Orono, Maine: National Poetry Foundation, 1982), 229–38. Karla Hammond's interview first appeared in *The Bennington Review*, 3 (December 1978), 18–20, © Bennington College, Bennington, Vt 05201. The interview is reprinted with the permission of Constance Hunting and the National Poetry Foundation. Karla Hammond conducted the interview at Sarton's home, "Wild Knoll," on 19 November 1977. Reprinted by permission of Constance Hunting and the National Poetry Foundation.

Q. Every poet creates out of a sense of a personal mythology. Does yours in part owe its impetus to regionalism?

A. My personal mythology has much more to do with the solitary and with nature in general. I've lived in New England, of course, all my life and I feel closely related to it. But I also feel closely related to Santa Fe, New Mexico. I loved the austerity of that landscape. I understand why Georgia O'Keeffe felt at home when she finally got there. Then for many, many years there was the conflict, never resolved, between Europe and America, when I went back and forth every year.

So I don't think that regionalism is applicable in my case. It would be better for me if it were. It's good if you have one region which is like Robert Frost's New England, say, or Yeats' Ireland. I think this is a strength rather than a weakness; but just by the configuration of my life it hasn't been true for me. I'm a New Englander, but with a difference.

Q. Can you speak of some of your early influences?

A. There's no doubt that my parents were enormously important. They were both extraordinary people—both very strong characters. My mother was an artist; my father, the great historian of science, George Sarton. I was an only child, and therefore I was very aware of them. They left me extremely free. I was allowed to climb trees, to

30

run away. I stayed at school from the time I got there in the morning until six at night. I got home after dark. My mother never said, "Don't do that" or "Don't do this." They encouraged anything I wanted to do which was reasonable. They let me go to Paris when I was nineteen for a year alone. Nowadays that would be nothing, but in those days people were chaperoned and it was really quite brave of them to allow me to go.

The Shady Hill School was undoubtedly a very great influence because of Agnes Hocking and the fact that poetry became the most important thing in my life before I was nine years old. By that, I don't mean writing but reciting poetry, learning poetry by heart and just loving it. My mother also read aloud to me from the time I was very small. She was English and had a beautiful voice. She read aloud very well. Things like "The Forsaken Mermaid"—"Children dear, was it yesterday?" haunt me in her voice.

Then, of course, the theatre. I joined Eva Le Gallienne's theatre as an apprentice when I was seventeen instead of going to college. After that I was thrown into too great responsibility, too young, when I had my own company. I don't think that it influenced my writing, but maybe it kept me from writing professionally too soon.

I was always writing poems. The first poems, sonnets, came out in *Poetry* magazine when I was seventeen. So there was no question that I was always going to write poems, but if I'd stayed in the theatre I probably wouldn't have written novels or memoirs. However, influence is very important. There are three kinds of talent, or genius, if you will, which people are born with: mathematical genius, musical genius, and poetic genius. If you're using form, the last is close to mathematics and to music. So influence is there; but, somehow or other, one is a poet—is born a poet.

Q. Which poets did you read when you were very young?

A. When I was very young I adored Kipling. I loved all the *Jungle Book* poems. This was when I was eight or nine years old. Once I found a five dollar bill in the snow and bought a beautiful edition of Kipling's *Collected Poems* on India paper. In high school it was H. D. and Amy Lowell, the Imagists, who were then very much *there* and who were possibly the avant-garde. Of course, at that time, Edna Millay, Elinor Wylie and Louise Bogan—whom I only came to know well as a poet much later—I admired enormously. There's no doubt that my early poems were influenced by Millay. This was not a good influence—not good because she was influenced by the Elizabethans. I remember a wise friend of mine saying, "Go back to the seventeenth-century poets, don't imitate Millay, go back to Donne." Later, I read Yeats, Herbert, Hopkins and Valéry.

Q. Did these poets influence the craft and structure of your early work? Was it a question of technique, sensibility, something else?

A. You do learn your technique by imitating, probably unconsciously. I always tell students you must read and devour what you love and build it into yourself. I don't think that one sits down and consciously imitates Millay, or whoever it may be, but you get it in your ear. Then if you're a good critic of yourself you're apt to look for another food, the opposite kind of food. For instance, at the time that I was most influenced by Millay I was also reading Walt Whitman with passionate love. So you put everything together finally into something which is yourself, which you've made out of the other people. There's no such thing as an uninfluenced poet. All poets are influenced. I've changed my style in the last twenty years because of Yeats. His influence made me tighten everything a little more and get away from the overly romantic and lush. I believe there are affinities and you go to the food that is going to nourish you. You're inevitably influenced by poets from whom you can learn something because of your particular talent and gift.

Q. Are you aware of any particular stylistic developments in your work?

A. I hope that it is less derivative than it was when I first began. I think that I have a style. Of course, I'm accused, even now, of being derivative and brushed aside as being more or less only a derivative poet. We'll let time do its work on that.

Q. Is free verse more difficult for you to write than traditional verse?

A. It is more difficult for the reason that the choices are infinite. At least with structured verse the choices are limited. In free verse the choices are so indefinite and immense that you can really go on revising almost forever. I never get the feeling that there it is like a block of stone as I do with a good poem, in form, when it's finished.

Q. Has the instruction of your immediate predecessor poets made it more difficult for you to write in free verse?

A. No, I don't think so. H. D. was one of my great influences when I was young—one of the first poets whom I really liked. There are a certain number of free verse poems all through the work, but never so many as in *A Private Mythology.*

Q. Would you discuss the working conditions necessary for your writing? Do you work best in isolation? Is music always a distraction? Do you write at a typewriter? Do you keep all drafts of poems? Are there certain hours in which you do your best work? Is it as easy for you to write in transit as it is here in York?

A. No, to begin at the end. I like to work at home; but, of course, I've done an enormous amount of work in hotels. This was especially true when I was young and lived abroad. It was inevitable, at times, that I live in furnished rooms or hotels.

I try to keep the drafts of poems. I find it difficult to do because I think that everyone wants to tear up what they're casting aside. For instance, I don't always keep all the drafts, but I think that it is a good idea to do it. Sometimes it's very interesting because you go back and see how it happened.

Generally, I get up at six—earlier in the summer—make my breakfast, go back to bed, and lie there for about an hour and think after my breakfast. That's my most creative time: before I put any-thing down, while the subconscious is still open from the night, before anything has started to interrupt—even good things. I enjoy watching the sun rise. It's very beautiful here. Then I get up and I'm usually at my desk by half past eight. I really don't work for longer than eleven or half past eleven; but I do it every day. Then I walk Tamas [the dog] and get the mail, which is a terrible onslaught and which almost always brings something that I have to answer at once. Then I have lunch and rest. At this point, I start a whole other day which involves household things, gardening and similar pursuits.

I work with records playing all the time when I'm writing. Only baroque music. I love nineteenth-century music, but I can't use it when I'm working at all. I write on the typewriter directly when I'm writing a novel, but not with a poem. A poem begins with a lot of jottings and then finally I put it on the typewriter and start revising.

Q. Is revision a desperate act or a creative act? Have you devel-oped a certain procedure for revising a poem?

A. It's a creative act. In fact, I wrote a piece called "Revision Is

Creation." I believe this. I don't think there is a procedure because every poem is different; but, on the whole, when I'm inspired—that is, when I feel that I really am a poet—lines run through my head. They're in meter. So the first thing I do is write down what has been given. Even when I've had a high fever and have been desperate, for instance, lecturing out in Idaho—as with the sonnet sequence "A Divorce of Lovers"—it just poured through me. I couldn't stop writing. It was amazing. Of course, what comes is only the notion. It sets the form. You know whether it's going to be a four-beat line or a five-beat line from what comes. Then there are the images which I jot down—everything that is flowing through me at that moment. After that I start fighting it out as to what I really mean. The subconscious brings a lot of gifts, but some of them are not usable. Some are really flotsam and jetsam. The struggle is to get down to the essential images. There are two things involved. First you have to break down the image, be sure that it's airtight and that it works on all levels. This is tough. Secondly, there's the form and the music. The good poems, my best poems, have been through as many as sixty drafts because I can go on revising when I'm really inspired. That's what I can't do when I'm not inspired. The critical self is just as alive and intense as the emotional self when you're truly inspired. So you can get things out of yourself that you really couldn't do except at white heat.

Q. Some poets speak of working on translations as a means of countering dry spells. What effective means have you found to counteract being "beached?"

A. For me, the writing of poetry depends on a Muse. So there's nothing I can do about it. Either I'm writing poems or I'm not. Fortunately, I write novels, memoirs or plays when I'm not writing poems. While I've not kept a regular journal, I've twice done it for publication: *Journal of a Solitude* and *The House by the Sea*. Some people think that *Plant Dreaming Deep* is a journal, but it isn't. It's a series of essays. So I'm lucky, I think. I mean it must be absolute— well, it was hell for me for five years not to write any poems; but I was very busy doing other things and moving into this landscape here by the sea. I kept hoping and one January I tried writing poems. At the time, I thought, well, you're sensitive, you have a lot of craft, you love nature and you must be able to write some poems. They were all what Bogan calls "imitation poems." None came in form. That's my test. These poems aren't bad and they're all coming out in magazines here and there, but they never pleased me as poems in form do.

Q. What is the greatest quality a poet can have? Is it formal technique or is it an attitude of mind and discipline?

A. The greatest quality a poet can have is to think in images, "to see the world in a grain of sand." That's the poetic thing because that applies to free verse as well. It applies to everything. If you don't have that, you're not a poet. If you think in abstractions you're a philosopher, you're not a poet. A poet always puts the abstract into the concrete almost unconsciously. That's the key. With teaching you can tell almost immediately that very few people do this: think in images. The poet does.

Q. Maxine Kumin has said that poetry is the closest thing that she has to a sense of religion. In "Because What I Want Most Is Permanence" you seem to be saying very much the same thing:

> Poetry, prayer, or call it what you choose
> That frees the complicated act of will
> And makes the whole world both intense and
>   still—
> I set my mind to artful work and craft, . . .

also—"Of Prayer":

> It is a mistake, perhaps, to believe
> That religion concerns you at all;

A. Yes. I always go back to that marvelous statement of Simone Weil's: "Absolute attention is prayer." Of course, you can't write a poem without absolute attention. Also, there's no doubt that anyone who writes poetry feels that he or she is an instrument, that her duty—her only duty is to be a good instrument for whatever flows through her. So there is a supernatural power or whatever you want to call it. I mean I'm not self-conscious about saying "God." But the subconscious, what Jung would call the "Collective Unconscious," is there in all of us. The poet has access in a way that other people do not. So he or she does have a sense of responsibility which is religious.

Q. You've said that one of the things that disturbs you about modern poetry is the self-indulgence and that some poets have only all the hell in their poetry.

A. I don't want to be shouted at in a poem; I really don't. Songs can do this. War songs. Music can do it much better—actual music, drums, trumpets, whatever you want; but I agree with Rilke that the great poem is the poem which, as he says at the end of the "Sonnet on the Archaic Torso of Apollo," "Here there is nothing that does not see you. You must change your life." That isn't going to happen with somebody screaming at you.

Q. The poems in "Landscapes and Portraits" seem to suggest Kunitz's conviction that "the supreme morality of art is to endure." Would you agree?

A. Well, this is "Landscapes and Portraits" in that very first book, *Encounter in April,* that you're speaking of, which, of course, was published in 1937—more than forty years ago. I don't really have a tremendous amount of interest in those poems any more. I can't see that it's particularly moral to endure. It *may* be the test.

Q. In *Mrs. Stevens Hears the Mermaids Singing* you mention confronting the enemy, in writing, as oneself. In *A Durable Fire* you state in "Gestalt At Sixty": "Have fought in this quiet place/ For my *self.*" How is this latter confirmation any different?

A. It's somewhat the same because the real enemy is not the critics. Mrs. Stevens is bitter, just as I am, because she's never had a real break from the critics. But she comes around to see that they aren't the enemy really. The enemy is oneself. The struggle, the authentic struggle, is with oneself, is to become what one can become. There's always a tremendous struggle involved. The self-realization of the person and the artist are very closely connected. I do think that "fought in this quiet place/ For my *self* " is a little different. You're right to suggest that it is in that it's more the acceptance, perhaps, of solitude, of making a life out of solitude. This is really what is now bringing me such a wide audience. Many people live alone. So there's a great interest in this, just as there's a great interest in dying. Solitude has some resemblance to dying.

Here I've discussed two different things really: the enemy as oneself, not what other people think of one, and then the finding of oneself in solitude, which is very frightening and certainly a challeng-

ing state to be in—to live in. Georgia O'Keeffe has said that she's
always lived on a "knife-edge." It's the conflict between art and life.
That's the "knife-edge."

Q. "I want good violence to find organic form" seems to be
poetic stance as well as verse.

A. Certainly. Absolutely. That's the whole point of the poem. It
concerns what I mean about form, which is that it's not static and
imposed from the outside as so many people believe. It is, instead,
good violence finding an organic form. A poem should be as alive as
a plant, Emerson says somewhere. I've always felt that. It has a form:
your idea and your emotion together—whatever you're trying to
say. The poem is born with its form and if form is imposed from the
outside then it's going to be a dead poem. So I want "good violence
to find organic form."

Q. Stanley Kunitz has said, "A poet needs to keep his wilderness
alive inside him. To remain a poet after forty requires an awareness of
your darkest Africa, that part of yourself that will never be tamed."
I'm reminded of your "Our wilderness gets wilder every day/ And we
intend to keep the tamed at bay."

A. Mine was a humorous poem, of course, I mean especially the
ending. I read it sometimes so as to lighten when I'm doing a
reading. I often bring it in to make people laugh at the end of some
rather intense poems. But I love what Stanley Kunitz says, I believe it,
and I think it shows in my work. It's apparent in the fact that Bogan
said a long time ago, and she was quite right, "You keep the Hell out
of your work." The reason I did that was because I believed in
sublimation. I still do. You may start a poem in anger, but it's not
going to end in anger if it's a good poem because by understanding
the anger, which you go through writing the poem, you come out
somewhere else. However, I believe she was right that sometimes this
gave the effect of something too facile. I'm beginning to learn how to
use the "Hell" also in the novels. I date the beginning of this with the
novel about the nursing home, *As We Are Now,* which on one level
describes a descent into Hell. Poems like the Kali poem or "The
Tortured" document Hell.

Q. You've said that "somewhere in his forties the poet reaches a
turning point, at which he either becomes a more public or a more
private person, that he has a choice, and on that choice depends the

kind of work he will produce, as well as the kind of life he will live."
Had you become a public poet how might your life and work have
been different?

A. Well, I think that was sort of whistling in the dark. I really went
to Nelson [New Hampshire] out of despair. At that point, I had
published ten or twelve books. I felt devastated by the lack of
recognition. I decided to go there and bury myself and work. I felt
that eventually *they* would come to *me,* which is what has happened,
thanks to God and a lot of hard work. So perhaps I didn't have a
choice. But one of the choices that I made consciously was not to
review. You see, at that time, I had suffered so much from reviewers
and critics, and I saw what terrible power they had. I decided that I
did not want that kind of power—for me it would have been too
costly. I also saw that if you review people well then they review you
well and it's a whole "patting on the back" thing. It made me sick.
It was out of rejection of the whole establishment and everything that
it represented that I went away. I reviewed for the [New York] *Times*
for awhile, but only books outside my field. I reviewed nature books
and biography, but never novels or poems. Then I decided not to do
that any more.

Q. A terrible power.

A. I saw it with Bogan at the *New Yorker.* She never reviewed
Muriel Rukeyser in twenty-five years. Now that's not fair.

Q. Was it because of the political impetus of Rukeyser's work?

A. She just didn't like Rukeyser's poems. Nobody should be in
that position of power that long. Every critic has biases just as every
poet has.

Q. Is there any one person who has given you advice that has
helped you to balance your life with your art?

A. Many people. Probably S. S. Koteliansky ["Kot"] more than
anyone else. Certainly all the people whom I knew . . . Elizabeth
Bowen . . . were a tremendous help. I've been very influenced by my
friends. I mean they taught me everything, you know. I never went
to college. I've learned everything through friends.

Q. What is the greatest risk in writing?

A. The greatest risk is, of course, giving yourself away; but this is
also true in prose. It's true for any serious writer that this is a terrible
risk. For me the risk was coming out as a homosexual, which I did in

Mrs. Stevens. It's there in the poetry once you know that, I mean the love poems are poems to women, but I believed at the beginning that poetry deals in essences not in sexes. Therefore, in "The Divorce of Lovers" I made the woman into a man. The lover has no sex. Louise Bogan, rightly I think, said that's wrong, you should have made the lover a woman. But I hadn't come out then and I really didn't want to. I came out long before most people did and it cost me jobs; but I was very relieved when I had done it. I think the work has gotten steadily better as a result, although the lesbian theme doesn't necessarily come into the books. It's there somewhat, but I haven't written a lesbian novel—nor shall I.

Q. Your journals and other personal statements suggest that for you poetry does not grow out of equilibrium but conflict and change. Would you agree?

A. Yes, that's true. It can come out of joy, of course, but certainly not out of equilibrium, no. Frost's wonderful statement that "a poem is a temporary stay against confusion," which has so often been quoted, I think is a marvelous statement. That is, for a time everything is solved by the writing of the poem, but only for a time.

Q. Are you presently working on a journal?

A. When I'm seventy, I'd be interested in doing a journal again about being seventy, about the change from sixty-five to seventy, because that's a big change. At sixty-five one still feels quite young. I mean the physical decay has not begun to the same extent as at seventy. So I think I'll have things to say that I'd like to say in a journal then. Not before. What I want to do, if I can possibly afford it financially, is to take a year off. You see, a book a year is a killing thing. This is what I've been doing for ten years. Either poems or prose, novels. The pace is a rape of the psyche.

Q. "My Sisters, O My Sisters" seems to echo Mrs. Stevens' statement concerning "psychic cost"—that women write at the *expense* of themselves. What do you see as the differing problems facing male and female poets? Is a dedication to art always an abdication of life? Could you explain the term "strange monsters"?

A. "Monster" was originally used in a letter to me by Ruth Pitter, who said: "We are all strange monsters." If you'd read it twice you might have got that the poem says women poets abdicate from life "or like George Sand suffer from the mortality in immortal hand."

The poem goes on, however, to say we, "who are writing women and strange monsters," are hoping to find a more subtle and warmer way of handling this. So the poem shifts in the middle to a totally different perspective which is finally to speak of "that great sun, the feminine power." It's interesting that the sun and the moon are different in Japanese and in German. The sun is feminine in Japanese and German and the moon is masculine. So I really reverse the whole thing at the end—women no longer have to be monsters. They can be warm human beings and still be great writers. There are a few now. I also think of the French "monstre sacré" which is used about great artists, genius, almost always. A "monstre sacré"—a sacred monster. You might think of Piaf, who was a "monstre sacré" in an entirely different world from that of poetry. Bernhardt was a "monstre sacré." You get it sometimes in poets. You might say this of Victor Hugo.

I think that it's much harder to be a woman poet—infinitely harder—for a great many reasons. One reason is that there is a real conflict between life and art which is much more intense for a woman because a man can marry and have children and he'll be a better poet for it. (I think of Dick Wilbur, for instance. He's a beautiful poet, has a beautiful wife, and children. Far from detracting from his work, Charlie [his wife] has been everything to him—has warmed everything, and made everything possible.) A woman who does this, however, is giving enormous amounts of energy, especially when the children are small, to family and housekeeping. I see it and speak about it: the terrible fatigue of my students who are now mothers and want to write. There are several very, very good ones who I'm sure are going to make it. But meanwhile what I see is the agonizing fatigue—the fact that they're always tired. So it's much harder. I don't think it's impossible. On the other side of this, which is what I always tell people too, is that, of course, the women who have had children and been married can say certain things which I, unmarried and without children, cannot say. There's a whole lot of experience which has still to be written about, which is only beginning to be written about. It's an exciting time because these things are possible; but the price is very, very high for a woman writer.

It's still a male-dominated literary world. The critics are on the whole anti-women poets, even the female critics. I mean there's tremendous savagery, it seems to me, in the way women critics treat women poets. Women poets are disliked. There's a certain jealousy of the essential creative power of the woman in being the person who actually carries the child, makes the child out of her flesh, if you will. Men have reason to be jealous of this. I think that it's far greater jealousy than penis envy ever was in women.

Q. Did you ever think of yourself writing in a feminist vein prior to the "Feminist Movement"?

A. "My Sisters, O My Sisters" was a beginning in coming to terms with what it is to be a woman. "She Shall Be Called Woman," which I wrote when I was nineteen, is really a feminist poem or at least it has to do with this whole feeling of not rejecting one's body, including menstruation. The latter is now being talked about a great deal, but nobody mentioned it in a poem then. That was an original poem. I wouldn't write it exactly like that now, but at least I was trying to deal with something. It wasn't consciously "feminist" because in a psychic, not physical, sense I'm afraid I thought of myself as a man. I felt it was the masculine part of me which was the creative part.

Q. Is the Muse androgynous?

A. For me it's feminine. I think the Muse is always feminine. What do women do who are in love with men?—I don't know.

Q. Why is the phoenix such a powerful symbol for you and does it symbolize the rift between life and art? Or is it a paradox?

A. I don't know that it's either. The phoenix symbolizes exactly what it does in the myth; that is, the act of rebirth, the power to be reborn. It is important to me because I have been reborn so many times out of so many disastrous experiences in my life, beginning with the failure of my theatre company. I've had disastrous love affairs and a very great struggle to get my work through. I have had to be reborn many times. Everyone does. Everyone who's alive and sensitive experiences tragedy here and there in a lifetime.

Q. What for you has been a memorable moment as a poet?

A. I think the most memorable moment was when I started writing poems again in a great flood after five years of silence. The Muse was there and it was just like being reborn. It's the phoenix again and it's unbelievable and marvelous. There we are!

A Further Interview
with May Sarton
Karla Hammond/1977

From *May Sarton: Woman and Poet*, ed. Constance Hunting
(Orono, Maine: National Poetry Foundation, 1982), 239–48.
Karla Hammond's interview first appeared in *The Puckerbrush
Review* 2.1 (Spring 1979). It has also appeared as "May
Sarton" in *American Poetry Observed: Poets on their Work*, ed.
Joe David Bellamy (U Illinois P, 1984), 198–206. Karla Ham-
mond conducted the interview at Sarton's home, "Wild Knoll,"
19 November 1977. Reprinted by permission of Constance
Hunting and the National Poetry Foundation.

Q. Maxine Kumin says that she wrote as a child to work out unhappiness and feelings of isolation and solitude. She says that she felt this
was true for most writers and offered the cliché that "behind every
writer stands an unhappy childhood." Would you agree? Has this
been your experience? In some way is this what you meant in saying
that "one of the springs in poetry is our strained relationship with our
own immediate past"?

A. I think the answer is no. In the first place I had a generally
happy childhood although I was an only child and although we were
refugees. It's true that my first four years were extremely disturbed.
But once we had come to America, I had such a marvelous school I
was in love with it. From the time I was six or seven I was in an ideal
school for somebody who was going to be a poet because the
founder of it, Agnes Hocking, was a marvelous teacher of poetry. I
tell all about that in *I Knew a Phoenix*, of course, in the chapters on
Shady Hill School.

What I meant about "the strained relationship with our own
immediate past" was more in terms of love affairs—the immediate
adult past, not childhood. Poetry springs, in my case, often from
conflict. The poem is a finding of peace by finding the truth through
writing the poem. Of course, no childhood is completely happy.
Childhood has everything in it. It's full of poignant experiences and

42

angers, and mine was like everyone else's. I would not say that it was an unhappy childhood.

Q. Do you believe that a sensibility for language is prehensile?

A. Do you mean that it's something that's in your hands?

Q. Yes.

A. I would think that any poet is prehensile in a general sense, is tremendously aware.

Q. Does the first draft of a poem generally offer the promise of several poems in it?

A. Once in a while, but I wouldn't say that that was usual with mine.

Q. Do you ever find that you have the beginning and the end of a poem but that the middle won't come?

A. No.

Q. Is titling difficult for you?

A. Sometimes, but not often. Often my titles come from the poem, as "In Time Like Air," for instance, which comes from the line "In time like air is essence stated." That was also the title of the book.

Q. Do poems come more readily to you now than when you first began writing?

A. No, because for me it's completely a matter of inspiration. When I'm inspired it's easy. When I'm not, it's impossible. And that has always been true.

Q. You've mentioned that "the tension between past and present" is one that you experience during the writing of a poem. Is retrospection and distance necessary before a poem can be written?

A. No, I don't think so. Everything is so highly charged when you're really inspired that the distance is forced by the kind of objectivity at white heat which goes into writing the poem. I always have to write the real poems almost at once. Oh, very occasionally it's been possible for me to work from recollection. There's a poem about the tremendous effect that Piero della Francesca's frescos at Arezzo had on me. His painting really made me re-think everything about art, and it has affected my prose style in terms of economy and space. I was finally able to speak of this influence in my Christmas poem entitled "Nativity" which is not for the frescos, but for the painting in the National Gallery—"The Nativity of Christ." It's a philosophical poem using that image, and so there was more space and time between the beginning and the end.

Q. Stanley Kunitz says: "A poet's beginnings are largely a generational phenomenon, a combination of accidents and influences, on which he builds. Maybe at a certain point he would prefer a fresh start, but the difficulty is that he has already established the condition of his art. Poets are always wanting to change their lives and their styles. Of the two, it's easier to change the life. Perhaps the style will follow. If poets lived long enough, they would become their opposites. No single kind of poetry is sufficient for a millennium." Would you agree?

A. Absolutely. That's beautifully stated. I think immediately of Conrad Aiken who was somehow caught in a style and good and marvelous a poet as he was he repeated himself endlessly. He was always trying new marriages, new whatever. He never extricated himself from this. Yeats is, of course, the obvious example of a man who changed his style in an amazing, vigorous way. I've changed my style in the last twenty years because of Yeats.

Q. Lowell seems similar to me in that respect.

A. I'm not sure. Because the curious thing about Lowell is that he began . . . it's a fascinating subject . . . with the very difficult baroque poems. He made his name with those poems. Lately the poetry has been almost obviously sentimental, almost too clear for me. The sonnets to Elizabeth Hardwick, for example. Well, he's dead now. God rest his soul.

Q. Is poetry the re-invention of our lives?

A. I would say "no," although I think we make myths of our lives. I would call it the invention of lives but not re-invention. I don't quite get *re-invention.*

Q. Well, re-birth?

A. Yes.

Q. Re-creation?

A. Yes. I suppose it is.

Q. In *Lovers & Tyrants,* Francine de Plessix Gray states: "Art is both a vengeance against reality and a reconciliation with it." Would you agree?

A. One doesn't have to take *vengeance against* reality. One has to accept it. Of course, she speaks of that reconciliation, but I don't feel that I have ever twisted reality in order to take it out on reality. Nor have I said this is the way it was, but dammit, this is the way it ought to have been. I don't think that I've ever done that. Perhaps some writers do.

Q. Vengeance and reconciliation don't even seem like opposites.

A. I don't think that they are. We ought to find a better word.

Q. Do you believe that historical consciousness can demean, freeze, or force the poet's art into a position of subservience? How can a poet protect against that?

A. I don't quite understand the question. It's a very interesting question, but I'm not quite sure what you mean. That is, do you mean imitating poets of the past, not being able to break from a form of the past?

Q. A structure or a form . . .

A. I don't think so, because all the time the poet is bringing his blood into a thing. It's never an exact imitation if he's a good poet because he's always changing it a little. Even if you set out to imitate Herbert, it's not the same thing. I use some of Herbert's form, particularly in a poem after my mother's death called "After Four Years." I was reading Herbert a lot at that time, but the tone is absolutely different from his.

Q. Stanley Kunitz has said concerning history and our conscious- ness of it: "We must be terrified by history if we are to write, if we are to be effective human beings. Yet at the same time, we can't be consumed by that terror."

A. You seek your affinities, and your affinities may be in periods of history as well as in specific poets, but you can't force an affinity where it isn't there. It was fashionable under Eliot's tutelage to dislike Milton and to like the Metaphysical Poets and I did not like Milton. I used to fight with Basil de Selincourt about this. But if Milton was your man, you know, it would have been dreadful just because it was fashionable not to like him. You've got to go where your heart is—where your nature is!

Q. Do you feel that you're still influenced by other poets, or do you feel that in having developed your own "voice" these influences are assimilated and unconscious?

A. They're assimilated and unconscious now, although I can imagine discovering a new poet, particularly in another language like

French, who might make me renew my style; but this hasn't happened.

Q. Have you ever felt any affinity between your work and Louise Bogan's, Kay Boyle's, Constance Carrier's, Ann Stanford's, Josephine Jacobsen's, Muriel Rukeyser's, Vassar Miller's, Marianne Moore's?

A. I haven't felt any affinity with any of these people except possibly Louise Bogan for the simple fact that she is a lyric poet, which is rather rare, and so am I. I admire Ann Stanford tremendously, and I admire Josephine Jacobsen. I love Marianne Moore, and I was a dear friend of Muriel Rukeyser's. I had great admiration for her and her powers of growth. Terrific woman.

Q. Would you agree with Marianne Moore that a writer is not fair with himself if he isn't hard on himself?

A. Absolutely. In much of feminist poetry today there is not enough self-criticism—I feel. People are much too pleased with what I would call half-finished work—full of talent, full of energy and everything else, but somehow it has stopped too soon. These poets think that the poem is finished when from my point of view it's only just begun. When you get down that strong feeling, that's just the beginning.

Q. There's one group that feels that any revision runs counter to the spontaneity and intent of the poem.

A. They think that's being spontaneous; but all art must *look* spontaneous. The trapeze artist must *look* as if it were the easiest thing in the world to fly through the air, but it's actually hours of work that brings this about. In sports, people recognize this. You couldn't play a good game of tennis if you just went running around batting the ball without any technique.

Q. In an interview by George Starbuck with Elizabeth Bishop (for *Ploughshares*, Vol. 3, No. 3&4, 1977), she said, "Sometimes I think if I had been born a man I probably would have written more. Dared more, or been able to spend more time at it. I've wasted a great deal of time." Do you share her sentiments?

A. That amazes me. I wouldn't say so for myself. Absolutely not. I'm very surprised, because she's a masculine poet in the sense that she's so objective. This is why she has appealed so greatly to the critics. She's a very good poet, but she's not disturbing and neither was Marianne Moore. I adored Marianne Moore, and I love her poetry, but the point is that it's never sexual, it's never disturbing, it's never the female speaking. So it's very acceptable.

Q. You speak of "becoming an instrument" when you write a poem. Do you equate "instrument" with "medium"?

A. All you can do is try to be a good instrument. That's my attitude. Give yourself space enough. This is the biggest problem. It isn't the writing time, but the space around the writing time that matters. I only work three hours, but I'm thinking subconsciously all day long about what I'm doing.

Discipline is necessary to make that space because everything in life conspires against it. Everything. For instance, I will not invite people here except one at a time. If it's a married couple, sometimes I'll invite two people; but I don't "entertain." It's too great a waste of time and energy. That's cost me a great deal because people don't invite you if you don't invite them. In other words, I have no social life in the ordinary sense. While I don't regret it, once in a while I'd like an invitation to a cocktail party and not have to return it!

Q. Has teaching influenced your writing? When did you leave teaching?

A. I left it because I'd never wanted to do it. I only did it when I had to for money. I love teaching, but it takes exactly out of you what writing does. So I taught three years at Harvard, three years at Wellesley, one summer at Carbondale—long ago before Southern Illinois University became as good as it is now—one semester at Lindenwood in Missouri, and in the Radcliffe Seminars for two years. I found teaching to be very rewarding. It helped in my work in that when I taught in Carbondale I decided to teach a course on the roots of modern poetry—Yeats, Hopkins and Eliot. I had never liked Eliot. I had simply never gotten inside the poems. I felt that even *Murder in the Cathedral* was almost unendurably depressing—no catharsis. Then by having to teach him, of course, I had to study him. Teaching helps clarify your ideas. There's no doubt that it does. It's a great discipline in itself. I left teaching when I was fifty-five.

Q. Has James Stephens' advice (as expressed in "A Letter to James Stephens"), been, in part, the discipline of your art?

A. No, because I think that I'm right in what I say in that poem, and he is *not* right. That is, I think that the deeper you go into the personal—the deeper you go—the more you hit the universal. I can't quote my own poems, but I say, in that poem, that if you write for one person and one person alone you really are talking to a multitude. Stephens was a beautiful lyric poet. I love his work at its best. In the end, I think that it became too pruned and too soft. Something went out of it. But I would stand by what I said then. I have the proof of it in that whenever I've written a poem which has seemed to me extremely strange—that nobody else would ever understand, that came from very deep in my own experience, these are the poems that bring people to me to ask, "How did you know?" One is the "Muse as Medusa," another is "The Phoenix." But you've got to go deep enough—way beyond self-pity and anguish. I feel that so much now is written out of self-indulgence. You may begin in agony, but you don't end in agony with a good poem because somehow the making of the poem is the solving. I'm very tired of primal screams in poetry.

Q. "Poets and the Rain" seems to be a statement of poetic balances: the delicate yet rigid balance between music and speech, incantation and evocation.

A. You mean the poem itself in the way it's written does this or by what it says?

Q. By what it says.

A. The poets in the "Poets and the Rain" are Rukeyser, Pitter and Yeats. Those three. It's really simply thinking over what they were, what they said to me and then feeling that now I've got to speak for myself. It's that. I don't know. I'd have to re-read it.

Q. Have you found any resolution to the question you pose in "Somersault"?

A. No. This is something one remakes over and over again—the perfect balance between grief and joy, and between the ecstasy of the moment and the burdens that we all carry which no one else ever knows. That's the image, I think, the best in the poem: that everybody is carrying these invisible burdens and that we have to balance them somehow. I don't think one ever finds that balance permanently, but it is found now and then. I've probably found it more now than I had when I wrote the poem.

Q. "O Saisons! O Chateaux!" expresses a theme central to your poetry on the whole: "We only keep what we lose." Would you elaborate on this?

A. You know, one doesn't really see one's work . . . I've written so much and over such a long period of years. I don't really look back very much except to read aloud to audiences. I don't go back and see what the themes were because that's the critic's work and not the poet's. So I would not have seen this—"We only keep what we lose"—although in a way I've always believed it and experienced it.

Q. I was just trying to think of an analogy to that. A very simple one would be "We lose ourselves to find ourselves."

A. There is something to that. The reason "We only keep what we lose," in that poem, is that the image is arrested, as in a snapshot. It's one of the things that I had in the back of my mind in the poem although I don't think that I ever used it. . . . Yes. I did. There was something about a woman on a balcony saying farewell. This was in Paris. I was thinking of a whole series of poems of Rilke's about windows and balconies and I think I say it in the poem: that the balcony or the window frames the moment when you leave, when you say good-bye. Something is arrested there forever. Whereas, if you, say, go on living with one person, life is changing that moment all the time so you don't get the sense of capturing it in the same way.

Q. Do you think that a poet ceases to *own* a poem once it is written? Is it a question of dispossession?

A. I think that's a very interesting question, but what do you mean? Do you mean that it should be free, that anybody should be able to use it?

Q. Once a poem is written, it is paradoxically the sadness and joy of the poem that it can no longer be owned. A painting you no longer own once the canvas is exhibited and sold; but a poem is ambiguous in the sense that certainly you have a piece of paper that it's written on, but the words or the speech or the import of it goes out and is no longer your own.

A. I don't know. I feel that a poem only begins to exist when somebody else has read it.

Q. Then it's communication?

A. Yes, in a way. So many people in our age have been in solitary confinement for months and even years. One of my friends, Herman

Field, was in a cellar in Warsaw for five years with only one other
person for some of the time. Imagine that! I know, had that happened to me, I would have gone on writing poems even if I thought
no one would ever see them; but I would not have written novels.
There is a difference. So I suppose you might say that it is communication first with *oneself*.

   Q. Is there a favorite poem?

   A. No, probably always the last one is. Then six months later you
see all its faults.

   Q. Are the journals sources of inspiration for the poetry, and vice
versa ("Plant Dreaming Deep" derived from the title for *Plant
Dreaming Deep*)?

   A. It's true that the title of *Plant Dreaming Deep* came from a
poem, but it's very different for me. I can't remember an instance
where I've turned a journal entry into a poem. Now I may be wrong
on this, but my notes for poems are very brief, you see, and they're
not like journal entries which are written out.

   Q. Do you ever conceive of an audience when you write? If so,
do you conceive of the audience for your poetry being different from
the audience for your prose?

   A. No. They're the same. I've always believed that the final
judgment would be made on my work as a whole. The poems, the
novels and the journals all are attempting to communicate a vision of
life. I never think of the audience while I'm writing; but, of course,
I'm glad when they're there afterwards. I really write for myself and
then it's wonderful if somebody's looking over my shoulder. I write
for myself and one other person, perhaps.

   Q. Do you think the reviewer's primary concern should be
whether the poet is reporting or inventing?

   A. The reviewer's primary concern should be whether the work is
good or not. Very good reporting poetry and very good inventing
poetry have been written; but they're perhaps different kinds.

   Q. Readers of prose look for morals. Do readers of poetry?

   A. As far as I know, readers of prose or poetry don't look for
morals. They look for enjoyment. Although there are all kinds of
enjoyment. There's the enjoyment of the "whodunit" which is
different from the enjoyment of Virginia Woolf's *The Waves*. People

really look for pleasure. That's the first thing they should get out of a work of art, and then everything else.

Q. What texts do you feel are constructive for a beginning poet?

A. There's a book by Jean Burden called *Journey Toward Poetry* which I have often sent off to people who send me poems. This is very helpful, but I would say that the best text is other poets. It's important to read not the poets who are fashionable, but the poets with whom you feel an affinity. The only thing a young poet has to concern herself with is finding out what she really sees and what she really feels and this is much harder than it sounds.

Q. Do you have any regrets in having left New Hampshire?

A. Yes, naturally I do. I invested an enormous amount emotionally and otherwise in Nelson. I'll never own another house and land. This was something that made me American—owning that thirty-six acres. I'll be buried in the Nelson Cemetery. My grave is already there. I miss the village. I've gone deeper into solitude here in Maine, which is not what I expected, frankly, but it's very good. The whole change to the sea . . . you see, the sea goes way back into my childhood. My passion for the sea. I looked first for the sea when I was looking for a house after my father died. . . . It's been a big life change, coming to live in Maine. I'm glad that I made it, but it was difficult.

Q. In looking for the sea, did you ever consider living abroad?

A. No. After I bought the house in Nelson, I felt that I really had become an American, and there was no longer that split. I go to Europe much less often because most of my friends, who were older than I am, are dead. It's going back to a lot of ghosts now when I go back.

I Live Alone in a Very Beautiful Place: An Interview with May Sarton

Robin Kaplan and Shelley Neiderbach/1977

From *May Sarton: Woman and Poet,* ed. Constance Hunting (Orono, Maine: National Poetry Foundation, 1982) 249–60. Robin Kaplan and Shelley Neiderbach's interview first appeared in *Motheroot Journal,* 1.4 (Fall/Winter 1979) 1, 10–11. Reprinted by permission of Constance Hunting and the National Poetry Foundation.

Q. In *A World of Light,* you state that one grows and changes, at least in part through the influence of friends. Among others, you singled out your father, George Sarton. How did he and other people in your life help you to develop as a writer, as a woman?

A. Enormously, I am what I am because of my parents. I learned from my father a discipline, worship of work, the fact that his work was his joy.

Q. He was an historian of science.

A. Yes, he really invented the discipline. He was a fiery scholar of enormous magnitude. Wherever I went in the world I felt that I was the ambassador of a great power, George Sarton—all through the Near East, Greece, Turkey, Japan. My father was very much not a father, not human, not a husband, but a child, a brilliant child.

Q. How would you characterize your parents' relationship?

A. My father was rather a childlike, very selfish man, whom, as I matured, I came to understand and love. But I took my mother's side, you see, against my father. My mother was a very remarkable woman who had been transplanted twice, which I think is very difficult. First, from England to Belgium, and then from Belgium to America. Never made the passionate friendships that she had in Europe after we came here. I was thinking about them when I woke up this morning. They were absolutely unsocial. I've never had

52

dinner parties because this is something that was not in the family tradition, but I was thinking of them sitting in the afternoon. My father came home from work usually with a huge briefcase full of books for mother, on Chinese Art. He would carry very heavy things—that's often one thing he did for her. He would walk with this huge briefcase with books from the library, and then they would sit in the garden having tea with the cat on my mother's lap. They would talk about the things that mattered to them, which were art and politics. They were both quite radical and really nourished each other in this way. He couldn't be tender and he couldn't be . . . he wasn't a good lover, shall we say, but he was a wonderful companion and they shared an awful lot.

Q. They were more intellectual companions . . .?

A. Yes, they were intellectual companions. Oh yes, my mother read a great deal, and she was a very extraordinary woman, but she was very human, the opposite of my father; a person to whom people turned with their problems, greatly loved as a human being, very mature, or she couldn't have handled . . . I mean she was a very deprived woman.

Q. How do you characterize her influence on you?

A. Well, I have a tremendous sense of responsibility towards people. For example, I answer every letter, and lives just pour into mine. I write about fifty letters a week, which is just charity, nothing else.

Q. Have you ever been mentor to another person? Have you felt *your* influence on others?

A. I guess so, in a mild sort of way. I think that I have believed as a teacher that you could always influence. I have not had great respect for teachers who had followings of adorers, you know what I mean, crushers, really, and I think that if you are wise, and if you know yourself, this can be turned into a good relationship which is not this adoring thing. What I love are the letters that say, "You've helped me to be myself," and the letters that say, "You've made me glad to be a woman," or, "Your book came at a time when I needed it desperately." These letters are really what keep me going. They're better than a good review.

Q. Do you think there's such a thing as a male literary establishment that controls which people get published and reviewed?

A. I think influence, unfortunately, matters, and one of my problems has been that I'm not good at buttering up the right people.

Q. Do you think that the resurgence of the Women's Movement has helped?

A. Enormously. There's absolutely no doubt about it. It's the Women's Studies people, in particular. Women are interested in women's work, so there is somebody backing you. It used to be that women were rather jealous of you. Louise Bogan practically didn't review me in the New Yorker, and it was very hurting, of course. You never mention this, it's a taboo subject, you never say to a critic, "Why don't you review me?" Oh yes, the whole idea of a Sisterhood, the idea of women helping each other, rather than one woman dominating another. The Vita Sackville-West relationship is a typical example of what I mean by the old-fashioned thing. It was a conquest. She was the man and even dressed as a man and pretended to be a man when they ran away, and danced in nightclubs where nobody knew Vita was not a man. Well, this has a certain childish charm, but it's not grown up. Now, it's different with a woman. I think that for a woman it's a mystical union, in a curious way. This, I think, has been under-emphasized.

Q. Do you think that there have been lesbian relationships well portrayed in fiction?

A. No. Very few, because the great books—Nightwood, for instance—make it into a horror. The Well of Loneliness is just a sentimental mush. I mean, it's a terrible book, I think, because we go back to that period when women wanted to be men. I think one of the big advances that has been made is that women now are glad to be women. You don't have to dress in a tuxedo and cut your hair short and be called Julian. That was role playing. Acting out.

Q. If you could write the ideal lesbian novel, what would it look like?

A. I think it would be hard to do, but I think tenderness and imagination would be far more important than sex. It seems to me that what women have to give each other is this ability to encompass the whole person, which is very rare with a man because we're very different. This is also the danger—women eat each other up. It's why I think lesbian relationships often don't last, and if they do last, it's often because they become more and more alike, like dogs, two

Scotties. I think it's not a life-giving situation except when you get a
rare combination like that famous couple in Wales, you know,
back in the 17th century, the Llangollen Ladies.
   Q. Georg Groddeck, a peer of Freud, said he felt that the essence
of homosexuality was narcissism. Do you agree with that?
   A. I think it's the danger, and I think that you see it in men
perhaps even more than in women. For this reason, physical beauty
for men is much more important—and very often in the homosexual
relationship, it's an older man with a young man who is beautiful,
and I think very rarely do you see this in women's relationships. I
don't think that women are primarily looking for physical beauty,
they're looking for understanding, and for emotions. I don't mean
that physical beauty is unimportant, but it doesn't have the primacy.
   Q. It seems that to write a good lesbian novel, one would have
had to have certain experiences, and be therefore somewhat older to
prepare for the writing by having lived it.
   A. And maybe gotten to the end of an affair as well as the
beginning of one. But I think the worst thing that's happening is the
fashion for lesbianism, that it's the "in" thing, and so, let's try it. And
this I think is dangerous, just because I think any sexual act boomer-
angs, if it doesn't come from feelings.
   Q. It seems to be a kind of contradictory problem, to start to write
when young and then discover, perhaps, one's sexual proclivities.
   A. Well, you see, anybody who's going to be that has probably
been attracted to women, and probably older women, from very
early, such as having crushes on teachers. I think that this is in the
real homosexual, you know, very early. I had marvelous crushes on
people when I was twelve. I was writing poems to people older
than I; I wasn't trying to go to bed with them—I was incredibly
innocent, I must admit. Now it would be impossible to be as innocent
as I was.
   Q. How do you account for the difference between female homosexual relationships and male homosexual relationships?
   A. It's partly sexual. It's inconceivable that a woman would pick
up another woman in a john and have intercourse. This happens
every day with men in New York. I'm not blaming men, or saying
that this is bad, it's simply that their sexual organs are outside the
body, which means that they're not taking somebody in, in a sense. I

think that it is very different. I don't think that the woman homosexual is at all like the man.

Q. Sex has come up several times in this interview. How do you see it as a force, and how do you consider it as part of your writing? How do you get it into the statement of the human condition, in poetry or fiction?

A. Well, everything is sexual in one sense or another. Only most of it is sublimated, if you are a writer. And it's been the fear, the emphasis that sexual fulfillment has to do with sexual intercourse, that's quite wrong, of course. If you love somebody deeply, this is part of the relationship, hopefully. We always hope it is. It doesn't always happen. If it doesn't happen, I don't think it's fatal, necessarily. And I think it's just that sex as a thing in itself is what disturbs me. For me, a woman, I think it is always related to love. And if you divorce sex from love, then to get any kick, it's got to be more and more manipulative, it's got to be different positions, and let's try this and drugs, or whatever, to get any kick. There's no kick without love.

Q. How can you relate this to a Muse?

A. Certainly, to some extent, there's sex involved in it, there's no doubt about it. I relate this to Robert Graves' *The White Goddess,* and *Mrs. Stevens Hears the Mermaids Singing.* I keep quoting parts of that poem, "Sister of mirage" is one of the phrases, I can't remember them all, but it's the last line, "Her nakedly worn magnificence." It's terribly hard to talk about because it's very mysterious. *Mrs. Stevens* has been rediscovered, of late.

Q. That book seems to be a statement about the woman artist. How much does that statement represent your own feelings and attitudes?

A. Somewhat it's a persona and somewhat it's my own feelings. But don't forget that my own feelings also change. We've all learned through the Women's Movement, and *Mrs. Stevens* is an example. She was portrayed as fifteen years older than I, when I wrote the book. I did this deliberately, because I thought it would be easier to handle looking back. She isn't altogether me—the parents are not my parents. There are a lot of things that are not me: I never married. It's a work of fiction, but in her essential vision of the woman poet, I think—I do believe in the necessity of a Muse, the fact that for me the Muse is feminine. This is completely in the spirit, because I have loved men, but I never wrote poems for them, I don't know why this is . . . you just don't will the poems. You don't say, "Darling Johnny is such a dear, I'll write a poem for him." The lines run through you and they only do that for me with a woman or for a woman, although they were often not lovers. That comes out also, I think, in *Mrs. Stevens,* in the case of Willa.

Q. In which form do you prefer writing, poetry or prose?

A. I'm glad you asked about it, because I feel very much closer to poetry. You see, form is organic and the fashion now is a spontaneous bubbling over of whatever runs through your head. Not changing, I think, leaves out one of the biggest weapons you have as a poet, which is music. I think that poetry is somewhere between music and speech in a highly mysterious region, in which sound is of great importance, and sound is being left out. Sound has also to do with meter and it's strange, because this is not the artificial, the French garden, it's exactly the opposite. Poetry began with dancing, in the subconscious with the beat. It's what gets people below the conscious level, and I cannot write in form unless I'm inspired. Far from being conscious and willed, form is what is given me when I'm inspired.

Q. So that the rhythm patterns and the rhyme patterns come out of the work themselves?

A. Lines run through my mind. The "Divorce of Lovers" sequence is a good example of this. I was on a lecture tour in the Northwest and I had the flu. I was really ill, and the effort was tremendous—it's really a little bit like being a singer. I was exhausted and I would get back to the motel with a temperature of 101 degrees and I would go to bed and then lines would come, and I would have to get up and write them down. And that's what I mean by being inspired. Of course, it had been a terribly painful love affair, but it lasted five years. This was the end and it was at the end that all this began to happen.

Q. Do you read other poets?

A. Yes.

Q. To kind of get you started?

A. Yes, I do.

Q. Do you use other poets as mentors?

A. Yes, I have, very much so. George Herbert, especially. The poem to my mother is written in a Herbert form. I never read it because it makes me cry. Yeats was the greatest influence. Valéry and Yeats, I would say, if I could name two. When I was seventeen, Millay, Elinor Wylie, Louise Bogan.

Q. Women poets?

A. Yes—women poets.

Q. You make a distinction. For all their accomplishments, they haven't the stature of Yeats and Valéry—

A. They don't—

Q. —in the world.

A. Somebody said a very valuable thing to me, an Italian friend of mine, a man. He said, "Don't imitate Millay—go back to the 17th century poets whom *she* was imitating. Go back to the source." In the first book, *Encounter in April,* which is out of print, there are a lot of sonnets and there's the influence. That is why I didn't put them in the *Collected Poems.* The influence is very clear. I think you build your style out of a lot of styles. I think you must admire and wish to emulate, and it's one of the ways you learn. You sort of eat up the poet. Gerard Manley Hopkins—I remember when I discovered him and read everything, everything. Then Yeats, more than anyone else, and I think because he was a political poet who succeeded, as well as being a very romantic poet. He disciplined his style; his whole style changed as he grew older, in middle age when everything really happens. Political poetry is considered a bad idea, but there is always some in every book of mine, because I think that you have to be part of your world. And write from where you are, and how can one not write a poem about the camps in Germany? "The Invocation to Kali" is being anthologized, so I've gotten through with one political poem. By political poem I mean something that doesn't come out of one's personal experience. And, of course, this is why it's hard to do, because it can be rhetorical, in a bad sense.

Q. Dated, rather than universal?

A. I don't know that it dates, if it's a good poem.

Q. Do you think that there's anything that's not material for poetry?

A. No!

Q. Seize it all!

A. Yes. I really think so.

Q. When did you write your first poem that you considered a poem?

A. When I was about nine. No, younger than that. It was about a pigeon. And I was very proud of it, it rhymed. But I was really writing poetry seriously from about the time I was thirteen. My first poems were accepted by *Poetry* magazine when I was seventeen. Five sonnets, and I was then at Eva Le Gallienne's as an apprentice. It was a wonderful training for a poet, because I learned to recite, to read, and to project.

Q. Is it the same Muse that keeps coming back?

A. No, it's always a different person. It's what Stendhal talks about as the crystallization around a person. For me, what it does is simply to focus the world. One person focuses the world and this person may be a lover, may be a distant person. I'll give you an extreme case. There was a person who became my Muse, who was the president of the college where I was teaching, whom I saw alone only once for twenty minutes in a large faculty dining room with a lot of other people around. I wrote a whole book (it hasn't been published) which was really a sort of argument to humanize this very scared woman. I mean, scared of anything *personal,* a workaholic. You see how far it can go—that you don't even see the person, but yet that's what I mean by mysterious. Or it can be a lover, which it has been and certainly that shows in "A Divorce of Lovers." Yes, I think that poetry is more important to anyone who is a poet at all, because it is given and not made on will, and so that makes it very precious to you, the one who is writing those poems. I always feel that a poem is a gift to me and hopefully might be a gift from me, eventually. But it is first a gift to me and this is not true of a novel. A novel is very hard work. In the design of a novel there is a moment when you see it, what it might be whole, and then comes the enormous labor of writing it, in which that original vision changes and you never really get it back. It's that—it's just the agony, very hard work.

Q. Is it as hard for you to write the non-fiction portraits?

A. Hard for different reasons. And I hadn't somehow thought that it would be.

Q. When do you get time to do your "work"?

A. Well, I get up at five. That's one thing. And I don't work more than about three hours and I don't think anyone can, at my pitch and intensity. That is, there are two kinds of writers. I think there are people who could work eight hours but whose tempo is very different from mine. Mine is quick and intense. Virginia Woolf didn't really write more than two or three hours a day. Of course, I live alone in a very beautiful place.

Q. Does that help, when you write? To have the time alone, the solitude? Or does the very fact of being alone, not lonely, necessarily, do something else?

A. Well, it does many things, there's no doubt about it. It can be extremely lonely, when I begin to feel starved, and one of the problems is that I see a great many people. Last year, for five months from May through September, I had somebody for a meal every other day. You see, that means my getting the meal. I have no help. Doing the dishes, hauling in the food, planning it, all this, and then giving a great deal because these are people who have written me or are coming to Maine, and also old friends, of whom I've a great many. But this is why the single person who focuses everything is so important. The place helps, and gardening. I have half a day out-doors in season.

Q. Do you think that being an artist requires at some level that you choose a life that is largely not self-centered, but centered around oneself in that lovers and spouses and friends are distractions or fillers?

A. Again, I was going to say, I think one person is terribly impor-tant, whether it be a husband or a lover, and without that one feels extremely deprived.

Q. In terms of personal growth and development . . .

A. I think you *have* to have goals. But when it comes to art, your goals have to be very much interiorized. I think it's quite stupid to say, "I'm going to have a show at Betty Parson's gallery before I'm twenty." I mean, this is silly.

Q. The talent of the poet is something inborn, and, like a musi-cian's, begins early on. Many of the women in the Women's Move-ment have begun to write fiction, prose, and poetry quite late in life. They seem to receive stimulation from other women writers.

A. I think that's probably true. However, I think there's such a thing as poetic genius. There's only one—no, three fields—in which I think this is true: mathematics, music in the sense of composing, and poetry. With mathematicians, you know you have a child genius before he is five—it's a thing, a reality. Mozart was composing symphonies when he was seven, maybe earlier—three. But this doesn't mean that somebody who starts at forty is not going to make a great writer. I think the best novels are written after forty. A novel requires so much understanding of people of different ages, it really takes maturity.

Q. Do you feel writing can be taught?

A. I've never taught for long. Three years at Wellesley, three years at Harvard when I was very young, English A. There, we were trying to get them to think clearly and to be able to write essays. It wasn't creative writing, it was freshman English. It wasn't creative writing in the usual sense. I think you can help people enormously. However, I think that poetic talent is very much like musical talent. It begins very young, the real thing. What you can do is help somebody not make bad mistakes and you can help them think things through, think through their feelings. I feel that the teaching of creative writing now is more therapy than it is anything else. In other words, several of my students have gone on to do well, but I don't feel any responsibility. I don't feel that it's because that they had me as a teacher—they would have done it anyway. But I think that I've helped people grow, which is after all what teaching is all about, for women to pitch their sights in a professional way or a developmental way is that kind of head start that you need. It's goal setting. The strange thing is that I'm not a success.

Q. Why do you think you're not a success?

A. Well, in the first place, my books don't sell. In other words, I have to write a book a year to live—that's the truth.

Q. Poetry or prose or both?

A. Oh, the poetry, of course, doesn't sell—nobody's poetry sells, but mine sells very well, as poets go. I'm supposed to be a sort of poetry bestseller, but the novels sell 17,000–20,000 copies. I don't make a living on that, I get $13,000 advance and I live on a scale of $30,000 so it means lectures.

Q. So you don't consider yourself a commercial success?

A. No. The point is, well, I'd like to make a million on a book, but I never will, because I won't deal in explicit sex and I don't want to—I couldn't, probably. It seems to me that most of us learned some time ago what it's all about and why do you have to read it over and over? I just don't know why this titillates people.

Q. But surely you consider yourself an artistic success?

A. Well, you have to talk about this in all kinds of terms. One is the literary establishment: I'm nowhere. I've never won a prize, I'm not in the anthologies. I'm not even in the *Norton Anthology,* my own publisher's, which is used widely in the United States for teaching. The trade department people have always backed me and I'm very lucky to have them—they publish whatever I write. I suppose that is success. If I write a book of poems tomorrow, they would publish it, unless they thought I had become senile or that it was going to do me positive harm; so they publish everything—the novels, the non-fiction and the poetry. It is the young people who are discovering me and saying, to the establishment people, "I want to do a dissertation on May Sarton," and they answer, "Who's May Sarton?"

Q. Do you think that you have better distribution in bookstores, or that you are being taught more now?

A. I'm taught more now because it's coming from the students more than from the professors, but also I must say the Modern Language Association has had seminars on me, and this is the beginning of cracking the establishment. These are women, again, who say, "I want to do a seminar on May Sarton." But not being in the anthologies has been extremely hard on me. I wasn't in the Untermeyer anthology and I wasn't in the reissue of it. I'm sure that I *was* in; then, at the last minute, there were too many pages and they had to cut, and they cut me.

Q. Do you think it's luck, or sexual politics or literary politics?

A. I hate to say sexual politics. However, I do think that male poets don't really like women poets, and never have.

Q. At this time of your life, do you find yourself reassessing what you've done in your adult life? One would think that the New York Public Library buying your papers is certainly a distinction.

A. Well, I was very thrilled. Not only that, it has helped me financially and that is why I haven't had to teach. Now I'm coming up against a bad time again, because I've got to finish this novel I'm on. It's really tough.

Q. Did you ever in your life consider another form of occupation for the sheer reason of making money?

A. Teaching. But I never wanted tenure. I never wanted to be caught in the academic world, which I think is very dangerous for a writer.

Q. But you make your living by the pen. Not many women do.

A. Yes. Not many women do.

A Conversation with May Sarton
Dolores Shelley/1977

From *Women and Literature* 7 (1979), 33–41. Reprinted by permission of Dolores Shelley.

I'd only recently discovered May Sarton myself, but when I began to read her a year or two ago, a single question came to mind again and again. Why has she received so little critical attention? And why has it come so late in her career? Although her works have always been reviewed (William Rose Benet, John Holmes and others favorably reviewed her first volume of poetry, *Encounter in April,* in 1937, while *The Single Hound,* her first novel, published a year later in 1938, was highly praised) and she has had an impressive audience of readers, scholars and literary critics have ignored her. That is, until the past five years when women in the "Academy" began to discuss her work. In 1973, '74 and '75, the Modern Language Association convention included seminars on "The Art of May Sarton"; nearly all of the papers presented were written by women.

Her first response to the question, during a phone conversation prior to our meeting, was that it was "partly ill luck." She said then, "I've had a good many favorable reviews, my books are read by many people, but I've not been a member of an establishment, or *the* establishment. I've never had any kind of power behind me."

Today we explore the reasons. "Well," she says, "I was not an innovator, certainly, and I think that's one thing that gets attention. Secondly, there was a very interesting paper written by a woman this year discussing me in relation to French culture and poetry, saying that my emphasis on clarity was very unfashionable and made the work look more simple than it is. I appeared on the scene just after the women lyric poets: Millay, Wylie, Louise Bogan. They were the generation just preceding mine. The fashion was Eliot when I was young, not lyric poetry, so I've always been unfashionable."

"I never went to college, which I have no regrets about, except that I notice that people who did are usually helped by their former

64

professors. Richard Wilbur had Matthiessen (F. O. Mathiessen of Harvard), for instance. The people who went to Columbia had Trilling. I've never been a part of any group, and groups help each other. I've been reading the new biography of Amy Lowell. One learns there how the Imagists backed each other, got each other published, wrote reviews for each other. The Bloomsbury group— another example. Virginia Woolf knew when a novel came out that E. M. Forster would review it; Strachey would review it. Imagine that!"

"The only group I've ever been a part of was a distinguished group of poets. This was when we were all young; John Ciardi, Richard Eberhart, Richard Wilbur, John Holmes, who's dead now, and I. We met about four times a year, drank a lot and read each other our poems. We all criticized each other, but I had the feeling the men were not very interested in my poetry. Not because it wasn't good, but that somehow when I got home, I just felt terribly lonely. That's what I'm really saying. And the proof of this lack of interest is that years later John Ciardi talked about our meetings in the preface to one of his books and failed to mention that I was there!"

I asked her about the support writers sometimes receive from each other at writers' colonies and her associations at Harvard and Wellesley, where she taught.

"I spent three weeks at Yaddo and was very unhappy there. I never went to MacDowell because about the time I might have gone, I lived fifteen miles away. At Harvard, there were people who were very kind to me. Archibald MacLeish and the Kenneth Murdocks couldn't have been kinder. They used to invite me to dinner parties, though I was never going to be great in the English department. I was only a lecturer, of course. I taught to make enough money so I could buy time to write. I never stayed anywhere more than three years."

"But to try to answer your question," she continues, "I don't think the kind of writing I did presented an exciting tool for intellectual analysis by young professors who might want to make a name for themselves. And I have absolutely no doubt that it's harder for a woman. And then, I'm bisexual and, of course, men don't particularly like this. Of course, I didn't "come out" for a long time. I'd written a great deal that I hoped would have broad, universal appeal. I want to be known as a universal, human writer. I dread being labeled, you see. I've never aligned myself with a lesbian group of writers, because I don't write only about that. That's a very small part of my work. I think it should be.''

In May Sarton's fiction, self-fulfillment is strongly emphasized and women often reject the passive acceptance of traditional roles. Hilary Stevens, in Mrs. Stevens Hears the Mermaids Singing, is an outstanding example of this sort of woman. The most profound satisfaction she experiences in life does not come through marriage but her own artistic interests, her own writing. The same could be said of the painter Joanna in Joanna and Ulysses, Lucy Winter, the teacher and protagonist of The Small Room and Caroline Spencer, the main character in As We Are Now. The traditional roles of marriage and motherhood are present in much of Sarton's fiction, but there are also new models for women who do not wait for their lives to be defined only by men.

"I'm very interested in the subject of marriage, though," she says. "I mean, anybody is; half the world is concerned with it. I've written about the marriage of young lovers in my third novel, Shadow of a Man (which is not my best), of middle-aged marriage in The Birth of a Grandfather (which I think is an interesting novel), and, of course, in Kinds of Love, an old marriage, people in their old age. Faithful Are the Wounds has quite a bit about marriage, though it also talks about a singular person who does live alone, the suicide, who was Matthiessen.''

She speaks again of the price she paid for admitting she was a lesbian.

"When Mrs. Stevens was first published, I lost two jobs right away. That was in 1965. You have no idea of the change since women's lib. Women's lib has made all the difference. I can now go on a television program and talk about this. People are much more liberal now, much more accepting. This in itself is good.''

She was silent for a moment and then came back to the question of recognition. "There is a third reason why perhaps I have not had a break from the critics. I have worked seriously in two mediums, and in the last years, three, if one includes the memoirs and Journal of a Solitude. That meant that the poetry critics tended to think of me as primarily a novelist and the critics of the novel as a poet. Then, because I was not born in America, I did not have the advantage of being 'placed' in a regional sense."

"In my father's house" are the first words of *I Knew a Phoenix*, the autobiography of May Sarton's early years. The opening pages are a daughter's loving tribute to George Sarton, author of *Introduction to the History of Science*, acknowledged even today, so many years after its publication, as one of the seminal works in its field. She writes of her birth at Ghent, Belgium, the birthplace of her father, her grandfather's house. And of her father leaving Belgium as a refugee of World War I, eventually to become the first American professor of the History of Science. She writes of England and Wales, her mother's countries and of conversations the two women have many years later of going back to Wales to find the valleys, farms and orchards of her mother's childhood. She writes of her parents meeting in Ghent, when her mother, Mabel Elwes, was a professional portrait painter and her father a student at the university.

By the time May Sarton was five, in 1916, her parents, ardent socialists both, were in America, where George Sarton taught a half course at Harvard in exchange for a room at Widener Library. Her parents lived in Cambridge, then, from that time until their deaths many years later.

"Was it through your father that you knew people or had introductions to people such as Virginia Woolf?"

"Yes, through my father I met Charlie Singer, the great historian of science in England. I was looking for a place to live in London. You could get a room with breakfast for a pound a week those days—horrible, with brown walls, but I didn't care, I was so excited to be there. The Singers helped me find a room in a cooperative house in Bloomsbury. There I made friends with John Summerson; he took me to Elizabeth Bowen and Bowen introduced me to Virginia Woolf. And the Huxleys were at Charlie Singer's, Julian Huxley, that's right, and *they* introduced me to Koteliansky."

A young May Sarton, twenty-five in 1937, paid a visit to Virginia Woolf, after sending her a copy of her first book of poems and a small bunch of primroses. She saw her alone in her drawing room, talked about writing poetry, talked about writing novels. When Leonard Woolf arrived, she impetuously invited them both to dinner at Whipsnade, thirty miles outside of London. Here tigers stalked the flowering hawthornes, but by the time they arrived, the tigers (caged, of course) had been put to bed and May Sarton had to hope that filet mignon and claret were enough.

From Virginia Woolf to Adrienne Rich, May Sarton has known many of the important writers of this century. When asked if she had ever met Carson McCullers, she replies, "No, she didn't interest me, because I think she was totally corrupted by the time she was thirty. It was fatal that she left the South. Here's an example of a person who was pushed by a group, if you will, and whom it ruined. That first house where she lived in Brooklyn with Auden and Gypsy Rose Lee, whom she was in love with, was disastrous for her. Carson was a sucker of people's marrow. She didn't give; she ate people up; she used them. I have a very terrible impression of an angel stuck in a monkey. She was certainly enormously talented, but I find somebody as neurotic as that not interesting. She was destructive to herself and to everybody who ever loved her. Destructive to her husband."

"But I think it's very hard for a woman to be married and have children and be a first-rate artist. If you try to think of the first-rate artists who are women, practically none of them have married and have had children except Kay Boyle who had three or four husbands and eight children, which is sort of like having none. She never has had a settled life. Katherine Anne Porter, you see, take her; take George Eliot, Jane Austen, Elizabeth Bowen, who was married but had no children. Look at the great women writers: Christina Rossetti, Emily Dickinson, Millay—she did finally marry, but Boissevain was a kind of nurse. Adrienne Rich married, of course, had children, but divorced. And Plath committed suicide trying to do it all. Now we are coming to understand that men can give more than they've ever been asked to give in a marriage, that a woman is not going to be expected to be everything; that is, to be all the time mother, all the time cook and also to be an artist."

"Do you think the woman artist is subverting her desires for a family, children, through art?" I ask.

"Not subverting, exactly, but perhaps it uses the same kind of creative energy. It's really a matter of energy. You can't do first-rate work and not give it your first-rate energy, I think. I write a fantastic amount, according to other people. I never feel this myself, because I

actually write very few hours a day. And I fight for the time, because
of the letters, keeping a house going. I do everything: garden, make
cookies, all these things. I don't have a secretary. I've been reading
Edith Wharton's life and I'm just mad with envy. She wrote in bed,
threw the sheets on the floor and her secretary picked them up and
typed them! Meanwhile, the cook came in and was told what to have
for dinner and the chauffeur took her out. I don't have any of those
things, nor do I really want them, frankly."

"For a while you had a column in—"

"*Family Circle*," she says. "Oh, that was heaven! I loved it. It was
like being Colette. Why did they ever have me? I mean, *FAMILY
Circle*? All the pieces were about living alone. They pushed the
column to the back of the book and surrounded it with advertise-
ments of bread so nobody could find it. But I enjoyed it. I thought the
pieces were quite good; they were casual essays about life as I was
living it in Nelson, New Hampshire. There are certain things I'm
gathering for my senility; I'll bring those twelve pieces together and
add a little, yes." "I'm very leery," she says, "of too strong a
theoretical structure before the novel is written. Forster talks about
this. My theory is that you have a theme and you put the characters
down into a strong enough situation so that they're going to work out
whatever it is you want to know about them. I write to a question,
not an answer. I think it's terribly dangerous to have too definite an
idea of what you're going to say before you say it, because your
characters teach you so much."

"With regard to the universal appeal of my work, I think it has to
do with the themes of family life and the woman. All the problems of
being a woman, which are dealt with in various ways in the books.
It's a generally humanistic view. This is another reason I haven't had
critical attention. Had I been a political writer, I might have. Had I
been more psychoanalytically oriented, I might have. But I love the
medium voice. I love Turgenev. I love Chekhov. Chekhov, Turgenev,
Trollope, of course Virginia Woolf, Jane Austen. This is what I call
the middle voice. It's not the screamer. It's not the extremely original,
except for possibly Woolf. By original, I mean the person who,
really, like Joyce, breaks through a whole new thing. These people
have not particularly moved me. I was influenced by Mauriac. As
a novelist, I think he's one of the greatest technicians there's ever

been. Incredible economy. Technically, I've learned more from the French, there's no doubt, than I ever have from the English or Americans. But French is half my language; I was born in Belgium."

"One of the problems of novelists is that any human life of *any* depth and passion is far more complex and more happens in it in even what *looks* like a fairly tranquil married life than one can readily accept. There are episodes. There are things that happen. Life *is* stranger than fiction and nobody would believe, really if nobody would believe, for example, the number of love affairs I've had. And I don't believe it myself."

"Why not?"

"I don't know. I mean, it just seems to be unlike me. But I think you have to live a lot before you can write. You learn from the person you love. You're so concentrated, really, that you almost become that person. And if you multiply this by thirty, or whatever it may be, then you have all these people you're made up of. It's great riches."

"I'm talking about women mostly. That's the whole thing for me. Women have been the muse and it's the more aggressive side of me which falls in love with women. I feel more able to write and more myself than I ever do at any other time. This is not going to happen anymore, and I don't even want it to, but when I was young, it was always people older. It was always people who had much to teach me with whom I fell in love."

"You wrote of a love affair in *Journal of a Solitude* when you were fifty-eight?"

"Yes, at least," she replied. "I brought out *A Durable Fire* then, the poems of that love affair, which ended badly as the book notes. I wanted to say to Americans, Don't think people are dead when they're sixty, because they're not. The more we learn about gerontology, the more it becomes clear that people go on having a capacity for passion, love, really, into their eighties. This shocks Americans to death, you know. They think that at a certain age, when you retire, you retire from everything. For me now, the stars, the horoscope, everything says more love affairs, but I say no."

"Do you think you have a particularly strong Freudian influence in your work?" I ask.

"No, I would not say so. Much more Jung. But I only came to Jung when I was fifty. I think Jung is for people who are fifty. Freud is for

the young because he helps them to understand. Nobody's pure
Freud anymore, not even Freudian analysts. They're all mixtures;
they're all eclectic. There are certain ways in which I think Freud is
helpful, but it's all being questioned now."

"I would be anti-Freudian in that I never believed that a homosexual was a cripple. I've always believed that there are neurotic homo-
sexuals just as there are neurotic heterosexuals. But the fact that
you're in love with your own sex does not make you sick. At the
same time, I think that it may be that you do not develop fully in that
life, the homosexual life, because you do not take in the stranger in
the same way. And there's no doubt that men are different from
women. There's no point in pretending they're the same. So that it's
much easier, I think, to love your own sex. It doesn't ask such a great
giving and taking in of the stranger and therefore you don't grow as
much. Often, homosexual relationships don't last for this reason. It's
all happened, you know, and then it gets thrown away because
there's not enough room for growth in it. It's too narcissistic."

"I started falling in love with women when I was nine or ten years
old and it's gone right through my life. I was in love with men. I
had a long affair with a rather famous man, but I always felt I was a
nurse. I always felt I was taking care of him. I was *exhausted* at the
end of the week by trying to do what he wanted. He was older than
I. I was trying to be a good wife, but I felt depleted and unable to
work. Or rather, since I'd given everything, there was nothing left.
With a woman, on the contrary, I felt very excited, wrote poems, you
see. And that's the only way I can judge."

"As you're speaking about this," I ask, "I'm wondering what your
feelings are in regard to the women's liberation movement, the
feminist movement. Many women in the movement must ally themselves with you whether they're homosexual or not."

"Yes. It's also because I live alone. I have proved that you can do it
and have a wonderful life, except that the day isn't long enough.
That's the only problem. I'm always in a state of guilt about the
letters that don't get written. That's the insoluble part of my life.
Because I love to get them, when they're intelligent, and I'd miss
them very much. But if you think of something that is never finished—see, a book is finished—oh, and that's a marvelous feeling—
but if I take two days off and don't write letters, it means there are

thirty there. Every single day I have to write letters. Otherwise, they accumulate. Do what can be done every day and don't let it get to you. Easier said than done, you know."

"I get letters from all over the world, all over the country, and this is what's exciting. People write who have read the works and so often they feel they've been made alive by them again. People of all ages and of every walk of life. Farmer's wives, old women out in Wichita, Kansas, and young people. The young are writing because of *Journal of a Solitude* and *As We Are Now*. Children write, of course, about the children's book and old people write a great deal. I got very interesting letters about *As We Are Now* and also about other books, *Kinds of Love*, for example, because many women are dealing with failing husbands and vice versa."

"Do people send you their own writing?"

"Oh, yes. I just received a story by a young woman who said she can't afford failure at this point. This is what I have to talk to her about. You *have* to be able to afford failure if you're going to be an artist. You've got to fail most of the time. It's inevitable. Nobody's going to produce a masterpiece every day. You *can't* say I can't afford to fail."

"Sometimes I get angry because I think people just don't realize at all how good you have to be to get there. What it takes in self-criticism and persistence—especially in self-criticism, being able to break down your own work and remake it because you see what's wrong. It takes guts."

"When you're writing, can you also rewrite at the same time?"

"In poetry, yes, because it's when I'm most excited that I'm able to criticize. I'm at a white heat critically as well as emotionally. I can put a poem through a hundred drafts and still keep working on it. With a novel, I don't revise that much. I usually put it through the typewriter twice, but then I revise a lot at the end for style and little things. Then you're helped with that by copy editors who really do a wonderful job because they pick you up with repetitions of a word, things like that, that you might not notice in a paragraph."

We turn once again to the question of the critics. "Of course," she says, "I used to feel as if I were underground. That's the image I think I used somewhere in *Plant Dreaming Deep*. As if I were underground and trying to push up a gravestone and say, 'I'm here,

I'm here.' It's started, though, and I'm not worried now. Now it's all very different."

"All I want now, which is very arrogant of me and vain, is a really big money success. I'd like to make a lot of money to give away and to not worry anymore. Now I have to write a book a year to live. And that's a lot, because it means you can never rest on your laurels. It's a precarious business at best."

"It sounds as if you're running a race."

"Well," she says, "that's it."

An Interview with May Sarton
Nancy Corson Carter/1982

From *Kalliope* 5.2 (1983), 36–48. Nancy Corson Carter conducted the interview at Eckerd College, St. Petersburg, Florida,
in the spring of 1982. Reprinted by permission of *Kalliope,*
Mary Sue Koppel, editor.

Carter: What is your sense of roots, for your writing and your
perceptions of the world?

Sarton: I was uprooted, physically uprooted, about five times
before I was four years old and often separated from my mother and
that explains why I attach myself very quickly wherever I am. I
learned to make roots extremely fast to protect myself, to survive.
Also, my parents' values are my roots. I got from both of them a
sense of the world, of concern about things like Hiroshima, Nazism,
the ghettos here. They were very aware of political issues and passionate in their convictions. They were Democrats by American
standards and they were also great believers in the arts and sciences—science not for inventions that would make money, but pure
science. I think their influence was the great thing I was given plus the
Shady Hill School, which was a simply marvelous school for somebody who was going to turn out to be much alone, to have work
which would be perhaps valuable but not popular. Shady Hill gave
me a sense of confidence in my capacities and who I was.

Carter: You spoke earlier today of Sappho as part of your literary
tradition.

Sarton: Yes. When I read Bowra's book *Six Greek Poets,* the
chapter on Sappho bowled me over because I too have been
brought up on the legend of Sappho as the great lover of women
(the poems say that, anyway), but I had never realized that for her
this was a religious vocation. She was training girls for marriage, and,
therefore, she had to learn to give up over and over again her great
loves. I suppose that came into my life at a time when I was
somewhat anxious about my being a lesbian, but, of course, I have
always fallen in love with people older than I, so I am not like

Sappho at all. That's been my problem. Now I'm seventy everybody teases me and says somebody will come along who's ninety. That'll be my great love. I've always been in love with older women, so where am I now? I'm stuck. Young women are in love with me, but that doesn't interest me very much.

Carter: Jean Dominique, whom you wrote of in *A World of Light,* was one of those important older women to you, was she not?

Sarton: She was such a marvelous woman, and she appears as Doro in my first novel *The Single Hound:* the young man poet comes to her, and she helps him understand himself. They're not lovers, but we were never lovers, you know. Of course, in her period women became old so much earlier. I figured out the other day that she was probably about fifty-five when I first met her, but she behaved and felt like a very old person and this is what's changed, you see. I mean, now, at seventy, I don't feel like a very old person.

Carter: I'm not sure where, perhaps in *A World of Light,* you wrote that maybe one of the reasons you started the journals was the wonderful intimate correspondence that you and she had, and lacking that after her death, you began them. Was that a source?

Sarton: I'd actually forgotten that. Could be. Could be because when I was young I wrote a great many letters, not more but better letters than now because I didn't have this enormous burden from the outside. When I was younger I just had many very great friends.

Carter: Jeanette Crane wrote in her *Evening Independent* article that the journals always seemed to be connected with love affairs and . . .

Sarton: And unhappiness over the lack of recognition of my work which has run through all the journals and which I certainly feel. I can't imagine another writer who appeals to so many people in such depth—people write to me and say, "You've saved me from suicide; you've changed my life; when I was mortally ill you brought me back; this is the year that Sarton saw me through"—but whom the literary establishment regards as having no value. Ask Penn Warren. Ask any of the people who are the establishment and you'll get "Who's May Sarton?" or "Oh, I don't know, I mean, she's a feminist, lesbian writer, I mean, I think." You won't get any response on a deep level.

Carter: Do you think that the forthcoming book of essays from the University of Maine is going to help change that?

Sarton: I hope so. Incidentally, at Colby I was given, thank God, a wonderful essay on *Mrs. Stevens* in one of the feminist journals called *International Journal of Women's Studies.* In another issue there's a good and stimulating essay on my treatment of old age which points out that in *Kinds of Love* I've been very romantic about old age and then have become realistic with *As We Are Now.* My answer to that is that there *are* some good marriages and there *are* some old people who have lived together for fifty years and still love each other and have an ongoing and growing relationship. But the problem in America today is that as far as serious criticism goes you have to be negative. One reason I've never had serious criticism is that I'm idealistic and believe in human beings and in their power to grow and change. This is not fashionable. So, it's been a strange life. I don't know any other writer like me at all. There are writers who've been discovered after they die, but they did not have the enormous audience that I already have. And there have been bad writers who have huge audiences, who would never get the kind of letters I get.

Carter: It's true. Last night when we were talking about what your work you were saying that sometimes writing the letters kept you from it. Well, isn't that really part of your work?

Sarton: Well, it is part of my work, except that it is temporal and won't last, whereas I hope the work will. This is like teaching in a way. Teaching is wonderful, but it is going to go into the people. It's not going to go into something which will be read 500 years from now, hopefully. You see, I don't have any illusions.

I think something that nobody has talked about yet is what the nuclear war threat has done to artists. Before, one always took refuge in the idea that things would last, but now the nuclear war would blow up the earth—finally we're through as a race. There won't be anybody to look at the works of art or play the music or to look at poems. So, in a curious way, since I have no children and am not married, my work, its influence on people, has been my immortality in my mind. And suddenly, I feel, but why bother? It's all going down the drain. I'm not saying this in self-pity, but every writer or artist must feel it, just as every mother must feel why have another child, it will just be blown up. That's why I think that women have to be the ones to do something about it. And if women just refused in some way—*Lysistrata*—we wouldn't have nuclear war.

Carter: Yes. So, if we talk about the function of art itself, what is it ideally to you?

Sarton: Well, I don't want to rush in where angels fear to tread, but all I can think of is the end of Rilke's "Archaic Torso of Apollo": "Here there is nothing that does not see you/You must change your life." And works of art have done that to me, for me. In Virginia Woolf's *To the Lighthouse,* I suddenly saw for the first time a vision of what a woman's life really is or was at that time. The book of the year for me this year was Isak Dinesen's letters. It was expensive, but I had to have it.

Carter: I was asking about the function of art, and you quoted Rilke. "You must change your life." Isn't that why people write to you, because they have read your work and have changed their lives?

Sarton: Maybe because one of the things is that people see a lesbian who is not a mess, who is sort of a dignified person, who is doing good work and lives a fairly reasonable kind of life, and it gives them courage. So many people have written me, I mean women from a small town where the word "lesbian" would not be understood even, who fall in love with another woman and feel completely alone and terrified. They think, "There's something terribly wrong with me; I should go and shoot myself." And then I have helped those people when they find *Mrs. Stevens,* when they read the journals, and I've had many letters from people like that who said, "You've helped me to be able to understand myself and to accept myself and to not feel awful or rotten or wicked," so there I think I've had value. I'm not an operator, and I'm unable to use people. I don't say this with pride entirely because I think you don't succeed in the big sense without being able to use people. I have known a lot of famous people, but I have never used them because I had a kind of shyness or a sense of knowing—having even in my small way been used, been asked to write blurbs for books—that it's a terrible burden, and I didn't want to do it to Elizabeth Bowen, to those people. I did it once with *Mrs. Stevens.* I was so angry with Norton for not advertising it that I bought a full page ad in the *Times.* For that ad I cabled Julian Huxley who was an old friend and said, "Would you write a blurb?" And he did, a very generous one, and that was printed in the ad. *Mrs. Stevens* was reviewed in *Time* magazine, the only book of mine that's ever been reviewed in *Time*. It was a short review which said Miss Sarton seems to be strangely interested in other women; I mean there was absolutely no review of the content; it never mentioned poetry or anything else. It was unbelievable. Otherwise, it wasn't reviewed.

The *Selected Poems* came out long ago. It was reviewed in the Sunday *Times* on Christmas Eve by Karl Shapiro, who said, "May Sarton is a bad poet." He never mentioned that on the back of the book were things by Louise Bogan and some very big names; he never said, "Other people think she's good; I don't." Nothing except that May Sarton is a bad poet, and it ended, "I'm very sorry to have to do this." You know, like, "It hurts me more than it does you." I thought it was dirty. Well, I was sick for a week. I threw up for a week. Then I was younger and I hadn't had as many bad reviews as I have now, so I was utterly ill-equipped to deal with it. It was terrible; it ruined Christmas. And in a way, I have never gotten over it. One of the things he had against me was I wrote sonnets. Since then he brought out a book of sonnets to his wife which were written in a very old-fashioned style, if *I'm* old-fashioned. He would go back on that, but you see what happens to you is that for the rest of your life and long beyond it, it is quoted that the *Times* says May Sarton is a bad poet—you see, that's the point really.

Carter: And I wonder do feminist presses and networking help change this?

Sarton: Yes, I think so. I am amazed now at how many people read the poems. This is very new; it's only in the last ten years. The last book, *Halfway to Silence* sold 5,000 in the first month, which is extraordinary since there were no reviews and no ads, none at all.

Carter: Yet isn't there an underground, if you will, which gives your work reviews?

Sarton: Yes, and that's very thrilling. At the same time I do not want to be known as simply a feminist and a lesbian poet. I want to be known as a universally human writer.

Carter: My friend's mother and grandmother know of you and they found you through their own channels—her grandmother's eighty-seven and her ten sisters all over the country also know who you are. It's wonderful, isn't it?

Sarton: Well, it is wonderful now. Wherever I go now I have big audiences, often standing room only. Just think of being seventy and having it all happen!

Carter: It's splendid. And you were telling us about Pat Carroll's working on a one-woman show of you and your work.

Sarton: Right. So I can't complain, but I just hope that some day there will be a serious critic who can show that there is literary value in all this.

Carter: At the end of *House by the Sea,* you quoted a French motto you said you'd used as your own device for a time: "Tout m'agite, rien ne m'ébranle."

Sarton: "Everything moves me and nothing destroys me." It's a tree—nothing uproots, nothing throws it (me) down. The tree is a good image because the leaves all are agitated by the wind, by the sun, but it's so strongly rooted that nothing will uproot it (though "uprooted" is not a literal translation).

Carter: I liked that so much because one of the things I keep remembering from *Mrs. Stevens* is the exchange between Mrs. Stevens and young Mar in which she tells him that no human encounter can be made without a great cost.

Sarton: Yes. Yes.

Carter: And yet, what you constantly show and say in the work is that you are willing to pay.

Sarton: Yes, that's right. And a lot of people are not willing to pay the price of being alive. I think being and remaining vulnerable is the thing that people are so afraid of; they must be in a position where they can't be hurt anymore. And if you get to that point, of course, you might as well be dead.

Carter: Would you talk some more about poetry or art, your art in particular, as healing?

Sarton: Well, I think what art can do is to make one look at the things that are too painful to look at unless they have been translated into art. I have a poem called "The Tortured" which took me a very long time to write because I couldn't find the form. I finally took it from George Herbert, I think. One of my relatives was tortured by the Gestapo in Belgium, never told, and died later because of the

torture. And it's haunted me. I'm sure that everybody of my generation and probably even of yours has asked themselves the question,
"Would I tell under torture?" I'm terribly afraid I would. I mean, how
do you know?

But he didn't, and so I had to write a poem about it. There were so
many being tortured—there are so many people being tortured right
this minute. I found that the way to do it was in ballad form and so
making it abstract in a way. Wisdom with a capital "W" answers the
cries of the tortured, and it ends, "And Wisdom wept. Now do you
understand, love, how you must live?"

Well, this is a hard poem for me to read, I must say, but occasionally I do, because it goes with the Holocaust poem and with political
poems or poems on the state of the world. It makes it possible for
people to take in the experience of torture and understand it without
being so horrified they can't take it in. That's what art can do, I think.
It makes the unbearable bearable, so we can look at it instead of
turning away from it and never taking it in. We've got to take it in.
Just as we were saying we've never taken Hiroshima in. We're
beginning to take it in now because we're so scared, but we didn't
take it in when it happened and when we did it. We really didn't. So I
think this is one of the functions of art, though only one of them; it
makes clear the essence of horror and pain and suffering and guilt
and everything else, but at the same time it transcends, and that's
why it's so powerful.

I used to argue with Louise Bogan about this, because she told
me, "You keep the hell out of your work." Actually I haven't, since
she died, I guess I've put the hell in more than I ever had before.
Maybe that sentence helped me, but I have believed in transcending;
I often would begin a poem in anger or in terrible grief, but it never
ended there, because in the course of writing the poem I transcended
the grief or the anger or the pain, whatever it was, and in writing the
journals the same thing happens. The problem is, how do you make
the reader go through it so that the transcending means something?
This is something I still don't know the answer to, because the poem
is the transcending on my part, but the reader doesn't see what was
back of it, all the drafts of the poem, all the battling it though to get
there. I think this is where the novel perhaps can do something that
the poetry can't. I don't know, I really don't know.

Carter: I feel your works are very spiritual, do you?

Sarton: I think they are, because almost every religious denomination in America has honored me in some way. The Catholic College of St. Catherine in St. Paul, Minnesota, gave me their Alexandrine Medal, the equivalent of an honorary doctorate; it's given, of course for life work, and it's never, I think, been given to a writer before. The Unitarians, I've told you about, and the Methodists asked me to be one of the three speakers, sort of gurus, at the yearly retreat for their pastors every summer, and I was absolutely taken aback. I said, why me? I also said, do you know I'm a lesbian? I thought I'd better not have this come from the back door, and they said, yes, that's quite all right, we want you to talk about vulnerability and self-healing. And I did. It was a most marvelous time. And the other people there were Sojourners, this truly Christian group in Washington. And Morton T. Kelsey, who has written a very good book on prayer, and I each had one part of the day every day, and that was a tremendous experience for me and enormously nourishing.

I do not believe in a personal God, but I certainly believe in some thing beyond our ken which is not purely materialistic. I can't go further than that. I think you have to believe, here I may quote Pascal, one has to live as if there were God. As if. And I must say that I go back to the New Testament in the words of Jesus: what you've done unto the least of these, you've done unto me. There's no other religion that I know of that has this in it. See, the Buddhists are passive. Nobody's been murdered or tortured in the name of Buddha, which is wonderful, but also it's so much personal salvation but not really caring about the other. I think the wonderful thing about the Christian religion as Jesus taught it was that—it's Mother Theresa. I mean, here is the perfect Christian as far as I'm concerned—the person who really lives it.

One reason I don't call myself a Christian is that I believe it too much. I believe if I really thought of myself as a Christian that I couldn't lead as comfortable a life as I do, that I would have to go somewhere into a ghetto and work among the very poor, and this I just can't do. I feel, perhaps arrogantly, that my work is what God meant me to do, so there's the other side of it. I mean that I have a talent and I should use it, like the man who says in *Chariots of Fire*,

God is pleased when I run. It's much better said than that, but that's
the essence of it, and I feel it very much so that I think I'm sort of a
religious person without a religion. I'm certainly concerned with the
soul, and I say this when I quote Chardin that our purpose of life is
making our soul. I feel this, and you know damn well when you do
something which is not making your soul. You know.

Carter: Yes. I wanted to ask some questions about your working
schedule: you get up at five o'clock in the morning and do three
hours of work, doing it then because early in the morning you feel
closest to that door to the unconscious?

Sarton: That's right. But I assure you it isn't immediate. You see, I
make my breakfast and I take it up to bed, and after I've had my
breakfast and given Tamas his tidbits and given the cat her cream on
the bed, then I think for quite a while and it's not a meditation in
the self-conscious sense. I just lie there and things come; I get ideas.
It's my most open time to what comes from outside me. And then I
get up about seven and then I've had my breakfast and I've done my
thinking—in the summer it's about half-past six—and then I wash
the dishes, water the plants, make my bed, sometimes do some
laundry, and get up to my desk about eight. I write from eight to
eleven, then I walk the dog and the day's work is finished.

Carter: That courting of the unconscious, how did you learn to do
that? How do you tune yourself?

Sarton: Well, I just think you do it—and it's awfully hard if you
have a family—by lying down and being quiet, just letting it come.

Carter: Sort of like remembering your dreams?

Sarton: Yes. I rest for an hour in the afternoon, at least an hour. In
the good times, I rest for two hours. The first hour I go fast asleep.
I'm exhausted by what I've done until then; it's about two o'clock.
And then, the second hour I'm apt to not feel like getting up and I
just lie there and then is when marvelous ideas come. I think, That's
what I'm going to do with that chapter. I know now what to do. And
then I get up and do physical work in the garden.

Carter: When you write, do you do it first in longhand or do you
go right to the typewriter?

Sarton: I do it on the typewriter with novels and make very few
notes, a few notes before, but with a poem I start in longhand and
put it on the typewriter about halfway through so I can see it in sort

of an objective way and then start tearing that apart. Yes, I start with writing a lot of notes, as I said, just sort of jotting down things and then I begin to feel it jell, then I start putting it in stanza form, then I finally put it on the typewriter, and then I start really working on it. I see everything that's wrong when I put it on the typewriter because it's slightly . . .

Carter: Colder?

Sarton: Yes, colder. And then I start saying it aloud too. I felt it was interesting today that the students read so badly, and I wonder if they ever read their poems aloud to themselves.

Carter: Very seldom, although when I did a poetry workshop this fall I had one of our theater people come over to show them how to read.

Sarton: Really! But how wonderful! That's what somebody should do.

Carter: Do you also do manuscript first with the journals?

Sarton: No, I type them, and I do that first before I do anything else at my desk, because I am also writing books while I am keeping a journal. The journals are almost too easy, but I think about them a lot. I think about that in bed before I get up, what I'm going to say. I'm already thinking about the first day of the seventieth year and I don't know what in hell I'm going to say, but it'll come to me. It depends on whether it's raining or the sun's out, for one thing.

Carter: If you were offering, from the seventieth year, advice to the young writer, what would you tell him or her about how to go about it, how to take care of the gift?

Sarton: The most important thing is to find a critic whom you trust and who really believes in your work and will tear it apart and help you. Because the hardest thing to learn is how to revise.

In a way you don't know what's wrong. You don't know how to go about it, and what you need is criticism of the kind that I tried to give today in the workshop. It's easier said than done. I'm amazed when I go to colleges at how poor the criticism is that they give each other. Over and over again it's one word, "why did you . . .?" instead of getting at anything that's essential or whole about it. They don't dare say, "I don't understand." This is one reason I do it. I think a lot of teachers don't dare say, "What did you mean?" because they've got to look as if they understand everything and are superior. Criticism should be severe enough and yet be exciting enough so that the student or you, whoever you are doing the writing, will want to go back and try again, want to make it better.

Carolyn Heilbrun did that for me on *Anger,* my new novel. I was so anxious about that book and so afraid it was bad. I was really upset. She said, "I'd like to read it, and I'll give you a criticism very fast." I have sometimes been quite cross with her and I don't think she's right about the journals, but in this case she wrote me a simply wonderful letter which made me revise it and know what I wanted to do with it and end it differently. She felt the end was too optimistic, and I think she was right. And anyway, even at my age and with everything I had back of me, I needed some criticism on that one, and I was so grateful to get it. Because there are very few good editors around now. So my first advice to the young writer is to find a critic you trust who will be severe enough to make you revise and make you excited about revising.

An Interview with May Sarton
Kay Bonetti/1982

This transcript was transcribed and edited by Elizabeth Meyer from an audiotape interview conducted on 26 May 1982 by Kay Bonetti for American Audiotape Library, 1015 East Broadway, Suite 284, Columbia, MO 65201. At that time, Ms. Sarton also read from her novel *As We Are Now* and from *Journal of a Solitude*. Printed by permission of Kay Bonetti and American Audiotape Library.

In the novel, As We Are Now, *is it a coincidence that Standish appears to be a lot like your friend Perley Cole, or was Perley Cole in fact the germ for that character and perhaps that novel?*

He was. It wasn't only Perley Cole. He was *in that place,* and it's a real place. And those two fat women were real, and I got it closed, at least to any one ill. I'm afraid it's still open for those who are old, but somebody as ill as he was should never have been there and he was sent there by the hospital without their ever having gone there or known where they were sending him. And it was really disgraceful. It was terrible. And then Caro herself [the novel's protagonist] was also there and this was a woman I only saw once. But she haunted me because she was wandering around crying, and she was obviously a different class from the other people there who were mostly farmers, old farmers. She was obviously, if you like, a lady. I thought of her as a school teacher perhaps. And the next time I went— which was quite a long time later, because it was such a long way from where I lived that I didn't go very often—I went with flowers from the garden and asked about her. They said—let's call her Miss Spenser—"Miss Spenser had to be put in a room with no windows because she became violent." And you see, *that's* what started the novel. I thought that could have been me, you see, that woman. And what would it have been like? That's how I wrote it. I got Perley Cole out of there, but he died two days later, so it was too late, you see, just as it is with my character, Standish, although he dies in the ambulance. I can't remember in the book exactly, but he dies very soon. So whenever I saw Perley Cole he would say, "Get me out of

85

here." But these fat women were always listening, and I had to shout. So I would say, "I'm *trying*, Perley."

Is it just my own middle age creeping up on me or do you think that there is a trend now in fiction finally to write more of death, and in more graphic detail, from diseases like cancer?

What I'm saying in *A Reckoning* is really that we've got to live as if we were dying all the time. That is, we've got to think about the priorities and the real connections. That's the lesson of that book, and some people felt it deeply. And it's only when Laura is dying that she begins to live her real life. And that's the power of the book, I think.

Well, do you think there is more attention now being paid to these issues in the world of fiction?

Well, it's probably because more people are living to be old, you see. I mean, seventy is not old anymore. In fact I'm *teased* by my friends who are eighty, who say, "You can't talk about being *old* yet." And I don't feel at all old. And it's the best time of my life. My seventieth birthday, I felt, was the happiest probably, except for one other, my sixty-fifth, when I was in love and was writing a book of poems which later came out, *Halfway to Silence.* One reason I felt older when I wrote *The House by the Sea* was that I was *not* in love and hadn't been in love for five years, and had not written any poems. I think that made me feel old and *now* I know that I'm going to go on writing poems until I die, and that probably the last Muse is the sea.

I wondered about that. In The House by the Sea, *you speak as though poetry had gone out of your life, but that's not true.*

It did for five years, but then *Halfway to Silence,* you see. That whole book of poems was written after I was sixty-five.

And after The House by the Sea.

Oh yes, long after.

I see. You said something in The House by the Sea *about the Muse and about love having changed for you, that you had moved from a position of love for one single person into a more generalized love for many. Would you care to elaborate on what you meant by that?*

Well, I felt that that was the only way I could go at that point, but as soon as I fell in love again at sixty-five, then I knew that was all a lie and that poetry is very much connected with one person for me. There's no doubt about that.

I have been writing some poems and that love affair is more or less over now, the love affair that created *Halfway to Silence.* It was like a miracle. I mean, poems just poured out, you see. The reason why I think the poems are what will last of my work is that if you're a poet at all it is the mystery, you see. It's given. You can write a novel on will; you cannot write poetry on will. It's given. It is a matter of inspiration. There is something divine in it, if you will, or something from the subconscious that you cannot control, and you *can* control a novel, and certainly a journal. If you have this gift [for poetry], which is very much like the mathematical gift or the musical, the composer's gift, you have to have it very young. And it's embedded in you; it's there very early. This is where poetry is absolutely different than any other form of writing.

An awful lot of bad poetry is being written today. People don't use form any more, and form is considered stiff. The point is that I can only write in form when I'm inspired; I can only write in form when form comes. I don't paste it on. It's there; it's organic. Therefore, if you're a poet at all, you realize that this is a gift. And, therefore, it's somehow more precious than the gift of writing novels. Virginia Woolf used to tease me and say that it's so much easier to write poetry. When I knew her I had only published one book of poems. And she used to tease me and say that novels are much harder. And I agree. The effort is infinitely greater. Of course, the form is much more complex when you're holding a great deal more in balance. But I think a great poem can be written by somebody seventeen or younger. You think of Keats dying at twenty-six. But a great novel probably cannot be written by a very young person because a novel implies an understanding of human relationships which you don't really have when you're that young.

Well, you did say that old writers do not fade away, they ripen.
Yes, is that in a journal?

I believe that's in Plant Dreaming Deep. *You felt that way—let's see that would've been at fifty . . .*

Fifty-four.

Fifty-four, fifty-five. Do you still feel that way?
Oh, absolutely. I've done my best work in the last five years. I
think *A Reckoning* is my best novel. And I think *Recovering* is good
as a journal; the poems I think are very good—*Halfway to Silence*.
Pure lyric poetry is extremely rare. I mean, rare, and very unfashionable, but it is what lasts.

*It's obvious from reading you that you make very clear distinctions
between the form of poetry and prose. What is the essential difference?*
Well, the poetry I write, which is mostly in form, is very close to
music, whereas prose, if it was that close to music, wouldn't be very
good. It would be too mellifluous, too "poetic." My first novel was
very poetic. It was highly praised for style. And I've worked very hard
to get away from that poetic style.

But the poetry deals with essences and the novel deals with
relationships. It's much more complex as a form. It never reaches, for
me at least, the sort of crystalline quality of a poem, which is there
forever. The very fact that poems are memorable, that they're short
enough so that they can be remembered entire . . . I've been
thinking so much these last days of Housman's "And since to look at
things in bloom/ Fifty springs are little room,/ About the woodlands I
will go/ To see the cherry hung with snow," and here I have maybe
only ten more springs. So every, every moment is precious. There,
you see, is a pure lyric which goes on ringing in people's minds.

"Loveliest of Trees, the Cherry Now."
Yes, that's it. I was influenced as a novelist most of all by François
Mauriac, the French writer, and his economy and clarity. There's a
good article in the book the University of Maine is doing on me, *May
Sarton: Woman and Poet*. One of the things I'm most pleased about
in this article, which was given at the MLA, is that it is called "May
Sarton and French Clarité." I've worked very hard for a very trans-
parent style. That's what I want, but it's most unfashionable. What's
fashionable is the complex style of Updike, whom I greatly admire.
But that isn't mine; it isn't what I want to do. I am, you know, half-
Belgian. French is my other language. Although I don't speak it

perfectly, I feel very much at home with it. I certainly was as influenced by Valéry, the French poet, and by Mauriac, as I was by anyone else. The poets who influenced me most were Yeats and Valéry. Both were poets who revised endlessly, and I believe in revision. But I think you can only do it when you're inspired. In other words, the poem goes dead if you don't revise it white heat. You can't revise it cold, as far as I'm concerned. It's like playing a very stiff three sets of tennis one after another.

In the Clark Lectures *you did say about the design of a novel that "one can always say I'm going to write a novel next year, but one can never say that about a poem." That does fascinate me. How do you know when an idea comes? You speak in there of a germ and how it goes down into the deeper self like a seed and it has to germinate. What's the distinction between a germ that comes out as a poem and a germ that has to work its way through to the longer form, to the novel?*

Well, I think it's more like lightning—the poem—it's like a streak of lightning, and the novel is more like a plant. It's a very complex thing that grows slowly, but a poem is something that you're shocked into it by joy or grief or whatever it may be, by some incredible happening. I'm only talking about lyric poetry, because I consider myself a lyric poet. If you're doing a different sort of poetry this wouldn't apply. But it's that, it's a whole different part of you that's involved. You have to *think* very hard about poems too as well as being in a state of high emotion. But the novel you have to *sustain* for so much longer. I used to say to my students that to write a novel was like taking an examination on which your whole future depends every day for a year. Every page has to be right. And the effort is immense. There's no getting around that. Every time I've begun a new novel I've really dreaded it. I've thought, I can't do it. It's too long and too hard—you know that push, day after day, dragging it out of yourself, sitting up in that room with nobody to drag it out of you. Teaching is so easy because the students are there. You may be very tired, but you get to class and there are all those faces saying, "Show me."

Do you ever write poems while you're working on a novel?
Oh yes. Oh yes. I would put everything aside if a poem came.

Are you working on a novel now?

No, but a new journal. I started the journal May third. I shall be working on a new novel as soon as I get out of the terribly pressured life I've been leading for the last two months.

So has this been your pattern, that you do in fact start working on an idea that you think is going to find its way to a novel and then you do rather in a workman-like manner say, "In June there will be time"?

Yes, when there's time. I'm now going to try to finish a novel I began two years ago called *The Magnificent Spinster*, which is really a biography of Anne Thorp. And I'm making it fiction so that I won't be tied down to facts. I mean, so that I won't have to spend a year just digging out *when* this happened and *when* that happened. She was a very great woman, and I want to celebrate her. But she was very rich. The reason I wanted to write it so much is that she was the only very rich person I've ever known who was not corrupted by money. The reason she wasn't was that she worked so hard and nobody even knew she was rich. When she died I suddenly realized that in fifty years nobody will remember Anne Thorp or know anything about her.

Who is Anne Thorp?

She was my teacher at Shady Hill. I mention her in several of the journals. Her family had an island, north of here, in Maine where I spent seventeen summers. I went for ten days every summer.

And you write extensively of that place in Journal of a Solitude, *as a matter of fact.*

Yes, that's it—about three pages. And anyway what I felt was nobody will remember so I want to make a work of art which will, therefore, perhaps be remembered a hundred years from now.

You've said that it's the poems that you think you'll be remembered for. Now is this a criticism of yourself? Is this your self-evaluation of what you think you'll be?

No. I just feel that poetry is so much more important than novels or anything else. Poetry, as I've tried to say, really does have something given in it which is very precious. Poets are rare, very rare, much rarer than novelists. There are an awful lot of poets around right now, but there's an awful lot of bad poetry being written: self-indulgent poetry, poetry which never transcends the moment, never reaches the universal, never has shown any self-criticism. The same thing with journals. I mean, I'm fed up with awful journals that people write and think are good. I do underrate my journals until I see what awful journals people are writing that they think are good. Then I realize that there is something in the balance in the journals between self-analysis and things happening. The journals are not entirely negligible. And I'm terribly grateful to them because they've brought me so many friends. They really have.

You've said one place that professionalism is only a husk in the writer, that the real person, the real writer has to be the lover of the work, the amateur. *How much of your work* per se *has been work to make a living for yourself?*

I didn't make a living out of writing until I was fifty-five. Now I make considerable amounts of money, more than I ever thought I would, but also by reading poems I get a thousand dollars, plus expenses. So you see, if I do that for two months of the year, that makes quite a lot of money. Then the paperbacks bring in money. But I had to teach. That's why I taught. I taught three years at Harvard, three years at Wellesley. I always did poetry readings, but I used to get very little pay—like $250 or something, and not always the expenses. But that's a lie when I said I've never done purely professional writing for money. When I was very young, before *The Bridge of Years* came up, between the first novel and the second, I sent a short story called "The Old-Fashioned Snow" to Diarmuid Russell. And he sold it for $600 to *Delineator*. All of these magazines don't exist anymore. There were a lot of magazines (slicks) that bought short stories. And for about three years I sold stories to the *Ladies' Home Journal*, to *Redbook*, well, to the good slicks. But I never knew how much I was going to make. They then paid about a thousand for a story. And maybe I sold three or four in a year. It wasn't quite enough to live on. It's terribly anxiety-making. And, I'm not really a short story writer. There are none of those that I would like to see preserved. Although I didn't do anything to a formula: I broke all the taboos. I wrote about a woman dying of cancer, for instance, which you weren't supposed to do. The *Ladies' Home*

Journal published that. I did a lot of things that were original, if you like, but I wouldn't like to see them among the bound books that you see over there, which are my books. But I did for awhile write for money, you see, in a sense. I was trying to. I think it's fatal. I mean, it *was*. It finally got so I sort of saw dollar signs on the typewriter, instead of the story I was writing.

I want to ask you want the germ of books like The Fur Person, Punch's Secret, Joanna and Ulysses, *and* Miss Pickthorn and Mr. Hare *is?*
  Well, they come from exactly the same place as all the rest—deeply felt. You know I borrowed a donkey and remade myself out of depression. *The Poet and the Donkey* is autobiographical, only I make myself into an old man in that. But *Miss Pickthorn and Mr. Hare* is one side of me. Mr. Hare was my neighbor. I mean, he's a real man and, of course, I just enjoyed doing it tremendously. I love those books.

I love them too.
The Fur Person has become a classic.

It was the first book by you I ever read.
  Oh really?

I wondered if in fact it has made you partially comfortable in your old age? I mean, that's a book that just sells and sells and sells, doesn't it?
  No. Well, it doesn't make me comfortable. All the others do; the journals do. I make now about, probably close to twenty thousand a year on royalties on the paperbacks—the Norton paperbacks. See, I've never been picked up, except once, for *Fur Person*, and now I think they bought that outright. I don't think they make any money out of that.

Well, I was wondering about the idea of play, writing as play. You say they're deeply felt, but in a sense are they . . .?
  Play? Oh sure they are. But then so is writing a poem play. It's only the novel that I don't find play. I find the novel very hard. Well, those books are novels, but they're fables, really. They're light, light in

texture, compared to the serious novels. I think they're among my best things. I like them.

One thing we need to go back to. You left home at seventeen to go join the theater. What happened? When did May Sarton the writer happen?

Well, I've been writing poems always. *Poetry* magazine took four or five sonnets when I was seventeen, the year I went into the theater and I knew that I'd always be writing poetry. But I was in love with the Civic Repertory. This was a remarkable theater and that's what I fell in love with, not the theater in the abstract, but *that* theater. And it's a long story and I tell it, somewhat at least, in that autobiographical book of memoirs, *I Knew a Phoenix*. But, of course, what it did was to spare me from becoming a blue stocking. I was supposed to go to Vassar. And Vassar was very political at that time. *That* would have been good for me, because I was very political too.

But, I think it was better for me to be thrown into a group of people who were absolutely different from any kind of people I'd ever known. Many of them Jewish, coming from New York, wonderful kids, poor. When I was director of the student group I was so moved by them. And, of course, there were very talented people there: Howard da Silva—people who have since become famous—Alexander Scourby. I learned a lot and I learned about failure before I was twenty-six.

I finally had the sort of first off-Broadway theater myself before I was twenty-five, and when that failed—it was the middle of the Depression—it was a tremendous blow, of course; it was terrible. But luckily my first book of poems came out that year. And from then on I never looked back.

When did you start writing in the novel form?

I first wrote short stories, which didn't sell, and Houghton Mifflin saw some of them—they published the poems—and said, "Why don't you try a novel?" I never thought of it. And so I wrote *The Single Hound*. They saw a hundred pages and gave me a small advance; then I went to Europe and finished it. And then I knew I would be a writer. For one thing I learned the bitter truth that the theater is an angel with its feet tied to a bag of gold. It takes *enormous* amounts of money and now even more than it did then, but I mean enormous amounts. So that you're scuttling around for money all the time; after all, you can sit and write if you have some bread and wine and you don't need an enormous amount of money. So that it's not a good thing. The theater is terrible. It's a terrible, terrible profession. I never go to the theater anymore. It was like a fever that took me and left.

But then the novel has become your form for thinking things through?
That's right. I write my novels to answer a question.

One of my favorites is Faithful Are the Wounds. *I love the figure of F. O. Matthiessen. He was a profound figure in my own intellectual life, and I've always been fascinated by his story; you know, when I found out about his politics and all those things. How close to his circle of friends were the other characters in that novel?*
They were *all made up.* I'll never do that again, because nobody believes me. But Cavan was Matthiessen; and Julian Huxley was Damon Philips. Nobody has ever recognized that, because Julian Huxley is over in England. I made the others up. I made up Goldberg, whom everybody thinks is Harry Levin, out of a man I met just once so I felt absolutely safe. I knew nothing about him—just the physical type: the bright eyes behind thick glasses, the stiff collar. I'll never be asked to Harvard, you see. They hate me. And I think wrongly, because Levin took it so ill—Levin doesn't want to be known as a Jew, which is so crazy—and Goldberg is really the only worthy antagonist of Cavan. I *admire* Goldberg. He's not a *monster,* you know. I mean it's not as if I *cartooned* him as a Jew or something, *not at all.* So, it's a very strange thing, but it has been very painful for me. And I got the Lucy Martin Donnelly Fellowship from Bryn Mawr to write that book. And they didn't like it. It came out to the best review I ever had in the *Times,* a very long, absolutely tremendously good review. I went to Bryn Mawr after it, sort of feeling they'd be so proud of me, and they said, "But we didn't like it very much; we thought it was poor," because somebody there had known Matthiessen and didn't like what I had done. And there are people who love it and people who don't, among those who knew him. Mind you, I didn't even know that he was homosexual then.

I guessed it, but I didn't know. I mean, so much has come out since. But it's just suggested in the book; it isn't rubbed in.

One thing about your life and the way you work that I find striking is that many writers, especially men writers, speak of the need to get away—that the only way they can work in this culture with the expectation of a sense that they're doing something to a purpose is to get out of the house. They rent a room someplace. They go to an office. That's the only way they seem to stay sane and work. And your life is so characterized by working where you live, in one spot. How do you do it?

Because I traveled; I used to travel a lot. What keeps me together is the routine, and I think when you live alone you have to have it; otherwise, you go to pieces.

But your routine involves staying at home to work.

Yes. Oh absolutely, because I have the whole top floor of this house as work space: three rooms.

Well, is there a psychological thing about having it up there on the third floor?

No. No. I wish it were downstairs. For instance, when I was waiting for you I could have done some work. In Nelson, it was right at the door so I could work up to the last minute. By "work," I often mean writing letters. You see, the one insoluble thing in my life is the letters. I answer fifty letters a week, from strangers. And besides that, there are all my friends who are scattered all over the world, very dear ones in Europe whom I can only keep in touch with by writing letters. But it's the routine that keeps me together. It is something about going to my desk and working. I mean, every morning I get up at five and have breakfast in bed and give myself about half an hour of just lying there—not willfully thinking anything—just lying there and often watching the sun rise. But just thinking a little. Not meditating in a formal way, but things come to me then because there's no door between the subconscious and the conscious early in the morning. You're still in that state of infancy of sleep—really. And things flow in. And then I get up and do the household things, which are not nothing. I mean, I have to make my bed, I often do laundry, often rearrange the flowers or go out and pick flowers, wash the dishes,

and get myself going. So I don't go up to my desk until eight—
although I'm up at five. An hour, you see, five to six in bed and then
about two hours doing odd jobs around the house. And by *then* I'm
really eager to get up there and get to work. Then I start walking
the dog at about half past ten or eleven. I take him on a daily walk,
get the mail, which takes me *one hour* to read. I read it before I have
lunch, with a drink, with some sherry to get me through it. And then I
have lunch and lie down, for two hours. And that is also a wonderful
time for ideas to come in. It's a very, very fruitful time. I may go to
sleep. Sometimes I don't. It's not always two hours, but an hour
anyway. And then I garden. And this is the ideal life which I almost
never have. But the ideal day (I think I've had two in May) is to be
alone all day and do that and then garden for three hours; then come
in, get my dinner, look at the news.

*But it's never given you a sense of a dull ache at the base of your
head to be doing everything under the same roof that you do?*
No. I don't get any ache. I love being here, and I loved it in Nelson
too. I have so much in my head, and so much is going on around
me—I mean, the flowers, all of nature around me. I'm extremely
aware of all this—besides which, I needn't tell you, living in New
England is like traveling because every season is different.
In April we had a colossal snow storm. I couldn't get out for forty-
eight hours. I finally managed to push open one door. And I couldn't
make an engagement. Well, that was a world apart from this, you
see. Look out now and you see the fruit trees in flower and the lilacs
in bloom, the daffodils; the field is green. It was white, snow white.
So I travel by being here, but I also travel, period, only less perhaps
than I used to. I went to Europe last year, to France, to see a cousin
of mine. It was very nice.
I used to go every spring to England. But that was when Virginia
Woolf was alive and the Huxleys; Julian Huxley was a very dear
friend of mine. And Elizabeth Bowen, whom I was very, very fond of,
too. I had a sort of glorious life then. And I don't know how it
happened; it was a lot of luck. I met all these people—how I don't
really know. I was only twenty-five, and there was no reason for
them to want to see me. But they were very kind to me. And it was
sort of glorious, glorious "bouquet" of people.

I don't know writers now. I really have very few writer friends now, almost none. I tried what many writers have done, that is, Yaddo, those places. I was at Yaddo for one absolutely terrible month in the middle of a winter. It was a terrible month because I heard that I lost my job at Wellesley, which was totally unexpected. You remember that; it's in one of the journals. The well—I had no water at Nelson— the artesian well had to be dug. And my agent thought *Mrs. Stevens* shouldn't be published. So I really was in hell. It was awful. And at the same time there was somebody there, who shall be nameless, the daughter of a very famous man, who took a tremendous dislike to me. I'm really quite likeable, and this has, I think, never happened to me before. But this woman just interrupted whenever I opened my mouth, and she sat at the feet of another famous writer—whose name I've forgotten now, but you'd know it at once—who lives in New York. Anyway, everything this woman said was listened to in awe and everything I said was just knocked over. And I began to think I was paranoid. I was so unhappy. But years later I asked Willard Trask, the translator, who was there, "Was this woman really so impossible as I thought she was, or was I sick?" He said, "Well, she was absolutely impossible." She was so rude. So the whole experience of being at Yaddo was so bad that I would never go back to another "colony," as they're called, a writer's colony, I don't think.

You've written about demons that come at you in times like this when you're in a low period and having a hard time of it. And one of those demons you've written about is the fatal division in loyalty between poetry and prose in your life. Now is this really a demon, do you think, something absolutely without basis, or do you think there is a grain of truth in this at all?

Oh, I think there is. It's a real conflict, of course. Now I thought you were going to say the conflict between private and public life, which I feel very much now, the conflict between being May Sarton in this public sense and the May Sarton who is still the very vulnerable child, really, and the artist. To preserve that child is the only way to go on writing until one dies, especially if one is a poet. You must keep the child alive. I was in a very great state of tension and despair a week ago because I didn't see how to handle my life. There's just too much in it.

Yes, you speak of the excruciating balance.

Yes. What are you to do if somebody writes you and says, "My daughter just threw herself out of the window of an eleventh-story building," and you don't know this woman. And she writes to you because she thinks you're going to help her. You can't just ignore such a letter. And I get a great many, from people who are depressed and think of me, as their friend, you see. And in a way it would be betraying my work, the trust that the work has created, if I just brushed them aside, and said, "I don't have time," because then the person who has come through in the work as real, as caring (I hope) and sensitive—it would all seem like a lie: "Well, I wrote her a letter and said my daughter died and she didn't even answer. I mean, so how human is May Sarton? She just talks about it." So this is the problem often for me. I do care. I mean I don't answer the letters just because I know I ought to. I do care, but it's very demanding.

Yes. You've said that "beyond even self-doubt, no writer can justify ruthlessness for the sake of his work because being human to the fullest possible extent is what his work demands of him. The conflict between life and art is bound to be acute, and the finding of a balance an excruciating daily struggle." And so I did want to ask you about that.

That's it. Every single day when I go up to my desk at eight I have this same struggle: but I ought to write to dear so-and-so who is depressed. And then I have to say, "No, Sarton, you've got to do your work first."

Yes. What about ruthlessness with yourself?

Well, that's it: you have to be ruthless with yourself too. And that's the hardest thing—to force yourself to keep on at it and not be swamped by all the demands and all the needs. You have to shut them out. But it's a daily struggle to do it. It really is. That's the thing I sometimes I think I'm going to die of. I'm going to die of the letters.

You said that there was a quote from Elizabeth Bowen that you had pondered a long time about and still do. And I wonder if you would do some pondering about it here for us. The quote is "If one is a writer one must regard oneself impersonally as an instrument."

Oh yes, I believe that, absolutely.

What do you mean by that?
Well, I mean by that—and that's why I think my journals are valuable—you've got to be able to look at yourself impersonally and for most people who keep journals it's a sort of vehicle for self-pity or self-adulation. I think Anais Nin's journals are terribly narcissistic. I find them unreadable, because here is a woman who builds up an image of herself as perfection—the saint. And it was only by accident that I heard in Canada from the woman who was writing the official biography, who said this in public, at a lecture, that when Nin, for instance, sacrifices her typewriter to Henry Miller and we're given to understand that this is a real sacrifice since she, Anais Nin, is a writer, and to give your typewriter is something; it's never mentioned in the journals that she was married to a very rich man. All the time of the journals it's never mentioned that she never had to worry about money. You see, that's what I consider dishonest and narcissistic, that she builds up this *myth*. What I've tried to do is to be terribly *honest* in my journals and in my life.

I wanted to ask you, though, from the standpoint of the craft and as artist, to what extent books like the journals and Plant Dreaming Deep *are "made" books? In what sense is the May Sarton in there a persona?*
Well, to some extent, I suppose. But I've tried to be extremely honest. This is why I wrote *Journal of a Solitude,* because I felt *Plant Dreaming Deep* had given a false idea. Don't forget that's *not* a journal, you see. It's a memoir. And it, therefore, is more of a work of art than the journals are and I think it's better than the journals as a work of art, for the reason that it's a distilled essence. The things had already happened. I sorted them out. Whereas in a journal it's on the pulse; it's what *just* happened. It's *that* day, although you sometimes think aloud of whatever has happened that day to make you confront, say, the problem of loyalty or whatever it may be. But, I say somewhere that we have to make myths of ourselves. Is that in *Mrs. Stevens* or in one of the journals?

That's in Plant Dreaming Deep.
Plant Dreaming Deep. And I believe *that:* because you have a certain idea of yourself you cannot do certain base things or certain easy things or certain self-indulgent things because it would not fit

your image, the image of yourself. I don't mean the image you project, but the image you have of yourself.

I think you have to be very clear about what you really mean about yourself. And you have to be able to be very dispassionate, to go back to Elizabeth Bowen. When I first heard that it struck me, you know, like a bolt of lightning, because I realized how important it was. The thing that destroys art is self-indulgence. And if you can be impersonal about yourself, to the extent of being able to see the reality, even when it's hard, then you have the capacity for growth, for one thing. You're not just defensive.

I have a friend who is very vulnerable, I think, but so on the defensive that she cannot take any criticism at all. She has to be right—always right. And luckily for me, I think, I've never had to be right. I've known that I was often wrong. I've spent a lot of my life being sorry for things I've done, but trying to find out why I did them or what was in back of it. Long ago, Jean Dominique—I quote this in one of the journals I think—said to me, "Pourquoi avoir raison?" [why be right?], in this gentle voice. It was a very gentle attack on me, and she was right, because I wanted to be right and I felt that I was right a lot of the time. I think I've learned to take that defensiveness off and just not have to be right anymore.

Another of the demons that you've written about, in the same context as that, is a fatal division in your loyalty between poetry and prose.

Yes . . .

And thus being disabled as a novelist. So I wanted to ask you if you still think that. But in that context I also wanted to ask about Plant Dreaming Deep *as being in a very noble tradition of books like* Walden *and the books of Henry Beston. Are you familiar with those?*

Oh, indeed, yes.

Were those at all models in your mind?

No. No. But, of course, Thoreau I practically knew by heart *(Walden)* before I was thirty. And Beston I haven't read as well. I have read him, but he certainly was not in my mind as a model. It's also very different, but I'm honored to have you put me in the same breath with them. They're both marvelous, marvelous writers and thinkers. But the point is that a novelist ought to belong to a society and I never have. Carolyn Heilbrun, who is my literary executor, has spoken of me as the "outsider." I feel it even here. I don't belong to any society. I don't. The easiest way to do that when you come to a new town is, of course, to join a church. And although I think I'm quite a religious person, my only affiliation is with Unitarians, but I never go to church.

But in what sense do feel that you don't have a society? This comes up over and over.

Well, I don't. I mean, what is a society? You see, class and all these things enter into what I mean by society. To some extent I belonged to a society when my parents and I both lived in Cambridge. But my father was a loner and he was an outsider, you see. He spoke with a French accent. I never *came out.* I never did any of the things that girls of my class did, you see, if you want to put it in class terms. I left home at seventeen to go into the theater. I never went to college. *That* is a group; *that* is a society. I see that with the friends my age. Think what their friends they met in college mean to them. When I went to Nelson I knew nobody. It was an extraordinary thing to do, really. To walk into a village where you had *no* roots whatever, knew nobody. I have nothing of New England in my background, nothing. My mother was English; my father was Belgian. I *made* roots, you see, but it could never be as though I had a family in the burying ground in Nelson where I will be buried, where I have my plot already. But, it's a big difference if you've been torn up from one culture.

But in so many ways, this is the American condition.
That's right.

And as a matter of fact, in the American tradition in literature this has been one of the major touchstones.
Well, except I envy the Southern writers because they have a society. I envy Eudora Welty, who stayed in Jackson all her life. I envy Faulkner, who could write about things that he knew that went back generations. That's what I mean.

But going back even further, both Hawthorne and James wrote of their not having an American past, by comparison to European culture, and they made that their fodder. And it seems to me that, in fact, that's what you've done.

I think it's just that I feel an outsider and a stranger in every respect. And I'm a lesbian. That also makes me an outsider.

Well, it does seem to be the American condition, that sense of no centuries and centuries and layers and layers of tradition.

Well, it's not true of the Southern writers. That's why they're better. There's a very big difference. You can't put a Northern writer, except Melville maybe, against Faulkner, Eudora Welty, Flannery O'Connor and so on. And the one who made the mistake of leaving, Carson McCullers, was ruined, of course. She could have been a great writer. She *left* the South, with fatal results. And, you see, in the South there was a culture which contained masters and servants—a whole richness, the badness of slavery, but also the richness of the black population. The North seems awfully empty in that way to me. It really does. There's Sarah Orne Jewett—there's the authentic one from Maine, certainly.

I've had problems because I belong to no group which backs me. Now, for instance, the lesbians don't back me because I don't want to be known as a lesbian writer. I want to be known as a universal writer. About six of my novels are about marriages, you see: young marriage, old marriage, middle-aged complexities of marriage, and what not. And yet I "came out" with *Mrs. Stevens* when it was very difficult to do that and I paid a very high price for doing that.

What was the price you paid?

I lost several jobs, immediately. I was to have been head of a summer poetry sort of school in a public high school in Bryn Mawr, Pennsylvania. And I was told by the headmistress of one of the schools in Bryn Mawr, who was running it, that she was afraid that because of *Mrs. Stevens*, as it was government money, she could not hire me. I think things have changed now. But, you see, I made that fight at a time when it was extremely lonely.

Now there's a huge lesbian nation, if you will, who is out to back anything that lesbians write. I don't approve of this. I don't think that just because you're a lesbian you're a good writer, or that people should pat you on the back if you're a writer and a lesbian and not pat somebody on the back who's heterosexual and a good writer. I mean, they're so narrow and so militant. And I'm not that. I want to be a universal woman. And women interest me. And I'm very pleased incidently, speaking of this, because the Unitarian women are giving me their citation for ministry to women this year, and they gave it to *Ms.* the first time. And then to the six Episcopal women priests who put up such a fight, and then to Maggie Kuhn.

And to Tillie Olsen.

And to Tillie Olsen. And it's very interesting and very moving to me that they're giving it to me. And they're giving it to me, it says, for "your courage and your honesty, and for your healing powers because of what you've written," which women find healing. I suppose they really do. It took me absolutely by surprise. I never expected such a thing.

What about the women's movement in general? Do you feel that this has done a lot to bring about what people write about as the rediscovery of May Sarton in the last few years?

Yes. I do. I do, indeed. And I'm very grateful to it. I myself am not a militant and in the first place I love men, and have been in love with men, though not since I was very young. I did have a love affair with a man when I was twenty-five, twenty-six. And I wanted to marry at that time. This was a married man, and there was no possibility of that. And I wanted to have children, but after that I was always in love with women (and even then I was in love with women). But, I shudder when I hear so much hatred of men. And granted that there are a lot of male chauvinists and granted that we have to fight for equal rights and all the rest of it, but there's a danger in the extreme militants, I think, of dividing the world into two and we've got to live together. I mean, we're one world. And just as blacks and whites have got to live together, men and women have got to live together.

Well, you've taken a lot of heat for the things that Mrs. Stevens says about this very issue in Mrs. Stevens Hears the Mermaids Singing. *And then you have written that this is a writer who is "somewhat like myself." You've also said that one of the problems of being a writer is that you can't answer your critics. Well, here you get the chance to answer your critics. How much of you is in Mrs. Stevens?*

Well, everything to do with the love affairs. Of course, I never
married. Remember, she's married in the beginning. Because I
wanted partly to point out what I had felt myself, which was that
when I was in love with a man I became a nurse. I mean, I never
wrote any poems. I was always taking care of *him*—it happened to
be a man a lot older than I who needed a lot of taking care of, but
still—whereas with a woman I feel inspired to write poems and to be
my real self in some ways. But where Mrs. Stevens is very different
from me is her parents. I adored my mother. My mother was my best
friend. And I made Mrs. Stevens's parents regular New England
people, rich New Englanders—nothing to do with my parents at all.
She's much less open to other people than I am, much less warm,
because you have to narrow things down in a novel. No character in
a novel is as complex as a real human being.

But what about the attitudes of women and art, and women as
women?

Everything she says in there about art and women I believe. I
mean, *there* she is my voice. The book was originally to be called
Naught for Your Comfort, because I was reacting then (already)
against the fashion for lesbianism. I would never proselytize. I would
never say that it's an adequate life. I don't think it is, compared to a
happy married life with children. In *my* case, that's the way I was
made. I am a homosexual woman. And it would have been very
false, I think now, for me to marry, and if I had I would never have
written. And there would have been terrible frustration.

But can one not get into the same kind of relationship with another
woman where these sorts of things happen too?

It's different. Women are too much alike. The challenge for the
man is that he's very different from you. I think there's more chance
for growth. The thing with women is that it's very narcissistic. They
are very much alike.

Twenty percent of the letters I get are from married women with
children who are terribly frustrated because they can't find time to
write, because they are unable to handle it. And the fact still remains
that when you think of the great women writers, none of them,
except Kay Boyle, who has six children, really has had a family life.
When you think of Virginia Woolf, Elizabeth Bowen; when you think

of the great painters, Georgia O'Keeffe; when you think of the
sculptors—it's very difficult.

But I have to be an optimist. I think it *is* possible. But it requires a
woman who has exceptional energy. There's *no doubt:* it is much
easier to be a man writer or artist or composer than to be a woman
composer or writer.

There's also the male chauvinism which is certainly very strong. I
mean that when it comes to reviewing women, they never get a
fair chance, or much less. For example, the *New York Times* has two
male reviewers and no woman. Now once in a long while there is a
woman, but she's not the regular. That's just one example. So
they choose the books they want to review, and *those* men are not
apt to choose women's books. They review *far* more men's books
than they do books by women. So the struggle for a woman still
remains. The very sad thing about it is that the worst reviews I've
ever had have been from women, the least generous. The most
generous reviews I've had have been from men. So you see, it's just
a difficult thing.

But, here is another example of male chauvinism. John Ciardi and
Dick Eberhart and Richard Wilbur and John Holmes and I used to
meet, thirty years ago or more, four times a year and read our poems
to each other and get very drunk and criticize each other. These
were very interesting sessions after which I always went home and
cried. In the first place, Wilbur was so astonishingly brilliant then.
Eberhart would arrive with a suitcase of material. Nobody really
wanted to listen to any criticism except me. I did. And sometimes
they were savage, and sometimes I learned a lot, but it was painful.
John Ciardi recently—I'm *told* this, I haven't seen the book—wrote a
book in which in the preface he tells about these sessions and never
mentions that I was there. That is an example of male chauvinism.

*Indeed. Do you agree with the criticisms that Miss Heilbrun levels
at you about your attitudes towards marriage and family life? She
accuses you of being a little bit soft-headed in this regard.*

Yes, I know it, of romanticizing marriage. I think she's wrong. And I
think if you take all the novels, including *Crucial Conversations* and
the one that's coming out now, *Anger,* which is about a fight between two temperaments, I don't believe that I've sentimentalized

marriage. She feels, for instance, that in *The Bridge of Years* it's wrong that Melanie adores her husband so and feels inferior to him. But the fact is that she is running the business. She is the masculine and he is the feminine in that marriage. And I think *that* is only true. It's true of *some* marriages. It was true of that marriage. It was based on a real marriage which I observed very closely. I disagree with her about a great many things. She's a little bit more of a feminist than I am; around her you can't say something like "women are different from men," but they *are*. I mean she's wrong, period.

What about her thesis—androgyny? You express ambivalence about that thesis in Journal of a Solitude.
Did I? Because I admire the book very much.

As I recall, in Journal of a Solitude, *you weren't rejecting it* per se, *but you had some feelings of ambivalence about how operative androgyny really was in the creative process with respect to your own work.*
Funny, because I feel that I am androgynous, and that every creator is. Are you sure that it was that? I disagreed with her treatment of Mrs. Ramsay in Virginia Woolf's *To the Lighthouse*. I disagreed violently and still do with that.

In other words, you do believe Mrs. Ramsay is an artist of life.
Yes, I do. Also I think it's the first time I ever read a book in which the life of a woman was made clear—the endless harmonizing of the endless chaos of life, that you make a beautiful table and cook a lovely meal, then a great mess is left and you tidy it up. The people who sit at your table all have their problems that clash with each other and you're the person, if you're Mrs. Ramsay, who is trying to make peace all the time and harmonize all this. Heilbrun sees her as a totally negative figure, really as a monster, a marriage maker and all this. So that's where I disagree with her.

But the theory of androgyny I absolutely agree with. It's only when men are willing to recognize the feminine in themselves and nourish it that we'll cease to have wars. I mean, it's a very important thesis. And women must not be afraid of the masculine in them. I object to Jung's definition of the animus as the male side of the woman because it makes it seem so negative. For me, the male side in me is the creator.

Not the female side?
Not the female side so much. The female side is the nurturer.

Thank you for taking time to talk with us today.
Thank you.

The Art of Poetry XXXII: May Sarton

Karen Saum/1982

From *Writers at Work, Seventh Series* by the *Paris Review*. Copyright © 1986 by The Paris Review. Used by permission of Viking Penguin, a division of Penguin Books USA Inc. Karen Saum's interview first appeared in *The Paris Review* 89 (1983), 81–110.

The author of a remarkably varied body of work, May Sarton lives by herself in York, Maine, in a former "summer cottage," quite isolated, at the end of a long dirt road. The road curves through a well-kept wood ending at *"The House by the Sea"* (the title of one of her journals). The house, formal in design, is of pale yellow clapboard fronted by a flagstone terrace. It faces, across a rolling meadow, the deep blue of the ocean marked here and there by a line of white foam. It is a late November afternoon and growing cold. The flower beds around the house, running along the fence and at the edge of the terraces, are all banked for winter. Her little Sheltie, Tamas, alerts her to the arrival of a guest, and she comes to greet me at the gate.

Possessed of that profound attentiveness characteristic of true charm, May Sarton has, at the same time, an exuberant nature. Her voice, full of inflection and humor, expresses the range of her personality. It has been called a "burnished" voice and it makes for spellbinding poetry readings, which she gives frequently—at places from small New England churches to the Library of Congress, and at colleges everywhere.

In the library, a fire is blazing, and Bramble, the once wild cat, is asleep on the couch. Sarton brings in a tea tray, complete with cinnamon toast and cookies. In this room, with the shelves of her work—novels, books of poems, memoirs, and journals—and the shelves of her father's works (George Sarton was the noted Harvard historian of science), under the benign gaze of Duvet de la Tour, "The Ancestor" ("always referred to as if he were the only one"), the interview begins.

Interviewer: Would you say a word about your work as a whole?

Sarton: My first book was a book of poems, *Encounter in April*, followed by my first novel, *The Single Hound*. There was quite an interval before the second novel, *The Bridge of Years*. And then *Shadow of a Man*. Then it goes on and on for a long time with a book of poems between every novel. That was my wish, that the poems should be equal in number, that the novels should not be more important than the poems because the poems were what I cared about most. Much later, when I was forty-five or so, I began to do nonfiction—first the memoirs and finally the journals, which came as the last of the forms which I have been using. Altogether now I think it amounts to seventeen novels, I don't know, five or six memoirs and journals, and then twelve books of poems, which are mostly in the collected poems now.

Interviewer: Has it been easy to shift amongst all these different forms?

Sarton: Sometimes the demon of self-doubt comes to tell me that I've been fatally divided between two crafts, that of the novel and that of poetry, but I've always believed that in the end it was the total work which would communicate a vision of life and it really needs different modes to do that. The novels have been written in order to find something out about what I was thinking, questions I was asking myself that I needed to answer. Take a very simple example, *A Shower of Summer Days*. The great house that dominates the novel was Bowen's Court. What interested me was the collision between a rich nature, a young girl in revolt against everything at home in America, and ceremony, tradition, and beauty as represented by the house in Ireland.

Interviewer: Is it safe to assume that the rebellious young woman is based partly on you?

Sarton: Not at all. It's a complete invention. The only person who is not invented in that book is the husband of Violet, and he is based on Elizabeth Bowen's husband. The house is, as I said, Bowen's Court. I stayed there.

Interviewer: And you knew Elizabeth Bowen.

Sarton: Oh, yes. I was in love with her. I've said what I really want to say about her in the portrait [*A World of Light*]. She was a marvelous friend. A very warm and giving person.

Interviewer: What intrigues me in your portrait of her is that although she had a tremendous effect on you emotionally, she had no influence on you artistically. You never emulated her work.

Sarton: No. Very little influence. None. Her style is too mannered. At her best, in *The Death of the Heart*, it's marvelous, but in the later books her style became too literary in a not very attractive way to me. For instance, a sentence is very rarely a straight sentence.

Interviewer: It's convoluted?

Sarton: It's convoluted and put upside down. "Very strange was the house" instead of "The house was very strange." Incidentally, Elizabeth Bowen appears in my novel *A Single Hound*, as the lover of Mark. I made her into a painter.

Interviewer: We were talking, before this digression, about why you write novels. You say you write them to find out what you are thinking, to answer a question. Could you give another example?

Sarton: In the case of *Faithful Are the Wounds*, the question was: how can a man be wrong and right at the same time? This book was based on the suicide of F. O. Matthiessen during the McCarthy era. At that time, people outside his intimate circle, and I was never an intimate of Mattie's, did not know that he was a homosexual, so that is only suggested in the novel. But what interested me was that Mattie believed that socialists and communists could work together in Czechoslovakia and had gone way out on a limb to say this was possible and was going to happen and might be the answer to world peace. Then the communists took over and the socialists were done in. It was a terrible blow to Mattie and some people thought the suicide came from that. I wrote the novel partly because I was very angry at the way people I knew at Harvard reacted after his suicide. At first, as always happens with a suicide, people close to him thought, "What could we have done?" There was guilt. Then very soon I heard, "Poor Mattie, he couldn't take it." That was what enraged me, because these people didn't care that much, were not involved. And Mattie did care. I'm sure the suicide was personal as well as political, and perhaps everything was all wound up together at that point . . . but he was right in the deepest sense, you see, only he had bet on the wrong horse. His belief that people could work together, and that the Left must join, not divide, was correct. It proved to be unrealistic. But he wasn't nearly as wrong as the people who didn't care. That's what I wrote the novel out of.

Interviewer: You've spoken of the novel. Earlier, you spoke of the body of your work as a whole. Would you talk about how the different parts fit together?

Sarton: The thing about poetry—one of the things about poetry—is that in general one does not follow growth and change through a poem. The poem is an essence. It captures perhaps a moment of violent change but it captures a moment, whereas the novel concerns itself with growth and change. As for the journals, you actually see the writer living out a life, which you don't in any of the other forms, not even the memoirs. In memoirs you are looking back. The memoir is an essence, like poetry. The challenge of the journal is that it is written on the pulse, and I don't allow myself to go back and change things afterwards, except for style. I don't expand later on. It's whatever I am able to write on the day about whatever is happening to me on that day. In the case of a memoir like *Plant Dreaming Deep*, I'm getting at the essence of five years of living alone in a house in a tiny village in New Hampshire, trying to pin down for myself what those five years had meant, what they had done to me, how I had changed. And that's very different from the journals. I must say, I'm not as crazy about the journals as some of my readers are. I get quite irritated when people say the journals are the best thing. God knows, I've struggled with certain things in the journals, especially about being a woman and about being a lesbian. The militant lesbians want me to be a militant and I'm just not.

But as for the vision of life in the whole of my work, I would like to feel that my work is universal and human on the deepest level. I think of myself as a maker of bridges—between the heterosexual and the homosexual world, between the old and the young. *As We Are Now*, the novel about a nursing home, has been read, curiously enough, by far more young people than old people. It terrifies old people to read about other old people in nursing homes. But the young have been moved by it. Many young people write me to say that they now visit elderly relatives in these places. This is the kind of bridge I want to make. Also, the bridge between men and women in their marriages, which I've dealt with in quite a few of the novels, especially in the last one, *Anger*.

So what one hopes, or what I hope, is that the whole work will represent the landscape of a nature which is not primarily intellectual but rather a sensibility quite rich and diverse and large in its capacities to understand and communicate.

Interviewer: How do you see your novels fitting into the tradition of the novel form?

Sarton: Well, they are quite traditional. I certainly haven't broken the forms. This is true in the poetry too. I think this may be one reason I have not had a great deal of critical attention, because the critics, I mean the real critics, not just the reviewers, are interested in the innovators. I suppose that *Mrs. Stevens Hears the Mermaids Singing* is innovative in that the material had not been dealt with as openly before, or at least not quite in the same way. But the technique isn't extraordinarily radical.

I have done all kinds of things with points of view in my novels, but I prefer the omniscient view, which I used in *Kinds of Love*. I think it's better for me, and perhaps for a poet, because you are able to describe things. In a novel like *Crucial Conversations*, the point of view is that of a friend of the marriage, an observer, and there is so much you simply cannot describe. You can't describe the atmosphere, the landscape, the interior of a house, say, without being quite awkward in the way you do it. "He walked in and noticed the roses were faded on the little eighteenth-century table." It's a little self-conscious. Ever since Henry James, there has been this big quibble about the point of view. As I say, I prefer the omniscient view although it's very unfashionable and is constantly pounced upon by the critics.

And the dialogue, of course. Elizabeth Bowen has said the great thing about dialogue: "Dialogue is what people do to each other." *Anger* is a perfect example. The war between these two characters is a war of dialogue. To some extent also in *Crucial Conversations* and even in an old novel of mine, *Shadow of a Man*, which I dipped into the other day because people are reading it now that it's in paperback, a great deal happens in the dialogue.

Interviewer: For which of the novels do you have the greatest affinity?

Sarton: *Mrs. Stevens*, I think, *Faithful Are the Wounds*, and *As We Are Now* would be my three . . . and *A Reckoning*. Those four. Of

course, they are all very different. *Faithful Are the Wounds* is a
passionate political book, and I haven't done that any other time. In
As We Are Now I think I did succeed in making the reader absolutely
identify with Caro, the old woman who is stuffed into a ghastly rural
nursing home and who is trying to stay alive emotionally. I look at *As
We Are Now* as a descent into hell in which there are different steps
down. The first is the person being captured, so to speak, and put in
jail. The final step is when genuine love is made dirty. Caro had
come alive again because a gentle nurse came into this terrible place
and she sort of fell in love with her. Then that love is made dirty by
the people who own the home. She tries to run away at that point.
That's the final step; after that she begins to go mad and suffers
despair. That's when she decides to burn the place down. She has a
long conversation about God with her minister. One thing I like about
this book is that there is a good minister in it. Ministers are almost
always treated ironically in fiction, or made into monsters of some
kind. This minister really listens. He isn't trying to tell her something.
He's interested in what she has to say.

Interviewer: So the end represents madness, not in any way a
cleansing.

Sarton: Well, it's partly a cleansing action for her. The end has
been questioned, and I myself question it because she burns up
innocent people in the fire. But I felt it had to end that way. The
innocent people were just vegetables, and so ill-treated that one felt
death was better, really. And Caro probably does feel this way, only
it isn't quite sane; she has all the inventiveness of the mad person
who has an *idée fixe* of how she is going to proceed.

Interviewer: At what point does the end become inevitable?

Sarton: When genuine love is defiled. That's when everything
goes. There is nothing left. Then she is in hell.

Interviewer: And the reason for your particular affinity with the
novel *A Reckoning?*

Sarton: The origin of the book is rather interesting. I wrote it
before I myself had cancer, and a mastectomy. But at an earlier date
I *thought* I had cancer, and for a few days while the biopsy was being
done I had an immense feeling of relief that I could lay the burden of
my life down, get rid of all the clutter, and for the last six months of it,
simply live and look at the world . . . look at the sun rise and not do

anything that I ought to do. And then when I heard that I was all right and had to pick up the burden again of answering letters and living my life, which is a very good one but very demanding, I cried. I went out to Raymond, the gardener, and said, "I'm all right, Raymond," and burst into tears.

That was the clue to the novel, you see. Then I thought, "Ah! I'm going to write it. What would it have been like if I had had cancer, and six months to live my own death?" Really, the book is about how to live as much as it is about how to die. From much that I hear about it, I know it has been a helpful book. It's used in the hospices, and in nursing homes, and often read by nurses and people who are dealing with the dying. It has been useful, there is no doubt, and that is a wonderful feeling.

Interviewer: Have any particular novelists been mentors?

Sarton: Yes. Certainly Virginia Woolf. She was the novelist who meant the most to me when I was learning. But she is a dangerous mentor from the technical point of view because she can't be imitated. It's too much her own genius. My first novel is written in a very Woolfian way. There's a description of a woman walking down some steps and it's summer and it's like a pastiche of Woolf. I never did that again.

Interviewer: You've written in your journals about your meetings with Virginia Woolf, but can you cast your mind back and describe the very first moment you met her?

Sarton: I had left my first book of poems at her door, with some flowers, and the darling maid opened the door just then and said, "Oh, won't you come up?" I said, "Oh, no, I wouldn't think of it." I just left the book. Elizabeth Bowen knew that I wanted to meet Virginia Woolf desperately, so she invited the two of us and a couple of other people to dinner. That was when I first met her. She walked in, in a "robe de style," a lovely, rather eighteenth-century-looking, long dress with a wide collar, and she came into the room like a dazzled deer and walked right across—this was a beautiful house on Regent's Park—to the long windows and stood there looking out. My memory is that she was not even introduced at that point, that she just walked across, very shyly, and stood there looking absolutely beautiful. She was much more beautiful than any of the photographs show. And then she discovered that I was the person who had left the poems.

She was very canny . . . she answered my gift of that book with a lovely note, which is now in the Berg collection, just saying: "Thank you so much, and the flowers came just as someone had given me a vase, and were perfect, and I shall look forward to reading the poems." In other words, never put yourself in a position of having to judge. So she never said a word about the poems. But she was delighted to find out that I was the person who had left them.

Then, later, we talked—Elizabeth and Virginia Woolf and I. The gentlemen were having their brandy and cigars in the other room. We talked about hairdressers. It was all like something in *The Waves!* We all talked like characters in a Virginia Woolf novel. She had a great sense of humor. Very malicious. She liked to tease people, in a charming way, but she was a great tease.

Interviewer: Did you feel shy?

Sarton: Of course! But she put me at ease and I saw her quite often after that. Every time I was in England I would have tea with her, which was a two-hour talk. She would absolutely ply me with questions. That was the novelist. I always felt the novelist at work. Where did I buy my clothes? Whom was I seeing? Whom was I in love with? Everything. So it was enrapturing to a young woman to be that *interesting* to Virginia Woolf. But I think it was her way of living, in a sense. Vicariously. Through people.

Interviewer: But you've written that you felt a certain coldness, in spite of . . .

Sarton: Yes. She was never warm. That's true. There was no warmth. It was partly physical, I think. She was a physically unwarm person. I can't imagine kissing her, for instance, I mean on the cheek. But she was delightful, and zany, full of humor and laughter. Never did you feel a person on the brink of madness. That has distorted the image, because she was so in control.

Interviewer: You were speaking of influences. Whom else would you add?

Sarton: The person who influenced me the most has been François Mauriac. I greatly admired the economy and thrust of his books. He was able to create so much between the lines. I was aiming for that. I was aiming to eliminate what at first I was praised for, a so-

called "poetic style." I wanted to get rid of that and to make the
poetry less obvious, to make it sharper and purer and simpler. I've
worked to get a more and more clarified style, but I think this has
been misunderstood in my case. Somebody said of *As We Are Now:*
"A ninth-grader could have written it"—meaning the style. I mean,
this person simply didn't get it! Other people did get it, fortunately.
Of course, the thing that is so tremendous with Mauriac, and isn't
possible for me because I don't belong to the Church, is the Catholic
in him, which gives this extra dimension to everything that he wrote. I
envy him that.

Interviewer: How was it that you began to write the journals?

Sarton: I wrote the first one, *Journal of a Solitude*, as an exercise
to handle a serious depression and it worked quite well. I did have
publication in mind. It wasn't written just for me. I think it's part
of the discipline. It keeps you on your toes stylistically and prevents
too much self-pity, knowing that it's going to be read and that it will
provide a certain standard for other people who are living isolated
lives and who are depressed. If you just indulge in nothing but
moaning, it wouldn't be a good journal for others to read. I also
found that by keeping a journal I was looking at things in a new way
because I would think, "That—good! That will be great in the journal." So it took me out of myself, out of the depression to some
extent. This happened again with *Recovering*.

Interviewer: You write for publication; do you have an imagined
audience?

Sarton: It's really one imaginary person.

Interviewer: Would you talk a little about this imaginary person?

Sarton: Well, I don't mean that when I sit down I think, "Oh,
there is that imaginary person over there I'm writing for," but . . .
yes! Somebody who sees things the way I do, who will be able
to read with heart and intelligence. I suppose somebody about my
age. It used to be somebody about forty-five; not it's somebody
about seventy. But then *Journal of a Solitude* brought me a whole
new audience, a college-age audience. That was very exciting because until then my work had appealed mostly to older people.

Interviewer: Isn't it true that lately you have been embraced by
the spiritual establishment?

Sarton: Yes, this has happened only recently and has been extremely moving to me. I have come out as a lesbian. And although I have no shame about this at all, I still feel it's quite extraordinary that religious groups would be so receptive to me, as the Methodists were, for instance. They asked me to be one of the speakers at their yearly retreat for pastors. The other speakers were religious in a way that I am not. Then, the Unitarians gave me their Ministry to Women Award last year and I was touched by what they said . . . that I'd helped women by my honesty. The Methodists also talked about honesty.

I must say it was quite brave of me to come out as I did in *Mrs. Stevens*, in 1965. At that time it was "not done." When I spoke at colleges I would never have stated, "I'm a lesbian." But this all changed in the seventies. It's marvelous now that one can be honest and open. At the time *Mrs. Stevens* was published, it was sneered at in reviews and I lost a couple of jobs. They weren't terribly important jobs but I did lose them. Now I don't think that would happen. It might if you were a professor in a college, but coming as a visiting speaker you can be absolutely open. Women's Studies have helped me enormously, there's no doubt about it. This is one way my work is now getting through.

I know of no other writer who has had such a strange career as I've had. When I started writing, the first novels were received with ovations. In 1956, I was nominated for the National Book Award in two categories, fiction and poetry. But after my fifth novel, *Faithful Are the Wounds*, the one that was nominated, this never happened again and I began to have bad reviews. I was no longer in fashion. I can't think of another writer who has had as hard a time with reviewers over a period of twenty years as I have but whose work has been so consistently read. It's word of mouth. It's people . . . every day I get letters saying things like: "I loved such and such a book and I'm buying five copies to give to people." That's how books get around. And then the public libraries. Without the public libraries, serious writers, unfashionable serious writers like me, really wouldn't have a chance. Again, I hear from people, "I was wandering around the library and saw the title *Plant Dreaming Deep*. It caught my attention . . . now I'm reading everything you've written." It's wonderful to have this happen at the age of seventy.

Interviewer: Will you talk about the relationship between the poet and the Muse?

Sarton: Many of my poems are love poems. I'm only able to write poetry, for the most part, when I have a Muse, a woman who focuses the world for me. She may be a lover, may not. In one case it was a person I saw only once, at lunch in a room with a lot of other people, and I wrote a whole book of poems. Many of these poems have not been published. But this is the mystery. Something happens which touches the source of poerty and ignites it. Sometimes it is the result of a long love affair, as "The Divorce of Lovers" poems, the sonnet sequence. But not always. So who is the audience for my poetry? The audience is the loved one for me. But usually "the loved one" isn't really interested in the poems.

Interviewer: You, and Robert Graves with his White Goddess, are perhaps the only modern poets to be so strongly and personally inspired by the Muse as a mythological figure. A literal figure. Do your Muses, diverse as they must be, possess any one thing in common?

Sarton: Maybe so. The word that popped into my mind when you asked the question was: distance. Maybe there is something about the Distant Admired Person. I had a curious experience in Berkeley recently, where I stayed with a friend I went to school with, the Shady Hill School, in Cambridge, Massachusetts. She had saved a book of poems that a group of us had written. We used to meet, four of us, and read our poems to each other and savagely criticize them. These poems were *passionate* love poems to our teacher, Anne Thorp, the person I'm now trying to write a novel about. I was absolutely floored by the intensity of these poems! We were completely inexperienced. In that generation there was no sex, I mean nothing like what goes on now. We were asexual because we just didn't know anything yet. But we *felt* so intensely. And I saw that I haven't changed that much. I'm not innocent in the way I was then, but my feelings have remained very much as they were.

Interviewer: If Anne Thorp had possessed all those qualities you worshiped, but had been a man . . . could you have been writing those love poems to a man?

Sarton: Yes, it's possible. I just don't know. The three other people did not become homosexual. Only I among the four.

Interviewer: You have spoken of poems as coming from the subconscious.

Sarton: It's not the poem that comes from the subconscious so much as the image. Also the single line, *la ligne donnée*. If I'm truly inspired, the line comes in meter and sets the form. But what comes from the subconscious is only the beginning. Then you work with it.

In the case of metaphor, it has everything to teach you about what you have felt, experienced. I write in order to find out what has happened to me in the area of feeling, and the metaphor helps. A poem, when it is finished, is always a little ahead of where I am. "My poem shows me where I have to go." That's from Roethke. His line actually reads: "I learn by going where I have to go."

Interviewer: So you write novels to find out what you think, and poems to find out what you feel?

Sarton: Yes, it works out that way. In the novel or the journal you get the journey. In a poem you get the arrival. The advantage of free verse, for instance in "Gestalt at Sixty," is that you do get the journey. Form is so absolute, as if it had always been there, as if there had been no struggle. The person who sees the lyric poem on the page doesn't realize there may have been sixty drafts to get it to the point where you cannot change a single word. It has been worked for. But something has been given, and that's the difference between the inspired poem and what Louise Bogan calls the imitation poem. In the inspired poem something is given. In the imitation poem you do it alone on will and intelligence. I mean, you say something like: "It might be a good idea to write a poem about a storm down here at the end of the field when the fountains of spray come up." And so you go ahead and do it. But the difference is simply immense, as far as the poet goes. He knows, or she knows, what is inspired and what is imitation.

Interviewer: Would the reader know?

Sarton: I think so.

Interviewer: What about the advantages and disadvantages of form?

Sarton: Form is not fashionable these days. What's being thrown out, of course, is music, which reaches the reader through his senses. In meter, the whole force is in the beat and reaches the reader, or the listener, below the rational level. If you don't use meter, you are throwing away one of the biggest weapons to get at the reader's subconscious and move him. The advantage of form, far from being "formal" and sort of off-putting and intellectual, is that through form you reach the reader on this subliminal level. I love form. It makes you cut down. Many free verse poems seem to me too wordy. They sound prose-y, let's face it. When you read a poem in form, it's pared down, it's musical, and it haunts. Very few free verse poems are memorable. You don't learn them by heart unless they are very short. But a lyric poem is easy to remember.

Interviewer: You have written poems in free verse.

Sarton: Oh, yes, a lot. I find it exhilarating.

Interviewer: How do you know when you're finished?

Sarton: That's the problem. I can go on revising almost forever. But with form, at a certain point it's all there. Another problem, or danger, with free verse, is that it depends almost entirely on the image, so you get people using what I call "hysterical images," images which are too powerful because you've got to hit the reader over the head with something big . . . like talking about love in terms of the Crucifixion. Or the Holocaust. A tremendously strong image to say something which doesn't deserve that intensity and only shocks the reader, but in a rather superficial way.

Interviewer: What poets have had the most influence on you?

Sarton: H. D., when I was young. It was the age of Millay. Millay was the great . . . well, everybody adored her. And I did too. I loved those lyrics. But I was fascinated by H. D. because of the freshness she managed to get into free verse. Then the other women lyric poets: Elinor Wylie certainly influenced me, and later on Louise Bogan, who I think was probably the most distinguished pure lyric poet of our time. There you get that marvelous economy and music and depth and also the archetypal images. And then Valéry, whom I translated with Louise Bogan.

Interviewer: Because your parents were European, and you yourself were born in Belgium, has that made a difference to you as a poet?

Sarton: I think an enormous difference. Because the things that touched me most, the literary things, were mostly in French, and later on, at fourteen, I came under the influence of Jean Dominique.

Interviewer: What about those very early years?

Sarton: During the first two years of my life we lived in a small heaven of a house in Wondelgem, Belgium. Then we were driven out by the war and went to England. In 1916, when I was four, we settled for good in Cambridge, Massachusetts. Even so, every seven years, when my father had a sabbatical, we all went to Europe. It took me until I was forty-five to become an American at heart. It was in 1958, after my parents were both dead, that I bought a house in Nelson, a small village in New Hampshire, and settled in for fifteen years and made roots. I describe that in *Plant Dreaming Deep*. I planted the dreams then and became an American.

But for very long, all my youth, from nineteen on anyway, I went to Europe every year. Although we never had much money, my father gave me a hundred dollars a month allowance, and an extra three hundred dollars, which at the time covered a boat round trip, tourist class. I either stayed with friends, or, in London, in one of those dreary one-room flats which cost £2 a week with an English breakfast thrown in. I felt European partly because—I still believe this—the emotional loam is deeper in Europe. People are less afraid of feeling. The lesbian part of me came into this because in the Bloomsbury society of the thirties there was no trouble about that. I didn't feel like a pariah. I didn't feel that I had to explain myself. And among my mother's generation there were passionate friendships between women that were probably not sexually played out, but it was common for women to be a little in love with each other. It was taken for granted. It wasn't a big issue.

One of the themes in all I have written is the fear of feeling. It comes into the last novel where Anna asks, "Must it go on from generation to generation, this fear of feeling?" I want feelings to be expressed, to be open, to be natural, not to be looked on as strange. It's not weird, I mean, if you feel deeply. And, really, most Americans think it is. Sex is all right, but feeling is not. You can have five people in your bed and no one will worry much, but if you say, "I've fallen in love at seventy," people's hair is going to stand on end. They'll think, "The poor thing, there's something awfully wrong with her."

Interviewer: Young people read *Halfway to Silence* and quote the poems . . . it goes so much against our cultural norms, the idea of a woman of sixty-five writing a passionate love poem to another woman.

Sarton: Yes, I know. And I have done it more than once. The poem "Old Lovers at the Ballet" is really about this: how is the sexuality different for an older couple, old lovers watching these magnificent bodies which they don't have and the grace which they no longer have? I suggest that what they do have is something else, an ability to communicate spiritually through sex. I believe that at its deepest, sex is a communication of souls through the body. That can go on forever.

Interviewer: Did you ever write poems in French?

Sarton: I wrote poems for Jean Dominique in French, but I didn't know the language well enough, the prosody, and so they have a certain charm but nothing more. I'd never publish them.

Interviewer: So the European influence is in the emotional climate more than anything.

Sarton: Yes. But as I said, the seminal influences in my writing were French; Mauriac for the novels, Valéry for the poetry, and also Gide at a certain time, particularly in the journals.

Interviewer: Would you talk about the poems you're writing now?

Sarton: I'm writing new poems now called "Letters from Maine." It's a new form for me. I've written so many poems in sonnet form, or in other forms, and I wish I could find something a little freer which is not free verse. These are a sort of loose iambic pentameter. They don't rhyme, and they flow. It's impossible for me to tell whether they're any good. In six months I'll look back and say, "That was a bad idea, it didn't work," or I'll say, "These are really quite good." Then I can begin to revise.

The poems come from a new Muse. A very distant one whom I probably won't see very much of. But it's opened up that mysterious door again. It's amazing, so mysterious, so extremely hard to talk about. Why should it happen that among all the people, the great many women whom I see and am fond of, suddenly somebody I meet for half an hour opens the door into poetry? Something is released. The deepest source is reached. Some of my best poems have been written for occasions which did not materialize, if you will. "In Time Like Air" is an example. "In time like air is essence stated" is the final line. Here is an example of an image which haunts for years, an archetypal image, *salt*, which I got from the French philosopher Gaston Bachelard. Bachelard has written a whole series of books analyzing images. In one of them he talks about the image of salt, and says it is a Janus material because it dissolves in water, crystallizes in air. I put that in a notebook and carried it around for years. Then I met somebody who started poetry for me again. I realized that salt was the image I needed. A metaphysical poem about love. And time. Love and time. There's only that one poem.

Interviewer: You've discussed the different forms, or modes, you use to express your vision of life: poetry, novels, journals, memoirs. Were you ever tempted to write short stories?

Sarton: I did at one time write a number of stories when I was living in Cambridge and making very little money. I sold some to the then slicks, a lot of which don't exist anymore, and also to places like *Redbook* and *Ladies' Home Journal*. There are about thirty stories. I broke some taboos. For instance, I wrote about a woman dying of cancer and you weren't supposed to do that—write about it, I mean. *Ladies' Home Journal* published that. But they were not wonderful and I wouldn't like to see them reprinted. They were just . . . well, I sold one little piece for $600, which to me was a fortune, so that sort of set me off. I thought—Well! This is great! I'll write lots! And I did write quite a few but I finally had to stop because when I sat at the typewriter dollar signs were floating around in my eyes. It was the money. I somehow couldn't handle it.

Interviewer: Could you write stories now?

Sarton: The form doesn't appeal to me very much. The short story is too much like a lyric, so that side goes into poetry.

Interviewer: You have spoken with great admiration of Yeats, who changed his style and grew in poetic power even when he was an old man. Earlier, you mentioned the new form of your latest poems. Using that sort of comparison, how does it feel to be seventy?

Sarton: For the first time in my life I have a sense of achievement. I've written all these books and they're there! Nobody can take that from me. And the work is getting through at last. For so long I felt there were people who would like to read me but didn't know I existed. So I'm more relaxed inside now, less compulsive . . . somewhat less compulsive.

Interviewer: You don't find that your past achievement acts as a brake on further achievement?

Sarton: Not at all. I feel much more creative now that I'm not carrying around that load of bitterness and despair because I was getting so little critical attention and therefore the readers weren't finding my work. Now they are finding it.

Interviewer: You once wrote that to be worthy of the task, the poet moves toward a purer innocence where "the wonderful is familiar and the familiar wonderful . . . ."

Sarton: That's a quote from Coleridge, of course. Where did I say that? In *Writings on Writing*, maybe. One of the good things about old age is that one often feels like a child. There is a childlike innocence, often, that has nothing to do with the childishness of senility. The moments become precious.

Ideally, one would live as if one were going to die the next day. I mean, if you were going to die the next day it would be well worth sitting and watching the sun set, or rise. It might not be worth doing a huge laundry.

Interviewer: Your aspirations for yourself when you were young were quite lofty . . .

Sarton: Where did you read that?

Interviewer: You told me.

Sarton: What do you mean? Of course my ambitions were lofty. I knew that I was a poet. This, like mathematical or musical gifts, you know when you are very young. My first poems were published in *Poetry* magazine when I was seventeen—five sonnets which open the first book, *Encounter in April*. Of course, I did think for a long time that I was going to be in the theater because I had fallen in love with a theater, the Civic Repertory Theater founded by Eva Le Gallienne in New York. She accepted me as an apprentice. I could have gone to Vassar, but I chose the theater. It was a difficult decision for my parents to accept, but in the end they backed the whole precarious plan.

Interviewer: If you could be the seventeen-year-old looking at the woman of seventy, what would you think?

Sarton: I think I would be proud of myself. I've done what I set out to do and without a great deal of help. I never took permanent jobs in the academic world, which most poets have to do, not that they want to, and this has cost me something because the critical acclaim comes from the academic world, which launches a poet. But yes, I think that if at seventeen I'd known there'd be twelve books of poems (at that time I never imagined novels at all), I would feel pretty good. I'd say, "You did what was in you to do."

But I don't sit here and think, "Oh, how wonderful you are, Sarton." I think, on the contrary, "Oh, how much there is still to do!"

Interviewer: You often see other poets and writers at conferences. Are you stimulated by this mixing with your peers, so to speak?

Sarton: I don't like writers. I don't like seeing writers. I'm not good at it. It upsets me. It's been too hard a struggle. I'm very competitive, and that side comes out. I'm uncomfortable with writers. I love painters and sculptors.

In relation to writers, the people whom I did love to see were the people who I felt were way ahead of me, like Louise Bogan and Elizabeth Bowen and Virginia Woolf. People from whom I had everything to learn and where my position was that of a neophyte. *That* I enjoyed. I have one very good new friend, a poet, Bill Heyen. He's a marvelously good poet, I think. But I really like to see what I call "real people"—who are not writers!

Interviewer: One theme I wanted to ask you about is the phoenix.

Sarton: The phoenix, yes. The mythical bird that is consumed by fire and rises again from its ashes. That was D. H. Lawrence's symbol. I've appropriated it. I think I have died and been reborn quite a few times. One renewal from the ashes, to stick to the symbol, is recorded in my latest journal, *Recovering*, which describes a combination of the end of a love affair, a mastectomy, and a third very hard blow: an attack on my novel *A Reckoning*. I knew this novel was going to have value for people who were dying, and for their children and friends and so on, and it was more or less damned in the *New York Times* as a lesbian novel. This hurt. So I was getting over a lot of things. Again, as with *Journal of a Solitude*, I used the journal as a way of coming to terms with depression, and that journal is helping a lot of people. I get many letters about it.

Interviewer: Have you been reborn recently?

Sarton: Yes. Yes, I have. I had gotten to a very sterile place because I was seeing so many people this summer and making so many public appearances, and yet at the center there was a kind of emptiness. I began to feel like a well that had gone dry. And then I did meet a woman who started the poems again, and has centered everything again for me. It's quite miraculous.

Interviewer: Would you talk about the theme of the creative woman as a monster?

Sarton: Ruth Pitter, the poet, said in a letter to me once, "We are all monsters," meaning women poets. *Le monstre sacré.* As I say in the poem "My Sisters, Oh My Sisters," I think that was to some extent true. It isn't now. Now it's possible for women to have much more complete lives, and that's what we're working towards, really.

But let me go back for a minute to the phoenix. You see, at twenty-six I had been in the theater for six or seven years, first as an apprentice to Le Gallienne and then, when her theater failed, I kept the apprentices together and founded something called the Apprentice Theater. We did a season at the New School for Social Research in New York—rehearsal performances of Modern European plays in translation that had never been seen on Broadway. We got quite a lot of notice. It was a kind of first off-Broadway theater. But then we had to go into production in order to be a theater. I was offered a small theater in Hartford and we did a season there which was not a great success. I was looking all the time for new American plays and didn't find one. Finally we opened in Boston the following year and failed immediately, having spent $5,000 that I had managed to raise. So at twenty-six I faced failure, the complete failure of my dream of making a studio theater a little bit like the Moscow Art Theatre Studio. This was one of the times when the phoenix died and had to be reborn again and I was reborn as a writer. I was very ill after the theater failed. I guess I had what used to be called a nervous breakdown. My mother announced, "May has to rest," and took over. I rested for three months, just lay out on a chaise lounge. I was exhausted. Emptied out. But one has extraordinary powers of remaking oneself. I learned it physically with the mastectomy. I was amazed at the power of the body to come back after such a shock. For that reason, the mastectomy was a thrilling experience, odd as it sounds. The body has this power, and so does the mind and the soul, to remake itself. That is the phoenix.

Interviewer: Given your experience in the theater, might you not have been reborn as a playwright? Especially since you have such a strong sense of dialogue.

Sarton: I've written two full-length plays.
Interviewer: Should I know that?
Sarton: No, you shouldn't. They were never produced, although Archibald MacLeish thought one of them had real possibilities and tried to get Robert Brustein at Yale to do it. The other one won a prize but I can't even remember what sort of contest it was. I wrote them quite fast, in about three weeks each, which is probably why they weren't better! But I wrote them long after the theater failed. Ten years, at least. Maybe twenty years.

It was like a fever, the theater, for me, but it was so closely connected with the Civic Repertory and Eva Le Gallienne and that marvelous theater which was so pure. The theater is heartbreak. I admire people who have the guts to take it.

Interviewer: Apart from the informal teaching arrangements, you've earned your living entirely by your writing, isn't that true?
Sarton: Yes. I've never had a bonanza, but my books have been consistently read and now many of them are in paperback. It's been tough at times, but my writing has kept me afloat financially.

Interviewer: Everyone wants to know about a writer's work habits . . .
Sarton: I do all my work before eleven in the morning. That's why I get up so early. Around five.

Interviewer: Have you pretty much stuck to the same kind of discipline over the years?
Sarton: Yes, I have. That I got from my father. I think the great thing he gave me was an example of what steady work, disciplined work, can finally produce. In not waiting for "the moment," you know, but saying: "I'm going to write every day for two or three hours." The trouble, for me, is the letters. They interrupt, and I give much too much energy to that. It's an insoluble problem.

Interviewer: Would it be helpful, say, if you were stuck in your work, to switch over to the letters?
Sarton: I sometimes start the day with the letters. Just to get the oil into the machine.

Interviewer: Do you have other ways of getting oil into the machine?
Sarton: Music. I play records, mostly eighteenth-century music. I find that the Romantics—Beethoven—don't work for me. I love them

to listen to, but not to work with, alongside of, whereas Mozart, Bach, Albinoni . . . Haydn, I love. I feel the tremendous masculine joy of Haydn. That gets me going.

Interviewer: It gets you going, but do you keep it going?

Sarton: Yes. It's probably a terrible thing to do to the music but it does a lot for me.

Interviewer: You have mentioned that you are writing a journal, and there are the new poems . . .

Sarton: And a novel. I'm hoping now to get back to a novel that went dead on me before I wrote *Anger*, called *The Magnificent Spinster*. I'm looking forward to doing it because it will be rather rich and poetic in a way that *Anger* was not. *Anger* was a novel like a blow, trying to get at things almost brutally.

This brings up an interesting point, I think. Here I have this novel, which I set aside for a long time and which I am going back to. In other words, you can plan for a novel. You can say, "I'm going to write a novel next year" and then go ahead and do it. Except that it might not work out, but still you can plan for it. You simply cannot do this with poems, they come out of a seizure of feeling. You can't plan for a seizure of feeling, and for this reason I put everything else aside when I'm inspired, because, as I've said, you can't summon a poem. You can try, but it won't be much good if it's written on command.

Interviewer: You've written movingly about your parents in *A World of Light.*

Sarton: That is a memoir recapturing twelve different people, a celebration of great friendships. All of the people were dead, or "gone into the world of light"—the Henry Vaughan quote—at the time I wrote it, except one. I included my parents because their friendship has weighed on me all my life. Their influence was the most difficult to deal with, and the most inspiring. I've spoken about the value of memoirs as the past considered, as essences. In "The Fervent Years," the chapters in *I Knew a Phoenix,* I talk about my parents' youth. It taught me an awful lot about them, and about a whole period. They were tremendously idealistic people. They had the nineteenth-century vision of life, the perfectability of man. Ever since the Holocaust, something has happened to people, to all of us. We've had to face certain things which make it impossible for us to foresee a much better future. We're faced with a whole lot of choices that are pretty depressing. Whereas my parents still had that well of idealism and faith in humanity which runs through all of my father's work.

Interviewer: What about your phrase "usable truth . . ."?

Sarton: This is the function of poetry. To make people experience. That's where it's completely different from philosophy, where you think something out but don't have to experience it in your whole being so that you are changed. It's perfectly stated by Rilke in the sonnet "To the Archaic Torso of Apollo." One must visualize this ideally beautiful sculpture with no head and no eyes. The poem ends, "Here there is nothing that does not see you. You must change your life." That is what art is all about.

Stopping the Sun: A Conversation with May Sarton

William Heyen and Mary Elsie Robertson/1983

From *Kentucky Poetry Review* 24.1 (1988), 56–65. This transcript was edited from a videotape interview conducted by William Heyen and Mary Elsie Robertson on 3 November 1983 at the State University of New York, College at Brockport, where May Sarton was a guest of the Brockport Writers Forum and Videotape Library.

[Sarton reads "Now I Become Myself."]

Now I become myself. It's taken
Time, many years and places;
I have been dissolved and shaken,
Worn other people's faces,
Run madly, as if Time were there,
Terribly old, crying a warning,
"Hurry, you will be dead before—"
(What? Before you reach the morning?
Or the end of the poem is clear?
Or love safe in the walled city?)
Now to stand still, to be here,
Feel my own weight and density!
The black shadow on the paper
Is my hand; the shadow of a word
As thought shapes the shaper
Falls heavy on the page, is heard.
All fuses now, falls into place
From wish to action, word to silence,
My work, my love, my time, my face
Gathered into one intense

Gesture of growing like a plant.
As slowly as the ripening fruit
Fertile, detached, and always spent,
Falls but does not exhaust the root,
So all the poem is, can give,
Grows in me to become the song;
Made so and rooted so by love.
Now there is time and Time is young.
O, in this single hour I live
All of myself and do not move.
I, the pursued, who madly ran.
Stand still, stand still, and stop the sun!

Heyen: The poem you just read opens up so many things. One of my favorite Sarton words is *centered.* You speak frequently in your journals of feeling "centered" or "uncentered." One of the efforts in the poem is to become "centered."

Sarton: That's true. It's a poem about getting centered over a long period of time, in terms of influences. It says that I've worn other people's faces. Any beginning writer, or any *person* for that matter, first imitates others. I was tremendously influenced by Virginia Woolf, Elinor Wylie, Ruth Pitter, Louise Bogan—poets whom I felt an affinity for. I didn't exactly imitate them, but when you're starting out, you wear the faces of others until you learn your own. Finally you come into this person who is yourself and the poet you really are.

Heyen: It's a poem about time, too—about stopping time, about memory.

Sarton: Of course, you of all people would get immediately the reference to Marvell: "Thus, though we cannot make our sun/Stand still, yet we will make him run." It's such a great poem that I shouldn't put it beside mine. But you *can* stop the sun, if you are an artist. This poem was written in the 40s, so it's very old already, but I feel it's quite fresh and I hope readers will too.

Heyen: And you still have, I know, that experience in writing the poem—that joy of stopping the moment while you're writing it.

Sarton: That's it! It's the one time in my life when time doesn't

exist. You're way out somewhere in eternity really, and it has nothing
to do with whether the poem will last. But while you're making it,
you're really centered, whole, happy, at ease in the universe.

Robertson: Is that your experience too in writing a novel, or is
writing a novel a different experience?

Sarton: *Very* different. A novel is infinitely harder. When I was
very young and all I had published was a book of poems, Virginia
Woolf teased me by saying, "Oh, it's so much easier to write
poems." Of course, I laughed then, and thought, You don't know.
But it's true, partly because you're carrying a novel over such a long
period of time. I try to write five pages a day, and to many that
sounds like nothing; but if you think that it's five pages a day, every
day for a year, then it's like saying, "I'll walk five miles a day for a
year." The first day is quite easy, but keep it up, keep it up, and it
gets harder every day. I find the writing of a novel an excruciating
effort. I almost never enjoy myself at all. I used to say to students,
"Writing a novel is like taking an examination on which your whole
future depends—every day for a year—because it's got to be as good
as your last novel. The more you've got behind you, the worse it is."

Secondly, not as much is "given" with a novel. The whole poem
isn't given; it's terribly hard work; but you're given this impulse to
write it. With the novel you may get that when you first conceive it,
but you never get it again while you try to get back to that wonderful
vision of what this novel might be.

Robertson: You have said, "All of my novels are in some sense
autobiographical," by which I assume you mean that you're working
through problems in them that have been compelling to yourself.

Sarton: Yes. Like the effect of form and tradition in a great house.
That's a good one to show what I mean by "autobiographical."
When I first went to Bowen's Court, Elizabeth Bowen's very formal,
eighteenth-century house—Anglo-Irish in the midst of the Ireland,
with all that means of having shut out the peasantry—I was absolutely upset by the formality. I was taken up to a very elegant room
where there were marvelous roses in an ancient, beautiful bowl and
there was a silk coverlet on the bed, but there was no desk. If you're
a writer, you don't care about the bed; the first thing you look for in
any room is a desk. "Where am I going to write?" I took that bowl of

beautiful roses off this little table and put my typewriter in its place so I could write there.

The aftereffect of that image was that I had broken a form, and somehow it haunted me. Out of that, I invented this girl, not me at all, who came there, angry at being forced to come to Ireland because her parents want to break up her affair with a boy in America. Gradually she comes to understand this great house which was originally an antagonist.

That's what I mean by "autobiographical": something happened to me which started a reverberation in the subconscious. Maybe three years later, it became a problem I was interested in: what this sort of formality or tradition really means, and why it's so powerful that as a guest in the house you feel guilt if you move a piece of furniture.

Robertson: Do you work out in advance what will happen in the novel? How much do you know when you start?

Sarton: Very little. The answer for me in the novel is to put characters into a situation sufficiently dramatic that something is going to happen; for instance, a man commits suicide, and the effect on his friends is bound to be very stunning. There's *Faithful Are the Wounds.*

I've always believed too much plot kills. It's theme that quickens. I'm trying to answer a question which troubles me by putting people into situations sufficiently dramatic that the answer will be given me through the long process of creating.

I have no idea how a novel is going to end. I didn't know how *Anger* was going to end; I did not know that the old woman at the end of *As We Are Now* was going to burn down the nursing home around herself.

Robertson: Did that ending come as a surprise?

Sarton: It came to me as an inevitability finally.

Heyen: I sensed in reading *Anger* the working out of two parts of a personality and wondered how the synthesis of the very conservative man and the very passionate woman would be found.

Sarton: It was very hard to get the synthesis, and maybe it was not quite right to use a problem with his father in his youth as one of the resolutions of the novel.

Critics can help one so much. I ended *Anger* very optimistically with the two protagonists, a married couple, kissing each other at the end of a long "war." A good critic of mine read it and said, "You can't end it like that; it isn't convincing." So the next morning I had another little "battle" take place, and I'm so grateful to her, because she was so right. There's where you can sometimes be very much helped by another eye, but it must be someone who understands your work and you, not some cold critic who is trying to put you down.

Heyen: I connect the theme in *Anger* in so many ways with you. You're here with us today giving us your energy and warm personality, when half of you certainly wants to be at home writing, centering yourself. There's the desire to receive mail while you are unable to answer all of it—so much of what I sense in you is in the novel—the conflict between the passionate, outgoing, performing personality, on the one hand, and the personality that just wants to sit still and get on with becoming herself again.

Sarton: You're quite right. I think that much art comes out of conflict, of course. If we attained the marvelous Zen peace and acceptance of everything, we would probably never write another poem, because it would be enough to sit and look at the sunset. This is interesting to me now, because I am more able to sit and do nothing than I've been. I'm sure it's part of maturing and the beginning of old age. I find that I can sit and look at the birds at the feeder almost indefinitely; and then something in me says, "Come on, Sarton, you have work to do." And so I tear myself away and go upstairs to my study.

Heyen: You said last night, "A poem can't be willed," so I'm sure something is building in you during that contemplation of the birds.

Sarton: We don't treasure enough the times when we are not working; those are real creative times, I think. I used to enjoy trains for that reason: you were in this space, moving across beautiful landscape so you could look out the window. In a plane, once in a while there are marvelous clouds, but most of the time it's boredom in the sky, and you're in this cocoon. I've written wonderful poems in trains, including the one about my father. But never in a plane!

Robertson: You've been so enormously productive. Isn't it seventeen novels and thirteen volumes of poetry as well as five or six journals? I have the feeling that no matter what you're doing, gardening or whatever, there must be this little voice in you saying, "I must finish this and get back to the writing."

Sarton: You're right. Of course, it's a compulsion. And *that* I inherited from my father—the idea that everything was forgiven you, if you worked hard. My father was not a very "good" man in the sense of being sensitive to other's needs; but we were taught to forgive him everything because of his "work." I can hear my mother saying, "But Daddy's great work is so important that you mustn't mind . . ." this or that. So I feel if I have terrible tantrums, then I've got to work and then I'll be forgiven.

Heyen: Would you tell us about your poem, "A Celebration for George Sarton," and read it for us?

Sarton: It was shortly after he died that I was hoping to write a poem for him, and it hadn't come to me how to do it. I was on a train, and that rhythm of the train—I've learned that whenever the subconscious brings lines to me, then I know I've got a poem. It may take years before I write it, but once that line starts going through my head, I know it will come.

These began running through my head: "I never saw my father old;/I never saw my father cold." Well, I thought, This can't do—he was a great scholar, world-famous; it sounds like a nursery rhyme. Then I said to myself, "Now, wait a minute. Think about it." Because what comes from the subconscious you have to trust. I realized that this complicated intellect was also a very simple, *child-like* man, and so the nursery rhyme was probably just right to write an elegy about George Sarton.

[Sarton reads "A Celebration for George Sarton."]

> I never saw my father old;
> I never saw my father cold.
> His stride, staccato vital,
> His stalk struck from pure metal
> Simple as gold, and all his learning
> Only to light a passion's burning.
> So, beaming like a lesser god,
> He bounced upon the earth he trod,
> And people marveled on the street
> At this stout man's impetuous feet.

Loved donkeys, children, awkward ducks,
Loved to retell old simple jokes;
Lived in a world of innocence
Where loneliness could be intense;
Wrote letters until very late,
Found comfort in an orange cat—
Rufus and George exchanged no word,
But while George worked his Rufus purred,
And neighbors looked up at his light,
Warmed by the scholar working late.

I never saw my father passive;
He was electrically massive.
He never hurried, so he said,
And yet a fire burned in his head;
He worked as poets work, for love,
And gathered in a world alive,
While black and white above his door
Spoke Mystery, the avatar—
An Arabic inscription flowed
Like singing: "In the name of God."

And when he died, he died so swift
His death was like a final gift.
He went out when the tide was full,
Still undiminished, bountiful;
The scholar and the gentle soul,
The passion and the life were whole.
And now death's wake is only praise,
As when a neighbor writes and says:
"I did not know your father, but
His light was there. I miss the light."

I miss the light, because although we didn't get on very well, I very
much understood what he stood for. He was a great humanist who
believed in the humanization of science. Now that we're in this
technological universe where it seems almost that humanist side of
science has been forgotten, I feel he's even more important than
ever.

Heyen: I think in the poem you make us, too, miss his light.
Your first book of poems, *Encounter in April,* came out when you

were 26. Now you have another coming out, *Letters from Maine.* You said that you're a lyric poet, that "most unfashionable of creatures." You've always been a lyric poet, but do you sense a change in your poetry over the years that you can focus on?

Sarton: Just as in my prose I hope I have tried to eliminate the obviously literary—I used to be praised for the "poetic style" in prose—in my poetry I have tried to move away from decorative lyrics in which the descriptive words were extremely important. One reason that the critics have never been terribly interested in my poetry is that you cannot endlessly analyze lyric poetry. A very short lyric is very hard to say anything about, and I've been writing many of those. I also use free verse more than I used to and enjoy it more, although I still suspect it. It's never the truly inspired poem for me. It's more something I'm making as a carpenter would make something, rather than a poem catapulted out on a stream of fire.

Heyen: Yeats said he wanted a poem to be a "cry of the heart," and he talked of the "enterprise" of "walking naked." That's what you mean, isn't it? A more conversational, less ornate style?

Sarton: Certainly less ornate. But you see, what's fashionable and what gives the critics a chance to explore is the baroque, the complex, the allusive, where you show your brilliance by recognizing that it's Marvell who's quoted in a poem. I hope, however, that this kind of unfashionable poetry can be memorable in the sense that people learn it by heart. You don't learn free verse poems by heart—very rarely, if they're very short: "The fog comes in on little cat feet. . . ."

Heyen: I think Whitman is difficult to memorize, and I love Walt above all other poets.

Sarton: What I always say about free verse is that you can revise indefinitely, and he did.

Robertson: Critics seem to have been remarkably obtuse in writing about your work, but you have an enormous readership, which must give you a real sense of satisfaction.

Sarton: What has given me a real sense of satisfaction in the last ten years—no matter what the critics say—is that I now know my work is useful, what Muriel Rukeyser used to call the "usable truth." I get so many letters from people that say, "You helped me through a breakdown," or "You helped me know how to be with my mother when she was dying." About five people came up after the reading last night and said, "I have to tell you what your work has done to help me."

This is some of the justification for writing. One of the things that I'm sure all artists feel is this terrible doubt: here I am giving my life to that which may be only an illusion; whereas if you're making tables and people need tables to write on and to eat on, you *know* you're achieving something.

My anxiety used to be so great that every single morning at my desk I would go through this awful argument with myself: "You ought to be out working in a slum with little children who are utterly deprived. What are you doing sitting at a desk indulging yourself in writing a poem?" Then I would fight it out, and say, "But this is one of the ways you can help people grow, and this happens to be *your* gift." Finally, I would say, "Now let's get to work."

Now it's the letters that bring another kind of awful self-examination: how can I do my book when there's a woman in Peoria whose mother is dying and I ought to be writing to her?

Robertson: But surely you feel that your novels and poems are a "writing to her."

Sarton: You're right. I've settled now on the belief that being loved is better than success, because I'm truly loved by a great many people I don't know. When I walk out on to a stage now—and it's tremendously moving—I feel that they're terribly glad to see me.

Heyen: Your journals especially have touched a deep chord in so many. Have you always been a journal-keeper?

Sarton: No. I started the first one, *Journal of a Solitude,* when I was in a bad depression and was looking for something to help me through—with the idea of publication. I would not go through the labor of keeping a journal unless it was part of my work, in the sense of something I wanted to communicate.

Robertson: I have difficulty with that. You are a very private person, and yet you choose to write journals for publication.

Sarton: But they are very reticent. I get letters all the time saying, "Why don't you say more about X?" X is my lover, is neither male nor female, has no name, no profession, no place of habitation, on purpose, because I knew it would be published and I had to protect this person. There is a great deal that is *not* said.

Robertson: That's true, and yet you do reveal quite a bit about your life.

Sarton: You've hit something very real. There are a great many things involved, and one of them is that I have a great responsibility to be honest, in writing about women, for instance. This has been very hard for me. A lot of the things in the later journals have been excruciatingly hard: I've lain awake at night over just how to say something.

Robertson: Could you give an example?

Sarton: I can't give a specific example, but it's the business of the homosexual and heterosexual in women. I want to be universal in the sense that I am not writing primarily for lesbians; I'm writing for women and women's problems.

Yes, I can give you an example. In the last journal, I talk about a woman living in a small town somewhere in America who has a family and who suddenly falls madly in love with another woman; she has given so much all these years, and although she had a husband who really cares for her he may not pay very much attention to what she's really about and never talks to her about *her* feelings. I suggest that it's very natural that she should feel suddenly here's somebody who understands, because she is a woman, everything about me and whom I can talk to. Is that wrong? I ask that in that journal. I'm trying to build a bridge between her and that imaginary town in which she lives. It would be different if I wrote about gay nightclubs—where I'm never seen and never would go. That would be another way, but it's not *my* way.

The responsibility on my part to be honest is very great, because I have no family. Most people who "come out," most people who talk about these things, have living parents or children, or even aunts and nephews, so they are going to make shock waves all around their intimate lives. Whereas I am free, and therefore I have a very great responsibility to talk, although you're right that I am reserved and reticent, and it's very hard for me to do.

The main value of the journals is not any of this, but making the reader realize that what's important about life is not the major calamities or joys but just living the day, just seeing the light on the wall, just seeing a rose open or the birds come to the feeder.

Robertson: Yes, the reader of your journals enters your world as though it were the world of novels.

Sarton: Yes, and that can be a problem, because they all want to come and see me.

Heyen: Even in the journals you have to develop that sense of "detachment" that you speak of in your relationships to your poems.

Sarton: Yes, and it's a good discipline for me in getting down to the nub, the essential. When I say in *Recovering* that "pain is a great teacher," I was learning that through a very hard time—a love affair that also appears in *Anger*. I grew so much, and I was 65 at the time.

One thing about my work that may be helpful is that so many Americans think a woman over 30 is past saving. Actually, as we know, life goes on, love goes on, feeling goes on, sex goes on, way beyond what people were willing to admit even 20 years ago.

It was good for me to have some very hard times, because Louise Bogan said to me a long time ago, "You keep the hell out of your work." That haunted me, because I believe in transcending. I would go through hell, but the poem the reader got was what I had fought through to. I would like it known that I am not all just "sweetness and light." At some point the iron went into me, and it was first shown in *As We Are Now* and *Crucial Conversations*. I began to look at the dark side in those two books, and in the poems "The Invocation to Kali."

Heyen: You've talked about the necessity of joy in the small things in life despite what seem to be calamities. In *The House by the Sea* you write: "Then, before the Nazi camps, we could still believe in the goodness of man." What can we believe in now? Do you sense anything building in yourself regarding these calamities? We're talking here in autumn 1983 shortly after the Russian jet shot down an airliner with 269 people aboard and all the young men were killed in Beirut and shortly after the Grenada invasion. What can writers do with all this material from that world pressing in on them all the time?

Sarton: It isn't going to do a great deal of good to go out screaming, except certain marches can be very important. The women's one in England is most impressive.

There, I would have to go back to my father, to the humanizing influences, to do everything we can. He used to say, "Religion, art, and science are the great inventions of man." We still have those three that we can build on and believe in.

Heyen: I sense in your work Auden's yearning to show an "affirming flame," to rescue or redeem something.

Sarton: In the Holocaust I and most thinking, feeling people recognized that we had inherited the nineteenth-century idea of the perfectability of man. We believed that people were getting more imaginative about others, more caring. But the Holocaust told us that man was still an unregenerate thing. Now we are perhaps confronted with something so terrible that change is absolutely necessary. Whether it will happen, God only knows.

The Governor in the Garden
Michael Finley/1986

From *The World* [Journal of the Unitarian/Universalists] (Jan/ Feb 1987), 24–28.

She has lived a score of lives at least—as actress, poet, novelist, teacher, writer of journals, scourge of critics, confidante of so many hundreds. At 70, sensing that the final act was being played out, she wrote a journal named just that, *At Seventy*.

Sometimes, with her vast correspondence, the pilgrimages of people from all corners to her cottage in York, Maine, and her passionate mastery of detail, and of the edifices of art she has erected to stave off the chaos of the world, she seems like the governor of an invisible state or province—a principality of flowers, friends and self.

Today, at 75, May Sarton is still a factor. Hampered late last winter by a stroke and "imprisoned" at home for another nine months with a heart condition, she has been unable, for the first time in 40 years, to begin her biennial novel.

Fan letters continue to arrive in bales. The ability to answer each and every one is not to be relied upon as it once was. This was a year without the daily workout in the garden, or the walk down to the water. The wild fur-person (the Sartonian designation for actualized cat) Bramble has died, and been replaced by a woolly Himalayan.

"It's a nuisance, all right," says May Sarton. But she went on tour in October, reading from her 12 books of poetry (including *A Grain of Mustard Seed, A Durable Fire,* and *Halfway to Silence*) and her fiction (*Faithful Are the Wounds, Mrs. Stevens Hears the Mermaids Singing,* and *As We Are Now*) and nonfiction (*Plant Dreaming Deep, Recovering* and *Journal of a Solitude*).

She will draw giant (for poetry) audiences, uplifting many and annoying several, for just as she has attracted friends so has she suffered fools with a minimum of solicitude. And she suffers critics hardly at all, not even at the allegedly serene age of 75.

142

It was not always thus. Born in Ghent, Belgium, of an artistic British mother and French-Belgian father (George Sarton, author of the massive study *Introduction to the History of Science*), Sarton hardly figured to spend the bulk of her life in rural New Hampshire and Maine as one of America's premier poets of fixed place.

She never went to college, choosing instead an apprenticeship in the midst of the Depression with Eva Le Galliennne's Civic Repertory Theatre, and tours abroad where she came to know many of the greats of the literary world, including Virginia Woolf.

Her first book of poems, *Encounter in April* (1937), and first novel, *The Single Hound* (1938), were hailed critically as the stirrings of a major new voice in American letters, and Sarton's future as a sleek modernist seemed assured. But something in her swerved away from mere stylishness, and she commenced a more inward journey, far from the fashionable, best-selling path through solitude, personal revelation, and a loyalty to the more enduring spirits—friendship, nature, and the perfectionist demands of her art.

Hear what the critics were saying even 30 years ago:

"When Miss Sarton talks to us we feel as though we were walking through a cultivated landscape in the early afternoon of a summer's day, with twilight far in the future."

She is: "serene-seeming despite her traumas"; "honest to the point of bluntness"; her work is "transparently about flowers and the seasons—but these are simply the backdrops for the agony of fading love, sorrow at a friend's death, fatigue from creating and the need to be alone."

Her works are like those of Flemish painters "whose bold brush-strokes make clear the troubled humanity in a face. . . ." Her tastes and styles: "immaculate and orderly, traditional, austere with over-tones of grace and charm."

Not much has changed, and yet everything has. Her style has transmogrified, from the profligate phraseology of youth to the biting clarity of one who knows the price of distraction. The critics, who were with her at the start, long ago gave up on her as unreformable.

(They complain that she has been too up front about her sexuality. That there is not enough sexuality in the books. She is too male. She is too female. She is too traditional. She is too radical. She is too intellectual. She is too emotional. Whatever you do, do *not* read a book by this vexatious person!)

She is not a girl any more—she is, as she puts it, old. ("I don't mind that, though," she says.) And always, her writing has been about the driving need *to be oneself.* The book which has had perhaps the greatest impact, *Mrs. Stevens Hears the Mermaids Singing* (1965), is about a woman poet in her seventies—an extrapolation of Sarton herself when she was 50. A startling fresh work both in language and structure, *Mrs.Stevens* probes the memories of outrageous novelist Hilary Stevens to learn where the irretractable choices were made—and relives the episodes of pain and love which were the seedbed of her witness.

The book was also Sarton's own tacit coming out as a lesbian—"I was trying to say some radical things about sexuality in a gentle way so that they might penetrate without shock." For Sarton, the Muse is not a disembodied occasional presence—the Muse is a friend, a lover, a special person who unlocks the cabinetry and lets light in on what has been stored away, unexpressed. There have been several.

She is an astonishing amalgam of contradictions—an intellectual entranced by nature; a formalist whose object is freedom; a friend to thousands who espouses the virtues of solitude; an exile who has grown her own roots. Not surprisingly, she is also Unitarian Universalist.

"My parents were not connected with any church, but when I was about ten I went to the First Parish, Unitarian in Cambridge, and I absolutely loved Mr. Samuel McChord Crothers, the minister there, at that time quite a famous man, a writer. A very wonderful preacher, and when I joined the Sunday School, I got a ribbon for perfect attendance! It was all my own idea, of course."

Sarton added that Unitarian Universalism was not that far removed from the beliefs of her parents. "My father and mother believed that, though Jesus was not God, he was a mighty leader and the spirit of Jesus, the *logos* of him, is the worship of God and the spirit of man. We Unitarians, after all, 'unite' in the spirit of Jesus for the worship of God and the service of man.

"I'm awfully proud to be Unitarian. I think the Unitarian Service Committee is marvelous. We're humanists, you see—the extreme right considers us devils, and that's something else in our favor."

Though there is no Unitarian Universalist church within driving distance of York—the closest is in Portsmouth, New Hampshire, twenty miles away, an hejira to downeasters—Sarton worships in her own way, with her own skills, writing letters to the very old and very sick on Sunday mornings.

There are some who say that, despite the lack of tacitly theological matter in her books, Sarton's thrust in fact is a religious one. A group of Methodist pastors asked her recently to be one of three spiritual advisors at a retreat. In 1982 Sarton delivered the Ware Lecture for Unitarian Universalists. She has taught at Thomas Starr King School of Religious Leadership in Berkeley. And when she travels to Indianapolis these days, she stays at the Carmelite monastery there—"they are great admirers of *Journal of a Solitude*."

Nevertheless, she says, she is less interested in religion than in something she sees as broader, or at least vaguer. Spirit? "Yes, or perhaps just humanity," she says.

Sometimes surface objects in her journals, such as fritillaria or dragonfly nymphs, are exactly that; other times they are something very different, a key to another level of being, a way of talking about things which otherwise are undiscussable. "For instance, flowers—I think very few people really look at Nature. I think I do, and I got that from my mother, a most remarkable woman.

"My last book, by the way, is not mine but hers—letters to me, called *Letters to May*, published by Puckerbrush Press here in Maine."

It was the Unitarian Universalists who, somehow or other, got Sarton "over the hump" from respectable small poetry audiences to the kinds of mass engagements she holds sway over today.

"The first one I remember was at Roy Phillips' Unity Church in St. Paul—a huge audience, the poor church was full to bursting. I heard it had never been filled before for any occasion. I really do not know why it happened as it did, when it did. But I have taken note."

Perhaps it is the sense of the individual as shrine that Sarton addresses, especially in her nonfiction, and particularly in her breakthrough book, *Journal of a Solitude*. From her earlier sense that an artist's art is the reason for her existing (perhaps even for the rest of us existing, too) Sarton suggests a less exclusive explanation—that the window to eternity is *this moment,* lived and felt honestly and with intensity.

"I try to live as if every day might be my last and yet, is eternal. You can only do this well in solitude," she writes. "Solitude is the salt of personality. I could live alone indefinitely and feel no need for company. Solitude can be very exciting."

Or perhaps it is the heroic combat she has maintained for so many decades against the chaos around her—in the turbulence of her own life and the lives of friends, the violence of world wars, the friction of cold wars, the grimace of political and sexual oppression, the growing sense of a mass culture seeking to obviate the inner quiet in the individual heart.

"My parents were both innocent and so am I, and this has perhaps been my undoing with the critics. I'm *not* a worldly person. I happen to be making a lot of money, for me, these days. But for years, until I was 65, I never did. That means that nature and animals and deep friendship are all extremely precious to me—being asked out to cocktail parties is not."

Sarton suspects that this innocence, and her disdain for the desiderata of the marketplace, may have contributed to the lack of attention she received from the front line of critics (read, the *New York Times*).

"It's true, I cut my own throat," she says, "I haven't been able by nature to use others. I've never asked any of my high-powered friends for help, for blurbs."

The result has been a perceived snubbing from the critics. Not the trade reviews or the secondary outlets, where her reputation has been solid through the years, but at the holy mountaintop—the *New York Times.* "After *Faithful Are the Wounds* (1955), I never got another positive review from them," she says. "And lately they've ceased reviewing my poetry altogether. I can't help feeling very bitterly about it."

One wonders about the bitterness of a woman in her seventies as honored as Sarton. Surely the books section of the *Times* is not one of those windows into eternity?

"No, it's not *that,*" she insists of the war between York and New York. "It's bigger than pride. It's the fact that they have stood between me and the audience I have so wanted for my writing. And not for me, either—my design has been that each of my books be *usable* in some way or other, usable truths that readers might apply to their way of seeing the world."

Sarton, while decrying her malfeasance, misfeasance, and nonfeasance at the hands of her critics, is still amazed at the audience she has managed to assemble, seemingly despite the sages of West 43rd Street. In addition to having sold at least a couple of million books over the years, many of them read over and over again, she is at the point where today three of her novels are entertaining film options, one of them in Great Britain. She has not been the dominant mailing address in York by hiding her lamp under the bushel basket, or by being ignored by the reading public.

"It's true, I have what many regard as a fairly large audience, gathered over many years and mainly through word of mouth. And they are an enviable lot—every day I get letters, sometimes from people who say I saved their lives. That I cherish.

"But then I ask myself what might that audience be, had I gotten the kinds of reviews Anne Tyler (whom I admire) has had? It's a maddening question, and I wish I could spare myself from asking it."

Bitterness may be a luxury that she cannot afford in the months ahead of her. She suffered a stroke in February, which she claims was "not so serious"; it is a fibrillating heart, and the medicine she takes for that, which has laid her as low as she can remember being in her whole life—worse than her breast cancer of six years ago which she described in her journal *Recovering*.

"Eight days after the mastectomy I was driving again," she says. "This time I was unable to do anything for nine months. It was prison for me, and even though I'm better now, the medicine still makes me ill. It's a difficult life, with no notion of making 'progress.' Still, I'm determined to make it like my real life."

Her current recovery has been so slow that she has been unable to begin a longer work, content to write entries to a new journal called *After the Stroke*. "People say I sound marvelous but they don't know how my poor head feels."

And of course, there are the poems. Sarton has never been one to play poetry against fiction against nonfiction. One is clearly superior in her mind, and that is the art of the poet.

"To me, if you're a poet you're a poet *first*. I've been writing poetry since I was 12 and getting published since 17. If you're a poet, it's a gift. Whereas you can start a novel on will alone, and intelligence and sensitivity—you can't do a poem with just that equipment."

The other side is that the novel is so limited by its length, she says. "How can anything so long be perfect? When I knew Virginia Woolf, before I had published anything but poems, she used to tease me, saying, 'It's so much harder to write a novel, too many ways it can fail.' She was right, of course, and I know that now, but on the other hand the poem has possibilities a novel can never have."

Which helps explain why, following the success of her first, lushly written books, she worked so hard to separate her poetic and fictional writing styles. "My first novels were poetic and got wonderful reviews, but I didn't want that. I don't want people to say, 'Oh, you've got such a wonderful style.' I want them to say, 'I can't forget that character.' Or, 'Your book changed my life.' "

In *As We Are Now,* she pared her style down to the point where an especially obtuse critic claimed the writing was at a ninth-grade level. The novel, a heartbreaking love story that takes place in a nursing home, was made deliberately spare.

"The book is a descent into hell, and the last rung on the ladder was when true love was made dirty, when Caro's feelings for Anna, which were not homosexual, but simply love, were made dirty by the awful women there." The story was strong enough to do the telling for her, Sarton says—writing it "up" would have only muddled the issue.

"I also like that there's a minister in the book who is not a caricature or hypocritical or cardboard. Ministers are seldom given respect in fiction, you know."

Sarton prefers formal poetry to free verse, although she claims to have enjoyed writing without form in "Gestalt at Sixty." She explains her defense of the art in her fiction above the less formal craft required of her journal writing:

"I do enjoy free verse, but how do I know when I am done with it? There are no brakes, and the process of revision looms eternally.

"I love the freedom that comes from form, not just in art but in life as well. I know that, as an artist, the form my day takes, which is my routine, is terribly important—you write for a certain number of hours every morning, not just when you feel like it. If you waited free-form for inspiration, you'd wait a long time."

A routine which looks confining is what actually refines one, she adds. Sarton's view of writing is that of an intellectual (novelist?) grappling with feeling (poet?)—and in her mature works the two forces have come into balance.

"What is good about the journal, I think, is that it is so much more spontaneous—it has no particular structure, but it requires an intensity of being. Therefore it is a very spiritual form of writing. People don't read journals for wise sayings but for the intensity of being that is approached, the life that is lived in them. When it is authentic it is very comforting, and very powerful, too."

In an address to students at Scripps College in 1957, Sarton laid down the rule she lived by, and expected other poets to live by as well. "Writing poetry is a life discipline maintained in order to perfect the instrument of experiencing—the poet himself."

Thirty years later, one wants to ask how that process of perfectibility, so innocent and impossible (so Unitarian Universalist?), has proceeded. Is the instrument, today, perfect?

May Sarton smiles, "I don't feel it is," she says, "but the process has remained remarkably intact and alive. And I truly do believe that a point can be reached, as in a poem, where nothing more can be changed, no paraphrase is possible. And that is a beautiful thing."

Looking back, would she wish to be a young writer just starting out, with the same brash head full of ideas, the same record (as at Sunday School) of perfect attendance, the same heart shining with passion?

"It's always hard, I think. There might be a few more grants and sponsors today, but I don't think I would make that switch. The truth is, I love being older, and I always knew I would. I dislike being sick—that's the nuisance, right there—but I would never want to go back. You pay a high price for emotional involvement, the love affairs and so on. I'm rather glad to be out of that.

"I know so much more, I'm more balanced. Things are less intense, but deeper."

A Conversation with May Sarton
Connie Goldman/1987

This transcription of Connie Goldman's interview was edited from an audiotape in the series "I'm Too Busy to Talk Now: Conversations with Creative People Over 70." Printed by permission of Connie Goldman Productions, 8888 Appian Way, Los Angeles, CA 90046.

Sarton: I've asked a great deal of myself. You don't write forty-two books without that, with having asked a great deal.

Artist George Braque once said: "As you become older, art and life become the same thing. What follows is a testimonial to that statement. The key to this series of conversations is the word busy. *That's why the next half-hour is called "I'm Too Busy to Talk Right Now: Conversations with Creative People Over Seventy."*

Sarton: My whole life could be defined as an acute conflict between art and life, between what art asks and what life wants. The conflict is what keeps you alive, in a way. It would be a very dull life—mine, I think—if I just did nothing but write up in that study and never saw a person. On the other hand, it would be an impossible life if I saw people all day, so it's a good balance, pretty good. I wish I had a *little* more strength now, physical strength, and didn't get quite so tired, but that's age. You see, I can't quite accept yet that I'm seventy-five; it seems—I don't *feel* that I'm seventy-five. But the fact is that I *am*.
    Goldman: Whatever seventy-five is supposed to feel like.
    Sarton: Well, the diminution of energy, I think, is the thing that is hard to work with.

The published works of May Sarton have been contributing to American literature for more than fifty years. Her many volumes of poetry, novels, and her personal journals depict her own struggles and relationships. At seventy-five, she has endured life with all its

150

hardships and joys. She works and lives by herself now in York, Maine, in a house by the sea. Her time is precious to her, and the planning of her days in this part of her life is best expressed in the last entry of her journal published under title At Seventy.

Sarton: "As I think over this year I wish I had a long empty time in which to think it over, instead of a few minutes before I take Tamas out into the wet, green world! In spite of the pressures of what is ahead—to clear my desk, sow the annuals, plant perennials, get back to the novel—I feel happy and at peace. My life at the moment is a little like a game of solitaire that is coming out. Things fall into place. The long hard work is bearing fruit, and even though I make resolves to see fewer people this summer than last, I know I shall be inundated as usual, be unable to say "no," but it does not matter, for I am coming into a period of inner calm. There will be months of seeing people and months of public appearances, but as surely as the dawn, there will be months of solitude and time to work. Who could ask for more? As Robert Frost says:

> I could give all to Time except—except
> What I myself have held. But why declare
> The things forbidden that while the Customs slept
> I have crossed to Safety with? For I am There,
> And what I would not part with I have kept.

Old age can be very beautiful, but it depends on what has gone on inside the face. In other words, wrinkles are of no importance at all, compared to the quality of the life lived, which is what you see in the face. So I'm not all worried, for instance, about the fact that I'm beginning to have wrinkles. I didn't for a long time. I looked much younger than my age. I *want* to look my age. I have a character in *Mrs. Stevens Hears the Mermaids Singing* who says, "I've *earned* being seventy. (She's seventy then.) Don't take it away from me by saying, 'You look fifty.' " So I feel I've earned being seventy-five.

May Sarton was born in Belgium and came to the United States with her parents when she was two. Throughout her adolescence her vision of the world was accented by long visits and schooling in Europe. Although her father was a professor at Harvard University, young May Sarton chose not to continue a formal education after graduating from high school.

Sarton: From the time I was seventeen to twenty-five I was in the theater. I was an apprentice at Eva Le Gallienne's, I fell in love with that theater. Then as a member of the first studio at that theater and then as the director of the apprentice group and then when her theater failed—this was the middle of the Depression—I kept some of those students together and we formed a little company called the Apprentice Theater, did ten European plays that had never been done in New York—at the New School for Social Research—and then went to Hartford. But money was the trouble—I mean, I was trying to keep ten people together in the middle of the Depression—and finally after three years it failed. I was always writing poetry, you see. My first poems came when I was seventeen in *Poetry* magazine. And I remember taking it to Eva Le Gallienne—I was so excited—because I was working there then. I *always* knew I was a poet, and nothing would ever change that, whatever I was doing otherwise. But when the theater failed—my company—in a funny way it was like a fever that had gone. I never looked back, and the next year my first book of poems came out, you see, when I was twenty-six. And then I wrote a novel, because the publishers said that they didn't think I was a short story writer; they thought I was a novelist, and this came to me as a complete surprise, and I'd never thought of it. But then I did *The Single Hound,* and from then on it was just a matter of getting a publisher, really. There was a gap between the first and second novels, which often happens, where I was really nearly in despair.

After overcoming the writer's block preceding her second novel, May Sarton went on to produce her many volumes and she became well known on college campuses, where she delighted students with dramatic readings of her own works. Her efforts have been rewarded with numerous honorary degrees and distinctions. As she aged, her following grew, and her success, despite some negative critical reviews, put her in a position of stature in the American literary community. Into her seventies May Sarton was still touring the country, delivering lectures and reading her work to her faithful followers. Then, at seventy-four May Sarton had a stroke. And, although it was mild, she also suffered from a fibrillating heart condition that was difficult for her doctors to treat. In the nine months that followed until the proper medications were regulated the life that Miss Sarton had carefully planned for herself was disrupted, and her view of the world changed as her own needs changed. The result of her recovery is evident in After the Stroke, *her latest journal, chronicling her illness.*

Sarton: Growing old is, I think, a very interesting process in which you begin to learn to give things up and to strike for the most important things in your life and hang on to them and just don't worry about having to give up a lot of other things. But when you're sick, as sick as I was, everything is taken from you at once. I say in the journal that I *jumped,* I *leapt* into old age suddenly, without having that slow preparation, by being so ill. But now, of course, I'm back again to where I was before, so I don't feel old at all.

Goldman: Analyze that with me: you leapt into old age, meaning not that you were really any older, chronologically, but you considered "old" as "unable to work" and "your health being out of control." It's interesting that what you really meant was you leapt into *sickness,* because you're older now and you feel better.

Sarton: Yes, that's true. But in a way sickness gave me a terrifying idea of what it might be to be old when you were too ill to do anything, if you have no family and you're not rich. But it's been wonderful to come back. The great advantage of going through something—and I've been amazingly well, really, in my life—is, of course, that just the ordinary things become so precious. The fact that I can garden again is just *heaven,* well, that I can enjoy life again. And that I dare to have a little puppy. You know, everyone said, "Don't do that. You're too old." I said, "I have to have a puppy; I have to have someone who sleeps with me." You see, dear Tamas who died at sixteen, a Shetland collie, I just adored him and I miss him every day. And I miss Bramble, my cat; they both died in that hard year. It was hard, like the break-up of a family. And now I have a little family again.

Loyal readers of May Sarton know that her animals are an important part of her life. Her writings have always included their affectionate presence.

During the time of May Sarton's illness, there was a void, the absence of her ability to even think about writing.

Sarton: That was the problem: I couldn't work, you see, and not a line of poetry ran through my head. I thought, I'm finished. I was terrified, partly because of—of course, I earn now enormous amounts of money for a writer of the kind I am. But if I don't produce, I don't have anything back of me—I have no family—so it depends on my continuing to be able to create. But now I'm back, back and able to do it and I've just finished a journal called *After the Stroke,* which will tell about my recovery. I think it will help some people, because there are a lot of things you learn about how to deal with it. At the same time, I must admit that I was suicidal at times, because I didn't see any way of handling it.

   Goldman: How did it come back? What did those first moments feel like when you knew it was going to happen again for you?

   Sarton: When I decided in the third month after the stroke that I was going to keep a journal. People kept saying to me, "You should keep a journal during this illness," and I would say, "It's like telling a man in a wheelchair, 'Why don't you go out for a long walk?' " At first I *couldn't,* you see. The letters were all mixed up, and the stroke was there. But it was when I began to keep the journal and realized that I could do it—just about a paragraph a day—*that* was a tremendous help.

   Goldman: You're talking about choices; you're talking about the years you have left after seventy-five and where you want to focus.

   Sarton: Well, certainly on writing and that means if any poems come—and I have written a few this last year—it's poetry that means most to me. But I have one more novel I want to write: a portrait of Judith Matlack, with whom I lived for fifteen years, and who was a very remarkable woman. She left me in her will a strange book of poems, much of which I believe she wrote when she began to have Alzheimer's. It's almost like automatic writing, but some of them are very interesting and beautiful; and I'm going to weave the portrait around them and her family will publish it—they're very anxious to have it done. But, of course, I've not mentioned yet the *work* of my life, which is answering mail. And it never gets solved. There's no solution to that. I mean, one of the choices I would like to make is, don't answer anymore. Everyone says that. All right, I have many, many friends. You see, I'm seventy-five and I've accumulated people for seventy-five years, so when somebody writes and says, "My mother is dying of cancer. I haven't communicated with you for so long, but I wanted you to know this. It's so hard," am I to say, "I'm sorry but I'm not answering letters anymore"? No. If it's a friend, I answer. The people I now answer less are the fans. And I wish I could answer, because I want to. I think there are about 400 letters unanswered upstairs in my study. Darling people writing, and you want to do so much more than you can. At the same time, you know you've got to learn that you can't and somehow take it without too much frustration. That's the great lesson of old age, I think: to learn to say, "It's all right. You just can't do it. Do what you can."

In her seventies May Sarton prefers to be more individual than part of a literary group. But there was a time in her early adult life that she was part of a writers' circle. It was in England prior to World War II.

Sarton: When Virginia Woolf died, I felt now there is *no* writer whose work I'm going to wait for, as I did for hers. And there hasn't been. Each book was new; I mean, she was constantly going further. And I saw her—I don't know why she was willing to see me—but she gave me about two hours of time whenever I was in London during those years before World War II, and we had tea, you see. Two hours is long. I know that, because I don't give people two hours when they come to see me. After an hour I say, "Well, I guess that's about all I have to give." She really did give. She teased me a lot about being a poet. (I had not published a novel when I first met her.) She said, "It's so easy to be a poet compared to being a novelist," and I think there's something in this, as I said, because of the very *long* time a novel takes and the anxiety you go through. She was a very great influence. I've had so many great friendships, and often with people older than I. Because I was always looking for masters, I suppose, or for people who could teach me something.

    Goldman: So older people have always been in your life and you haven't had a fear of aging, or a feeling that older people are used up and disposable, like Kleenex.

    Sarton: On the contrary. I think it's almost too romantic—now I'm beginning to realize it was too romantic—I *loved* old people, and I looked forward to being old. I really did. And in some ways I'm glad to be old: you have solved so many of the problems which are agony when you're young, like the sexual problem. You've come to terms with your life and therefore it's much easier to lead it than when you're nineteen and you don't know who you are or what you want. I mean, I was in love with men and women, and it took me a long time to sort it all out. I just loved *people*. I had many love affairs; I mean, I sometimes look back on my life and think how shocked some people would be if they knew how *many* love affairs I had. It's all in the poetry, you see. The muses were not always lovers, but they were always very important to me in the influence they had. Sometimes the ones who were *not* lovers were really the important ones, I think.

Goldman: You see, you've told all—everybody does know. If everybody read your work from one end to the other, they would know it all. And just so they shouldn't miss it, I mean, you "came out," and you said, "I'm a lesbian," and you've even alluded to two men you would have married, although we don't know who they are. You've kept a couple of secrets, but you haven't kept very many. You've been very up front.

Sarton: I want to be open. "Transparent" is one of the words that comes through *all* my work, and "vulnerable." If you can't let pain in, you see, you'll never know joy, for one thing. You really won't. You may be happy, but you'll never know joy.

Goldman: Let's dispense with this whole business in one question: what made you "come out" and tell the whole world you were a lesbian, and what have been the repercussions since? I mean, has it made any difference?

Sarton: I thought about it for a long time, but I could not write *Mrs. Stevens Hears the Mermaids Singing*, which is the book in which I "came out," until both my parents were dead. I think they *knew*, you know, about me; but we never discussed it. And especially for my mother, I felt I didn't want to. I guess it was just lucky, in one horrible way, that they died when I was fairly young—I was forty-five when my father died—and it was just about then that I did *Mrs. Stevens*. My agent didn't want me to publish it even, he thought it would do me so much harm. And I said, "Let's not just throw it away." I think it's a very good book, partly because I projected myself—I was then fifty—into seventy. Now I'm seventy-five and much older than Mrs. Stevens. But I thought it would be easier to handle with an older person looking back. I've empowered the people who are lesbians, who've been scared of themselves and have been ashamed, to be aware that you can be a good *person*. *That's* the important thing. And that love is very difficult, whether it's heterosexual or homosexual. It's very difficult to handle.

For now May Sarton prefers to be alone with herself, rather than put in the time and work involved in another love relationship. With her health back, she views her solitude as an opportunity to develop the richness of self. And she is excited about the work she has yet to do.

Sarton: If a poem is running through my head, everything else is put aside while I write it. And this happens to me now maybe only twenty times a year. I'm not writing floods of poetry. I think they're quite good. They're very pure lyrics—that most unfashionable form—but they're memorable. By that I mean I can learn them by heart, which is one of the lovely things about a pure lyric. I like them, and I'm very happy that a small book is coming out of the new ones. How do I write a poem? Well, it may be three days in which I may write a hundred drafts. I revise a great deal; but you're in a state of high tension. I mean, it's when the emotional and intellectual parts of you are linked like two racehorses and are running together. That's what makes a good poem—the intensity.

    Goldman: What about the journals? Where did you get the idea that what matters to you personally might matter to the rest of us?

    Sarton: I was fifty, you know; I started the journals very late. I started the *Journal of a Solitude* because I was in a serious depression and I thought it would help me sort of define what I was all about and whether it was worth anything by recording it and what I was thinking of. It's helped so many people, that journal, I'm just amazed. It's the best, I think, partly because it was the least conscious that there was an audience for it. Now I'm very aware that people are waiting for the journals. I somewhat resent the fact that so many people like them best because they're so easy of access, compared to the novel or the poetry. But never mind. I think I have created something of a work of art with the journal, and I'm proud of that. For a long time I brushed the journals aside and said, "They're just nothing," but I don't think that now.

There are priorities and order to the life that May Sarton leads. Her work, her daily schedule, her animals, and of great importance her garden.

Sarton: I couldn't live without flowers. Even when I was very poor I used to always have one rose or something, a bunch of daisies, in my room wherever I was.

Goldman: What do flowers mean to you? I mean, that's a pretty heavy statement, "I can't live without flowers."

Sarton: One, of course, they're so beautiful; it's a tremendous aesthetic pleasure. And secondly, they have the whole sequence of life in them, from the bud to the death. And then, growth, everything about growth is in the flower. In a way, it's all of life: each day has this cycle for me. I mean, I wake up young and I go to bed old, in a happy way, tired, glad to go to bed, very early, having had an extremely active and complicated life for a whole day. But it's a rich life. I think about that when I get very upset and badgered by various things; I think, Well, how would you change it? Would you like this to be different, or that? and I realize that I'm living the life I've chosen and I love my life—especially because I can garden again. I'm Taurus, you see, the earth. Not having been able to dig in the earth last year was very hard for me psychologically. I lost something, some strength, psychic strength, because I wasn't close to the earth anymore.

Goldman: How often do you garden? Tell me what a day might be like for you.

Sarton: Well, my *ideal* day is I get up at five—this is always, now with the animals there are various things to do, I let them out, I feed them, I make my breakfast, I take it up to bed, and then I have an hour where I try to really think out what I want to do with the day, so it's sort of meditation; then I get up and I'm very busy for an hour, just washing dishes, making the bed, watering the plants. Then by about eight is my ideal I get to my desk and I don't work more than three hours; in fact, rarely—and that's all Virginia Woolf ever did;

three hours of intense work is a lot—then at eleven o'clock I get the mail, have a drink of sherry, because I'm very tired by then; you see, I've been up since five. Then all of life comes crashing in on me: somebody's in need, somebody's dying, somebody needs money, should I give it, or not? so all that's buzzing around in my head. Then I have my lunch, which I have to get, then I rest for an hour and a half. At three I get up and it's a whole different day. I put on my gardening clothes before I rest, because it's such an effort to change—if I'm already I go out happily at three and garden for two hours and a half. Then I come in and have a bath, and then I have to get my dinner. And this is the hard thing, because then I'm very tired, from the physical work; then I go to bed at eight and read—eight or eight-thirty, sometimes nine because people call me, then I can't get to bed. The little dog is very anxious to get to bed too, and the cat, and then we all go up.

Goldman: You're looking forward to your tomorrows, aren't you?

Sarton: Yes, I am, I am. I am, indeed, if I can keep my health. Of course, that's what everybody feels. As long as one can maintain at least the *structure* of one's life, then what goes on within it does change but you have the form, if you will, and you can fill it here or there, or not fill it. Some days you can say, "I am just not going to work today." But the structure is there. I go up to my desk every day, whether I work there or not. Sometimes I just sit there and think—not often, but I do.

Goldman: From what you've learned and what you know now and what you've gone through and coped with, are these maybe the best years of your life?

Sarton: I think they are, without any doubt.

Creativity is a mysterious thing. It's an attribute of every human being, not just the great and the gifted, not just the young. Each can bring an enriched sense of self, and often people are more creative in their later years. Creativity is the expression of the human spirit, to be studied, cultivated, and cherished.

For May Sarton there is a sense of contentment now, a feeling that she is at a comfortable place in her journey through life.

Sarton: Well, I think I feel happier now than I've ever been, because I do feel that I have served whatever small talent I have, as well as I could.

May Sarton
Martha Wheelock/1987

This transcription was edited from Martha Wheelock's conversation with May Sarton in Los Angeles, California, following an
award ceremony on 10 April 1987, proclaimed "May Sarton
Day" by Mayor Tom Bradley. It is printed with the permission
of Martha Wheelock and is not to be reprinted without her
permission.

Wheelock: We would like to ask you what has transpired since you
made the film *World of Light* and what your life has consisted of.

Sarton: And can I talk a little bit about the film, since I didn't get a
chance to do that today? Every time I see it, I become so grateful, all
over again, to you and Marita. It is such a beautiful job. When I first
saw it—I'm sure I've told you this—I cried, and I thought, Now I can
die, because here's this record which is so deep, really, and so
beautiful. Of course, seeing the animals made me cry this time,
seeing Tamas and Bramble who are both dead. That's one of the
things, Martha, that's happened, of course, the death of the animals—who were my *family!* And I am going now, on my seventy-fifth
birthday, to get a puppy, and I have a Himalayan cat, who was given
to me, so it will be a little family again. And that I'm looking forward
to very much. I miss the animals terribly. I miss Tamas. You remember what a *saint* he was—the dog, the Shetland.

And there's only one thing I would change in the film now, and
that is, smoking had not become a criminal act at that time, and I
smoke all the way through it. I would certainly not have done that—
now, if we were making it now. I would've gone off into a corner and
had a cigarette, but I wouldn't have done it on the film. The only
bad time is when I have it in my mouth at the Library of Congress.
The other thing is I don't think that it really shows that it's the Library
of Congress, that people don't realize, because there's no way they
can tell.

Wheelock: They wouldn't let us. Remember?

Sarton: Yes, I know. It's not that important.

A lot has happened, of course. Eight years is a long time. After it came the mastectomy, didn't it? The film was made before the mastectomy, and therefore it was made before a journal of mine called *Recovering,* which tells about how you and Marita came and helped me. I'll *never* forget that—because we had become very intimate friends from making the film, and I have no family. It was just so moving, the way you came and brought me the mail every day to the hospital and flowers from the garden. That was just darling, and I'll never forget it. And then you cooked, on the first days when I came back and you stayed—it was just marvelous, it was marvelous. I'll never forget it. That was a real bonding of a friend-ship. Now I'm recovering from a stroke and a fibrillating heart, all this is now in the past, but I didn't think I was ever going to recover at this time last year. So it's marvelous to feel well. It's just *incredible,* I can't believe it, because I couldn't believe I'd ever feel well because the medicine for the heart made me so sick. With a mastectomy you get better all the time: you have an operation and either get worse and die or get better, so you have the feeling of working toward some-thing. And the psychological problem that I had with this illness I've been through now was that there was no change. Every day I had to take a medicine that was poison to my system but kept the heart from fibrillating. Psychologically, I think it's the hardest thing I've ever had to do.

Wheelock: How did you conjure up enough strength to do it?

Sarton: Well, because if I hadn't, when the heart fibrillates then the lungs would fill up and then they'd have to drain the lungs. The fibrillating heart is terribly nerve-wracking; it would be much too fast, so it would be better to be sick and unable to eat. In one way it was wonderful, because I lost thirty-five pounds. I was so *elegant.* I've now almost gotten it back. That was the best thing about it. I was almost as thin as Marita. That's very thin.

Wheelock: Tell us about the other books you've been doing [since *World of Light*].

Sarton: Well, I was thinking. *Recovering,* then the novel *Anger,* which has meant quite a lot to people—I was amazed at this— was very hard to do, and very good things have happened out of this—people's marriages have been helped by it. I'm *glad* I made it a heterosexual marriage; it could've been a homosexual novel, between two women. But I didn't want that, for various reasons: one of them was that I wanted it to be as universal as possible, but the other was that I didn't want, if I was going to write a lesbian novel of this sort, to make it a *war* the whole time, you see. I want to do the book about the women's bookstore that I mentioned in the film. That's one thing. Then other books: *At Seventy,* the journal; a book of poems called *Letters from Maine;* and a lovely book of my mother's letters to me, which has a preface by me. I was so happy that Constance Hunting at the Puckerbrush Press wanted to do that. It was because I was reading my mother's letters, which will go to the Berg Collection with my papers—I hadn't been able to read them for thirty-five years, you see, and I made myself do it, thinking I'd cry the whole time. *Instead,* I kept feeling that she was such a wonderful woman, you know; I was just overwhelmed with joy. And I was talking to Connie about this and she said, "I'll publish them." I'd never thought of doing that. Then I thought, Yes! I chose letters not so much about our relationship but to show what a wonderful person she was, and what a great writer. You see, that's where I got it.

Wheelock: A catharsis, you mean.

Sarton: Yes, it was. It was really thrilling.

And now there's a new journal in the works. It's finished and it's just gone to Norton, *After the Stroke,* that I kept for nine months of that year, until the anniversary of the stroke, which was February 22. And I'm pleased about it, because I think it may help some people, although I did have a very mild stroke. I still had a lot of things to overcome, particularly that I couldn't do my work, you see, anymore for a long time. I couldn't type. Everything was scrambled. It's a hemorrhage of the brain. The brain, you know, takes a while to recover.

Wheelock: Is there any advice you can give to people?

Sarton: Well, I think the main thing is to live in the present as much as possible—in the actual *small* things of the present, like light on a curtain or on flowers, like watching an animal play, playing with your animal. I couldn't walk because I'd get so out of breath. I couldn't garden. That was also very hard. I had to pay someone $3,000 to do what I do as a regular part of my life for fun.

And there have been quite a few poetry readings. I was in Indianapolis; I stayed with the Carmelites, a great experience. They invited me because they've used *Journal of a Solitude* in their meditations, for years. And I was received, really, as a member of the community; it was very moving. I had dinner with them every night, and they would talk, ask me questions—such a marvelous group of women, so various, so independent, so radical. The most radical women in America today are nuns. I'm convinced. I mean, they go down to El Salvador, they go to Nicaragua; they're violently against our policy in Central America. We got on very well. I had a wonderful time with them.

Then I gave—with my terrible memory now I can't remember the name of it—I gave a series of lectures at Indiana University where my father had been invited to lecture thirty years before. That was very thrilling to me; it really was. They asked me to read *As We Are Now*, as one of the two lectures, and then poems. You see, I don't lecture; I have a rule about that. I only read my work. This was a problem for them. My father, bless his heart, wrote a whole book called *Six Wings*, about science in the Renaissance, whereas here I was a cheat, really, being paid an enormous amount of money to read work that I'd already written. But it was lovely just the same, and he would have been pleased, I'm sure. And going to Belgium for my father's centennial, which was two years ago—that was very thrilling, you know. Scholars came from all over the world. They had a beautiful show of his Belgian life. He left Belgium before he was thirty—we did, refugees of World War I. But it was his youth there, and wonderful photographs, and quotations from *I Knew a Phoenix*, of course. That was a great experience for me.

Wheelock: You're certainly a symbol of the writer who writes about aging and wisdom-gaining and all of that. Do you have any new perspectives?

Sarton: I feel I should do less and less of it rather than more and more. I mean, I don't really want to write now about being old. Maybe in time I'll do more, but I doubt if I'll do another journal for a long time. Maybe when I'm eighty, if I'm still alive, I might do one last one then—which would be real old age—because, you see, actually this last one is not old age, it's illness. There's a big difference— although I feel much older as a result of this, no doubt. I feel a lot older than eight years ago, obviously. It would be strange if I didn't. I mean, it wouldn't be normal, really.

I think I can be valuable from this point of view, because there are increasing numbers of old people that we live with and that we want to help have as good lives as possible.

Wheelock: You can show your vitality.

Sarton: Well, yes. And I rest a lot. That was always true. A performance like even the short half-hour here is very costly in energy, as I don't need to tell you. I rested the whole afternoon to have the energy for that. I did a radio interview this morning which lasted too long. It took energy too. I don't have infinite amounts. I rest a lot, but then I always did. I did when you were there for that week, you remember. I think we never shot in the afternoon, or before four. What a wonderful time it was! And what a great result. It's just marvelous to think about it.

Castaway's Choice:
A Conversation with May Sarton
John McNally/1988

This transcript was edited from an audiotape conversation conducted by John McNally on 1 July 1988 for the "Castaway's Choice" series of Radio Station KCRW, Santa Monica Community College, 1900 Pico Boulevard, Santa Monica, CA 90405. Printed by permission of Ruth Hirschman, General Manager, KCRW.

McNally: Welcome to Castaway's Choice. Our premise is, if you were to be cast away, which ten recordings would you take and why? Our castaway is novelist, keeper of journals, and poet, May Sarton. Welcome, May.

Sarton: I'm happy to be here.

McNally: How would you like the idea of being all alone on a deserted, tropical island?

Sarton: Well, actually I wouldn't like to be on a tropical island *at all*. But I *am* all alone on an island, in a way, because I live alone, in Maine, and look out to the ocean. And it's very much my life. So these records I've been playing on my own desert island, in a way.

McNally: So you enjoy living alone?

Sarton: Oh, very much, yes. Solitude is an absolute necessity for me, actually, and I've written a lot about it. The *Journal of a Solitude* is one of my most popular books. The point is, as I've said and as it's often been quoted to me, loneliness is the poverty of self and solitude is the richness of self. I don't think you can be happily live alone when you're very young, because you don't have enough inside you. I started really living alone when I was forty-five and bought an old farm in New Hampshire. From them on, I have been *happy* to be alone.

McNally: So you think you would survive quite well all alone on a tropical island.

Sarton: Well, I would if there were food around, if there were bananas I could get.

McNally: How did you go about choosing your ten recordings?

Sarton: Well, I had very little time, as you know, and I just lay down and said to myself, "What are the records that I've played many times; in other words, that are really in my bones?" Whenever I'm involved in a book, whether it's poetry or journals or a novel or memoirs, I'm apt to play one record over and over again. I don't mean thousands of times, but the year I'm writing that book I'm apt to play the record fifty or a hundred times. It becomes almost the theme of the book—for me. So these are all records that I have listened to a great deal.

McNally: So music is very important to you.

Sarton: Yes, it is.

McNally: Where shall we begin?

Sarton: Well, we're beginning, I think, with Monteverdi, conducted by Nadia Boulanger, whom I very briefly knew—never studied with. I'm not a musician at all. But these are marvelous songs, I think.

McNally: Why this particular choice?

Sarton: Well, it's the poet in me, partly. The actual language is magnificent, the poems, and then the music. These hit me as the most modern definition of love that I'd ever heard, not old, not way back there, you see. And I was in love at the time, and I played them over and over again. Music is very important to me in New England, partly too, because we have these long winters. After all, here you are never without flowers.

McNally: May, were you born in the United States?

Sarton: No. I wasn't. I was born in Belgium. My father was Belgian, a famous historian of science, and my mother was an English artist. We were driven out in 1914. I was only two, of course. I started with French; French was my language first, and then English.

McNally: Do you still continue the French?

Sarton: Oh, yes, and it's influenced me enormously in my work. Mauriac, for instance, influenced me tremendously as a novelist; Paul Valéry as a poet. And I read—I used to read a great deal of French. I don't anymore, partly because I haven't been back to France and able to buy books as often as I used to. I used to go over to Europe every year when I was young—for two or three months—and then I would buy books, you see, and read. So I'm not as much in touch with what's happening in France *now* as I was in the thirties and forties.

McNally: What were your parents able to do when they came over to the United States?

Sarton: Well, my father was dreaming of writing a history of science, which is what he finally did, though only after the fourteenth century. The Carnegie Institute gave him a fellowship which lasted for twenty years or so. He had to learn English; he was over thirty; He had taken lessons—Berlitz School, you know—and they'd said, "We won't issue any more tickets, George Sarton; you really *never* will be able to learn English." And the poor man, here he was landed in America and *having* to learn English. There my mother was a great help. And we always spoke English at home, which was a pity for me because then I forgot my French and had to relearn it.

McNally: And your mother, was she able to get along quite well in the United States?

Sarton: Well, she was a designer. Her career was, in a way, broken by 1914, because there was to be an international exhibition and she had designed a series of furniture, very beautiful, and that had to be put in a cellar, since the exhibition was postponed. But she designed clothes later, which were bought by Nieman-Marcus, Lord & Taylor, the great department stores—yes, she was a very wonderful artist. But *her* career was not fulfilled by being in America, whereas my father's was, because in Europe there was no such thing as this sort of fellowship that he had. And for me, I would have had to be a poet writing in French in a country divided in language between Flemish and French, where it was much better for me to be a poet writing in English. And also I think it's the best language for poetry, because it has all the Latin words, beautiful words like *charisma* and *lucid,* and then all the nice Anglo-Saxon words like *pig* and *earth,* and combining is what makes English poetry so rich. So I'm very happy to be a poet writing in English.

McNally: What do you remember about your early days in the United States? Where were you?

Sarton: First we were in Washington, D.C., where we were none of us very happy and then I really began to become an American in Cambridge where I was sent to the Shady Hill School, a marvelous school which I've written about in *I Knew a Phoenix.* The school

emphasized creativity, really, especially poetry; now this was a piece
of luck for me. We learned a great many poems by heart. The whole
atmosphere was that of bringing out that which was in each child, but
it was also very disciplined. This is what people don't remember
about the so-called "progressive schools." They think everybody
went haywire and did what he chose. We were given the ability to
find the tools for anything we wanted to do and to have enough
confidence to do it. So it was a great education.

McNally: You've chosen a selection from Bach's six cello suites,
performed by Pablo Casals. Why this choice, May?

Sarton: Because I think they're like meditations, and you could
listen to them forever. It's a sort of geometric meditation, very much
like form in poetry for me. It does the same thing for me as a
beautifully constructed poem, and I could listen to them forever.

McNally: May, when did you know you wanted to be a writer or a
poet?

Sarton: I think I knew that I wanted to be a poet—and I think that
if you're a poet you're a poet *first*—when I was about nine years old.
The first poem I ever wrote—and I was very proud of it—was about
a pigeon. I'm proud of it because most people start writing poetry
about themselves, you know: *I'm so unhappy*. And the first poem I
wrote—I wish I knew it by heart, it wasn't that good—was a description of something. It was looking out at the exact—I remember "its
coral feet" came into the poem; that's the only thing I remember
about the poem. But I always wrote poetry, from the time I was nine
or ten. My first book of poems came out when I was twenty-five. My
first poems were published in *Poetry* magazine when I was seventeen. At the same time, I was falling in love with the theater. I never
went to college. I went into Eva La Gallienne's Civic Repertory
Theatre as an apprentice right after high school. I'm an "ill-edu-
cated" person, although I've taught at Harvard University, because I
only have a paper from the public high school in Cambridge.

McNally: And of course that's most important to have all the
paper.

Sarton: Yes, it is. Well, now I have twelve doctorates, honorary
doctorates, so I guess I'm doing all right.

McNally: Why did you decide to go on the stage?

Sarton: Well, because I fell in love with that theater. You see, that theater, which of course doesn't exist anymore, was a *real* repertory, which we've never had in America; that is, not the same play ever twice in succession. A typical week would be Chekhov's *Three Sisters* on Monday, Ibsen's *Hedda Gabler* on Tuesday, *Peter Pan* on the Wednesday matinee, then again *Hedda Gabler* and then *The Three Sisters,* you see, so there'd be three plays in the week. We had a repertory of twenty-six plays. And I was madly in love, really, with Eva Le Gallienne—everything that she stood for—a most remarkable woman and a great actress. I've never seen anyone who could communicate soul as she could on the stage. In parts like Masha in *The Three Sisters,* she was extraordinary. So I learned a lot, of course.

McNally: What *were* you learning, in fact?

Sarton: I was learning—I wanted to be a director and an actress. I did have small parts. I was made head of the apprentice group at the age of nineteen. Then the theater failed; it was the Depression. All she needed was $100,000 a year to keep that theater going and keep eighty people alive and give these marvelous plays to audiences. It now costs a million to put a play on Broadway with one set and five actors. It's just dreadful. You see what's happened to the theater: it's an angel with its feet tied to a bag of gold. And when the theater failed and I was head of the apprentices, I decided to keep them together and make a company of my own, which we did for three years. Then, for the same reason, I couldn't go on—the money. It was the Depression.

McNally: But you survived the Depression.

Sarton: Well, yes, but I had a nervous breakdown when my company finally failed. At twenty-five, you see, I had experienced tragic failure, and I think it was very good for me. I mean, I approve of it as a method of learning: you know that you'll never fail in that way again. And then my first book of poems came out, and I went to England and I met Virginia Woolf, Elizabeth Bowen, and all these marvelous people. I never looked back.

McNally: May, you've chosen an excerpt from Beethoven's "Emperor Concerto." Why this choice?

Sarton: This is very romantic, and it's associated for me with a marvelous woman, the mother of one of my fellow students at the Shady Hill School, Edith Forbes Kennedy, who was a genius at bringing people together and drawing them out. I can remember an evening when Elliott Carter—the composer—was there, I was there—the poet—and a young man who was slinging hash in some sort of joint but who was a great expert on jazz was there. She had no money; she had a salon without any money or any appurtenances in just a little room in Cambridge. We would sit and listen to records and talk about music. She had the widest frame of reference of anybody I've ever known: she knew everything about art, about music, about literature. And then her genius was drawing other people out; she didn't dominate, but she made everybody there feel brilliant by the way she drew them out. I listened to this with her many times, and it's associated with that room, with that person. It's very romantic. I read one poem that I had written really for her, called "Evening Music," which ends "And there would be no music if you left." And she left forty years ago.

McNally: You mentioned that when your first book of poems came out, it made a great difference in your life. How did they come about and how did they come to be printed? You make it sound very simple—that they came out and you were immediately acclaimed.

Sarton: Well, I wasn't "immediately acclaimed," because nobody is with a first book of poems. But I did get some good reviews. They had been coming out in magazines, like *Poetry* magazine, and various little magazines. I made up a book of them and sent it to Houghton Mifflin, and they sent it to Conrad Aiken, whom I did not know personally, for his judgment, you know, Is this any good? Should we publish it? and he said yes. That *was* very lucky for me. They did publish it, in a beautiful edition, I may say, with an engraving from a drawing of me by a Boston artist. I was launched, really, *then* as feeling I was a professional; that's what it did. Writing was going to be my profession—which is a big difference. Then I wrote a first novel which Houghton Mifflin also published. I first started writing short stories, which didn't sell—later I did stories that did sell—but my editor at Houghton Mifflin, said: "We think you're a novelist, not a short story writer." It never occurred to me to write a novel. But then I became *immersed* in a novel—*The Single Hound,* my first novel—and I found it a fascinating form and went on, you see, seventeen novels now.

McNally: What were your poems reflecting?

Sarton: Love affairs, or I mean, *a* love affair. The book is called *Encounter in April,* and they're sonnets. They were greatly influenced by Edna Millay, who was *the* poet of the time. And they were derivative. A very wise friend of mine said, "Go back to the Elizabethans. Don't imitate people who are imitating the Elizabethans." He was right, you know. But there are a few good poems among them—enough so that the book did make a little splash.

McNally: So you went to England and immediately entered the literary circle.

Sarton: Well, somehow, a piece of luck, really. I stayed with the historians of sciences first in Cornwall; it was spring and the grass was strewn with camellia petals—it was like a dream. You know, the English spring—absolutely incredible. Julian Huxley happened to be there, because he was trying to find out whether they could grow eucalyptus and have koala bears at the London Zoo—he was then the secretary of the London Zoo—and so I had an entry to them. He said, "Be sure to call us when you come to London." I've forgotten all the things that happened, but people knew each other and there was a young man in the same rooming house where I was—John Summerson, who has turned out to be a great writer on architecture and now been *knighted*—and he knew Bowen and asked one day, "How would you like to go to dinner at Elizabeth Bowen's?" I almost fainted with pleasure. *She* found out that my dream was to meet Virginia Woolf and arranged *that,* and so everything sort of came together. It was a dream. I could dream. Because I had been working so hard in the theater, I had never had any youth—I'd worked from the time I was seventeen, you see—I'd never danced, things like that. I'd never "come out." Then I suddenly became a young woman, attractive—much to my amazement, because there had never been any time. And I had a marvelous few springs in England, before World War II.

McNally: You've chosen an excerpt from Albinoni's "Adagio." Why this choice, May?

Sarton: This piece of music meant an enormous amount to me while I was writing *The Journal of a Solitude,* the first of the journals and I think the best perhaps. Still I get letters about this journal, oh, once a week, from people who have discovered it and say, "This is what I've needed. This is the food I've been waiting for. You've changed my life." It talks a great deal about being alone and how you handle it, about being lonely, about being depressed, about being creative, about what it's like to come to a village where you know no one and reclaim an old house and start living there. The only bad influence it's had is to make *young* people think, I'm going to be like May Sarton and go and live in a village somewhere alone, and, you see, at maybe nineteen or twenty you don't have enough in you. I was forty-five when I went to Nelson. I played the Albinoni, a great deal. I have getting over an unhappy love affair, and it had something to do with that perhaps.

McNally: What a beautiful piece of music, May.

Sarton: Isn't it? It really is. I started to cry, listening to it again. I haven't heard it for maybe twenty years, and it all came back.

McNally: You seem to be very romantic.

Sarton: Well, yes, I think I am. It's the romantic in a classic form, if you will, and this is why all these people like Mozart, Monteverdi, Bach appeal to me so much, because you get all the feeling there but you also get the wonderful form. And I think that's what I am: a romantic in a classical form.

McNally: You seem to have been falling in and out of love all of your life.

Sarton: Oh, yes, I have. I think it's inevitable. People who have moved me and who are the muses of the poems have always been women. Well, you can't find what you might call a "lesbian poem." Somebody tried to, somebody who was pulling me down in a review in the *Times,* she couldn't find a lesbian poem. There's no such thing in my work, because I think love is universal. It's not primarily in poetry, which transcends sexuality; poetry is not primarily sexual.

McNally: After your trip to England, what course did your life take then?

Sarton: Well, it came World War II, of course, and I just went on writing. I had a hard time between my first and second novels, and that often happens. I couldn't get the second one, which was called *The Bridge of Years,* and was about Belgium, about family life—it's a very good novel, actually. When it came out, it was recognized; but I couldn't get a publisher for that for a long time. I worked for O.W.I., writing film scripts—propaganda, really. You tried to be rather subtle about it, but things like the T.V.A., about what it had done for that part of the country, and a wonderful one on schools, called "All the Children," in New York, for instance, about schools for deprived children, for deaf children, and all that. It really was true of New York then. So that's what I was doing.

McNally: You were living in New York.

Sarton: Well, yes, during that time. Then I went back and lived in Cambridge. I lived for years with my great friend Judith Matlack, who taught at Simmons College. And we had a wonderful life together. Then I felt that I needed finally to be alone. My father had died, and there was all that old Belgian furniture rotting in a cellar. I think that partly made me feel that I must have a place for this furniture. I went to Nelson, partly to rebuild a life of my own. Judy came for all the holidays. We didn't part as enemies at all. I mean, we stayed very dear friends.

McNally: So you enjoyed being in Nelson.

Sarton: Yes, very much. Then I began to read poetry.That started a long time back, partly just to earn money. You can't earn money as a poet, and my novels didn't sell enormously. So I started going out and reading my poetry in the colleges. I do it rather well—there the theater was a great help: you see, I learned to read well and to project to an audience—so I was much in demand. For forty years I've been doing that, in the fall and the spring going out on tour. I learned a lot about America, because colleges are so often in small towns and you *see* so much. I wouldn't have given it up for anything.

McNally: You've chosen Mozart, an excerpt from the "Flute and Harp Concerto in C."

Sarton: Well, if I were to choose one composer, and I could only have one, it would be Mozart. Mozart has everything; it has all the feeling, the infinite invention and imagination, and enormous tenderness. I couldn't live without Mozart—period.

McNally: May, you wrote a small tribute to Mozart.

Sarton: Well, it's not exactly that. Let me read it and then you'll see what I did. It *is* for Mozart. It's called "Mozart Again," and it's really about the spring.

Mozart Again
Now it is Mozart who comes back again
All garlanded in green.

Flute, harp, and trumpet, the sweet violin—
Each sound is seen.

Spring is a phrase, repeated green refrain,
Sound of new leaves springing.
I see the wind flowing like slanted rain,
Wind winging.

I learn this loving fresh, in ancient style
(Lightly time flows),
And mine a green world for pure joy awhile.
Listen, a rose.

Leaves are glissando. A long, haunting phrase
Ripples the air—
This harpsichord of light that the wind plays.
Mozart is there.

McNally: May, how do you approach poetry writing? What do you look for? What are your subjects?

Sarton: Well, you don't "look." Poetry *comes.* What you do is try to be a good instrument for poetry, which means keeping yourself very clear, very transparent, *not* cluttered up. This is partly why I live alone in the country. And then poems come, but they don't come all the time. This is one of the reasons I'm very glad I'm a novelist and a memoirist, because I always have another string to my bow, that I can be playing while the poems are gestating somewhere. Poetry always begins for me with a line, a single line that runs through my head. I pick out of the air a poem about my father that began, "I never saw my father old, / I never saw my father cold." Those two lines *came* to me, and I remember thinking, It's like a nursery rhyme; it isn't right. But then I realized that my father, like many great scholars, was a very innocent, childlike man and that this nursery-rhyme poetry was *exactly* what the poem required. You have to trust the subconscious and then work with it, of course.

McNally: Is this true as far as your novels go?

Sarton: The novel is different, because it's a tremendous labor, much harder work. Virginia Woolf used to tease me—when I knew her I hadn't written a novel—and kept saying, "It's *so easy to write* poetry compared to writing a novel." You see the novel in its big shape before you and you get a moment of vision about it; but then it's a tremendous daily effort for a year to write it. I used to say to my students that writing a novel was like taking an examination on which your whole future depended every day for a year. Every day you have to bring up from yourself this tremendous aliveness and to project it onto a page. I mean, it's very hard work.

McNally: So you have to be quite a perfectionist and very disciplined.

Sarton: Well, yes, and full of juice. That's the hard thing, you know—to get yourself back into the imaginative world every morning. Yes, I think that discipline, routine, all these things which I learned from my father are very important. You can't wait for inspiration; you've got to make it happen—in writing a novel.

McNally: Can you afford to be particularly moody when you're writing a novel?

Sarton: You're bound to be, because so much of the time you feel it's a total failure. You never believe in it. Every morning you have conquer the demons who say, "This will *never* be any good. This will *never* be what I saw when I dreamed of it." But you just have to say, "Keep on, keep on," and finally it gets through.

McNally: And you've been able to do that for quite a few novels.

Sarton: Seventeen, yes.

McNally: Were you ever tempted to give up?

Sarton: Oh yes. Every novel I've written, I've had to overcome terrible anxiety and fear and self-doubt. But then some of them are quite good. Some have become classics. What's nice is that novels of mine written twenty years ago are being taught *now* in the schools. They're absolutely *alive!* That's the good thing about my work.

McNally: Are you able to make a "Sophie's Choice" about your creations? Do you have a favorite?

Sarton: No. I think it's a little like asking people about their children, because my books are my children, and I would hesitate to say, "That's my favorite child," for fear the others' feelings would be hurt.

McNally: You've chosen an excerpt from Duparc's "Songs with Orchestra."

Sarton: This is a poem by Baudelaire, "D'invitation au voyage," "An Invitation to Go Away." It's a magnificent poem I used to read in the Luxembourg Gardens in Paris when I was nineteen. Le Gallienne's theater had to take a year off because she was nearly burned to death in an accident, and so I spent a marvelous year in Paris, alone, studying the theater *ostensibly*, but what I was really doing was walking the streets and reading Baudelaire and other French poets. So "D'invitation au voyage" takes me back to that time in Paris. Also, because I'm a poet, the marvel of the music being so perfect for the poem. People have written music for my poetry, and it's *never* seemed to me that you got the words—it was a big clash of cymbals and things and it was probably wonderful music, but it didn't make the poem seem wonderful.

McNally: I'm intrigued by the title "keeper of journals." What exactly does that mean?

Sarton: I'll tell you why I said that—I said it off the cuff—because "journalist," you see, doesn't mean someone who is keeping a journal; it means someone who is writing for newspapers. I've published five journals, and there'll be a new one next year called *After the Stroke*, which I've just handed in to my publishers. The last one was *At Seventy*, one celebrating my seventieth year, which I kept for a year—you see, a journal of the day-to-day life. That's what they are.

McNally: You seem to be a remarkably spry person. Have you always been like this?

Sarton: Well, I think I've been lucky in having an enormous amount of psychic energy, which I got from *both* parents—my mother had it and my father had it. I don't have great physical energy and I get very tired, but I can summon this physical energy when I'm working and when I'm on a show like this—having a very good time.

McNally: You mentioned that you recently had a stroke. Did that make a great deal of difference to your life?

Sarton: Well, it certainly taught me to be much more sympathetic with people who have real disabilities. It was very frightening. And I was made more ill by a fibrillating heart, for which the medicine made me sicker than I really was made by the stroke. It took me nine months to get over the two things, nine months in which I couldn't do anything. I couldn't bury the ashes of my cat whom I adored. People came and put up a little monument for her and I was supposed to come out and we'd have a formal burial. I couldn't go because I was panting so. That means I was very sick because I loved this cat, you see. It was a bad time. But I think I learned something about living in the present, intensely in the present, watching light on flowers, and just being. I learned something about just being and not being so driven.

McNally: Apart from the journal, have poems come from this experience?

Sarton: Yes.

McNally: And does an experience such as a stroke automatically mean that a novel dealing with that experience will be coming?

Sarton: No, I don't think so, because I've written a novel about dying already. The thing was that I couldn't write poems at all during those nine months and I couldn't play music, records, which I've lived on, because I would burst into tears—because I thought I could never write again. The poetry *finally* came back, but it was a long time. You see, it affects your head. Frankly, it was a hemorrhage of the brain, and so you feel very queer for a while.

McNally: You've chosen an excerpt from Benjamin Britten's "War Requiem."

Sarton: It's particularly the part where Peter Pears with his wonderful voice sings—again I'm on poetry and music—a poem by Wilfred Owen, the great poet of World War I, the words of which, if I remember, are "move him into the sun." This is a dying soldier, obviously. It's just a tremendously moving requiem for all the war dead, for all men who die in wars. I don't know whether Benjamin Britten will last forever, but I found this requiem very moving.

McNally: May, when did you become "May Sarton"? When did you establish yourself, do you think?

Sarton: Gosh, it's hard to say. I think about twenty years ago, because it was cumulative and that's been the whole thing with my career: it's everything together which is finally going to be seen as a statement, as a vision of life. And I think that began to be clear about twenty years ago, when I'd published perhaps twenty books in these various genres. I've never won one of the great prizes like the Pulitzer. It's been a very slow process of people telling each other about me—they discover me and they tell their friends. Or, they go to the library and see a book called *Journal of a Solitude* and think, That's an interesting title, pull it out, and then say, "I'm going to get everything she's ever written." I get letters that tell me this very often. So it's *nice*. It's been sort of a difficult career in some ways, because in some ways I've never "made it." But I'm greatly loved, and maybe that's better.

McNally: You consider the memoirs as a genre as well.

Sarton: Oh yes! It's very different from the journal. You see in the journal life taken on the pulse, as you live it, and I've made a point of honor of not adding to the day's journal later. But the memoir is a distillation, perhaps, of the whole life, the portraits of my father and mother, for instance, and the people I've loved very much in a book called *World of Light*. That's memoirs. A book called *I Knew a Phoenix*, which is about my childhood and about my mother and father's youth—that's a memoir. It's a distillation, then, whereas a journal is something taken on the pulse.

McNally: While you've decided not to choose among your favorite novels, how about between the genres?

Sarton: Well, I think poetry comes first. It would if you're a poet at all, I think. I think you're born with it, just as composers and mathematicians know very early that they are—composers or mathematicians. Those three—including poetry—you know very young, I think.

McNally: Along the way is there anything that you would like to have done that you've not yet done?

Sarton: Well, I've done it, but it hasn't succeeded. I'd like to have a play produced—I've written two long, three-act plays, which have never been produced. But I probably will never do that. It's just an idea I have. But it would be nice.

McNally: You've chosen an excerpt from Fauré's "Requiem." Why this choice, May?

Sarton: Well, I've played this requiem, lately, in the last ten years very, very often, because when you get to be in your seventies people begin to die, people you're very fond of. And it's such a tender requiem and it's such a consoling requiem that I've found it very valuable as the losses pile up. And I think I first began to play it when my mother died, which was a long time ago, thirty-five years ago. It reminds me of her.

McNally: May, you've been very prolific in your life, many poems and many novels and many journals and one or two memoirs as well. How do you handle criticism? After all you've stuck your neck out.

Sarton: Well, I've not only stuck my neck out, I've had no luck. I'm nowhere with the literary establishment—except now students are going to their professors and saying, "I want to write my Ph.D. thesis on Sarton." And the professor says, "Who is Sarton?" And the student says, "You'd better read her!" And the professor finally says, "Well, yes." You see, it's coming, but it's taken a very long time. I used to have good reviews, but the *New York Times*, the most powerful, single publication, has not given a good review for twenty years. Meanwhile these books have become classics, are taught in the colleges. So I've had to handle an *enormous* amount of criticism, of negative criticism, and I think most people would have committed suicide. I'm very proud that I didn't.

McNally: It made you stronger?

Sarton: Yes, I think so, in some ways. Well, it's hard—there's no doubt. I think I got cancer from a review in the *Times*, from rage. You see, you can't answer. You have to sit there and be slapped in front of five million people, and you can't answer.

McNally: And you do resent it.

Sarton: Yes, of course, you do! I mean, if you were making automobiles and they said, "Don't buy this car. It's no good," you'd resent it.

McNally: But you seem to have overcome the minds of the critics.

Sarton: Well, partly because of the enormous following I have, and this has always been true. I do have hundreds of people—they can't believe it, wherever I go, these huge audiences come up from the boondocks, you know; they come from little towns, way off somewhere, when they hear that I'm there. So there are thousands of people who live on my work and love it, and *that's* what sustains me, of course. And the hell with the critics! They'll be dead.

McNally: And your work will live on.

Sarton: I hope so.

McNally: You seem to be in quite a position of power.

Sarton: In what way?

McNally: Well, if you have many people waiting for you to write and waiting for your words.

Sarton: I suppose that's power of a kind, yes.

McNally: You must be able to influence many people. Have you ever been tempted to consciously . . .?

Sarton: No, but I think that what I'm doing all the time is project-ing a vision of life, of values, that success and money are not the important things, that maybe looking at a flower is very important. An old man of eighty, a recent fan in San Francisco, told me that he'd never looked at flowers before and that this had absolutely changed his life now when he goes for walks. He said: "I'm eighty and I've discovered you and I carry your books in my pocket and give them away. Perhaps when I was seventy I wasn't yet ready for you."

McNally: You've chosen the Beatles, a little change of pace. Why this choice?

Sarton: Well, I loved the Beatles. I remember when they came on the Sullivan show the first time and he sort of shyly said, "Here are some English boys." One was simply overwhelmed by the vitality, the charm, the wit of these boys. And then there is something else, which is in the one that I chose, "Let It Be": it's very religious. It's about Mary. I played this when I was very depressed some years ago. I've gone through many depressions and come out. And I remember this was an extremely comforting thing to me, this record. I love it, I still love it.

McNally: When you are "all alone on this deserted, tropical island," is there anyone or anything you would be glad to be away from?

Sarton: Noise, noise. I live in a very silent place where I only hear the ocean—rarely a small plane going overhead. But coming here and being in the city, I must admit that the noise has been an assault upon me.

McNally: If you're allowed one person from history to drop in and visit you, who might that be?

Sarton: Chekhov.

McNally: Really, why?

Sarton: Well, I love his work, and I love the man. I think he's one of the very few writers whom one *knows* was a remarkably—again the word *tenderness* comes in—tender and compassionate person as well as, of course, a genius.

McNally: And if you're allowed to have a luxury item with you, something that's not at all applicable to your survival, what would it be?

Sarton: A pet would be wonderful, but, of course, how would you feed it? But how would you feed yourself? This is an imaginary world. So the luxury would be a cat.

McNally: And if you're allowed a book, excluding a religious book and excluding Shakespeare?

Sarton: The dictionary, without any question, a really good dictionary because you get so much in it. You can sit and think about words, you know, and the dictionary would take you long distances, without ever boring.

McNally: Would you continue to write?

Sarton: Oh yes! Well, poetry. I've often thought about it. So many people have been in solitary confinement in my time, and if I were I would not write novels, I would not write memoirs, but I would write poetry, because I think poetry is between oneself and God. And that relationship continues, would be there. It isn't that you write religious poems, you understand. But I think I'd go on writing poems.

McNally: Are you a mystic by any chance?

Sarton: I think I am, yes. That is, I am religious in a very minor way, but I am religious. I suppose it's summed up in Schweitzer's phrase "reverence for life." And if you have that you must realize that it's full of mystery and grandeur that we have to admit is there outside ourselves and more important than we are.

McNally: You're going to leave us with something which seems very applicable to your life—Frank Sinatra singing "My Way."

Sarton: I'll bet a hundred people have chosen that, because it expresses so many people's view of their lives, people who've made it on their own, have had a hard time and have somehow come through—without the critics or without the help they might've had.

McNally: If you were to lose nine of these recordings and could only keep one, which one would that be?

Sarton: That's a hard question. I think I'd keep the Fauré "Requiem."

McNally: And if you were to leave one of these recordings for the next castaway?

Sarton: Well, maybe the Monteverdi.

McNally: May Sarton, thank you for allowing me to cast you away.

Sarton: Thank *you* for casting me away in such a rich way, such a joyful way.

May Sarton
Lois Rosenthal/1989

From *Writer's Digest* (March 1989), 44–48. Reprinted by permission.

May Sarton has openly shared so much of her life with her readers (her bouts of illness in *After the Stroke,* her feelings about growing older in *At Seventy*) through her long career of writing poems, novels and journals, and has built such a strong bond with her avid audience, that visiting her in her house by the sea in York, Maine, feels like a homecoming. Those who have pictured her yellow-shingled Cape Cod, surrounded by the flower gardens she writes of tending with so much love and effort, will find it just as she has described it in her classic *Journal of a Solitude* and *House by the Sea,* as well as in one of her collections of poems, *Halfway to Silence.*

Now in her seventy-sixth year, plagued by health complications caused by a fibrillating heart, recovering from a stroke that kept her in near seclusion for most of the past year, Sarton is determinedly in the midst of a new novel—her nineteenth. In addition, she has written two children's books, fourteen books of poetry and nine books of nonfiction, which include the journals that have earned her a huge following.

She continues to live alone, fiercely protecting her independence, and she still rises at six each morning, writes from eight until eleven when she feels well enough, then drives—through fog, freezing rain, snow or record heat—her Ford Escort station wagon over York's bumpy back roads to the post office to collect her mail. Though Sarton is small and now rather stooped, her presence is commanding. Her voice is rich and resonant, mirroring her Cambridge, Massachusetts, upbringing and her early adult years spent as an actress. When Sarton settles into a chair and begins to talk about her writing life, it is easy to see how her poetry readings captivate crowds from coast to coast.

"I never had any doubt that I wanted to be a poet," she says. "I wrote from the time I was nine or ten, and was part of a family that encouraged deep thinking and creativity. My father, George Sarton, was a great international scholar. He was a pioneer in creating the subject of the history of science, and he wrote extensively about it. He was Belgian and my mother was English—an artist and an extraordinary woman. My parents were very radical, enormously idealistic in a way that no one has been able to be since World War I. Both of my parents read avidly and we discussed books all the time at home. It was an exciting atmosphere.

"I was supposed to go to Vassar and get a good education as my family expected. But while I was in high school, my father took me to see Eva Le Gallienne—one of the most famous actresses of that era—and her Civic Repertory Company perform Maria Sierra's *The Cradle Song*. I haunted the theater in Boston where her company was performing other plays. I knew immediately I would never be the same. I wanted to become an actress, join Le Gallienne's company as an apprentice rather than go to Vassar—which, at first, made my father furious. Finally he agreed to let me have my own way and go to New York."

Though life in the theater was close to survival level for Sarton, she speaks of those years in New York with passion. "The company performed a different play every night, and Ibsen's *Hedda Gabler* might be followed by Barrie's *Peter Pan* and then perhaps Chekhov's *Three Sisters*," she says. "I had an amazing education in the theater. There is nowhere in America today where it could be obtained to that rich and exciting extent."

However, in the middle of the Depression, Le Gallienne's theater failed. Sarton, as director of The Apprentice Group, tried keeping these earnest young actors together by forming The Apprentice Theatre, which was based at the New School for Social Research, and offering ten modern European plays as a course at this school. Because no scenery, makeup or costumes were used, critics were impressed that such illusions could be created with such meager means. Even so, after two more years of struggling to make ends meet at other theater locations, this troupe failed, as well.

"This was the Depression," says Sarton. "Though I only needed $5,000 a year to keep 12 people together, money finally ran out. But I will never regret that I experienced failure so young—I was twenty-three. I had done more extraordinary things than I would have if I had gone to Vassar. Because I learned about failure, it would never again frighten me so much. And during all of that time, I never stopped writing poems."

Those poems were collected in a book published by Houghton Mifflin in 1937. Though they were critically acclaimed, Sarton was unable to live by writing poetry any more than she was by acting. Her father kept her going with an allowance of $100 a month.

"I lived on that $1,200-a-year allowance and the little bit I earned as a writer during the '30s and '40s. The New York women's club where I stayed cost $11 a week and included two meals a day. Though I never had any money left over, I was always able to make ends meet.

"I thought that a good way to supplement my income would be to sell short stories to popular magazines, but the ones I wrote were continually returned. Finally, my editor at Houghton Mifflin told me he felt I was a novelist rather than a short story writer, and he offered me a $250 advance to try one, which I eagerly accepted. *A Single Hound,* which was published in 1938, is about a poet I knew in Belgium and two of her friends. I was pleased because this book, too, was positively reviewed."

Poetry, however, seems to be at the core of Sarton's creativity. To Sarton, a poem is the result of a collision between an object and a state of awareness that registers sensation. This means poets must develop a sharp state of mind, must become an instrument to transform what they see around them into images about which they write poems. They must see what they see as if it had just been created, and they must write about it in such a way that it seems readers have never seen it before.

Sarton writes in her book *Writings on Writing* that poets must use discipline to create an extraordinarily sensitive state of mind. "I myself have found that a good deal more solitude and a good many empty hours than are usual in our 'busy' civilization are one of my own requirements. I have to induce the state of awareness by renouncing some pleasures—the pleasures of society, for instance. If I do go to a dinner party, I know that the next morning the edge will be a fraction less sharp. What is inspiration, so-called, but the successful wooing of a state of mind? You cannot write a poem by wanting to write a poem, but only by becoming an instrument, and that means not being knotted up to a purpose, but open to any accidental and fortuitous event.

"Here's an example of what I mean," says Sarton. "At the end of a very painful and marvelous five-year love affair, I found myself in Pocatello, Idaho. I was on a lecture trip in the middle of the winter and I had the flu. I was in an absolutely miserable motel and was so sick I had to cancel my reading. But even though I had quite a high fever, I was forced out of my bed to write ten sonnets. They just came to me and there was nothing I could do except catch them as they poured out.

"I had been thinking and feeling about this major love affair for about six months and suddenly all of this came out. So these poems were about transcending an experience. I was somehow above what I was writing about and deep inside it at the same time.

"But people must realize that although deep feeling is important, you must also think a poem out, so it's the mixed combination of being able to think and feel at white heat that makes good poetry. And writing poetry can be quite a long process.

"So many people say, 'Oh, I feel everything so acutely and I've put it in my poem' and think that makes it a good one. But because you've felt something doesn't make your poetry good. There's the craft. There's the making. The beginner hugs his infant poem to him and does not want it to grow up. But you may have to break your poem to remake it. You must think and feel at the same time so that the thinking part of you can see why that particular line doesn't work, why it's too trite, that you will have to work it over and over again.

"The revision process is fascinating to me. Some of my poems have gone through 60 or more drafts by the time I'm satisfied. I think it's very important for poets to have others read their work, get all the criticism they can as well as be extremely self-critical."

If Sarton's poetry comes from internal white heat, her novels come from questions to which she needs to find an answer. *Faithful Are the Wounds* is a good example of her trying to write about a subject she wanted to better understand. "This novel's main question is how can a man be wrong and right at the same time? It's set in the academic world of Harvard and Cambridge in the 1950s, and Edmund Cavan, the novel's main character, is an English professor who believed communists and socialists could work together in Czechoslovakia and was proved wrong. Yet his idealism and his belief that all people must work together was right. I was desperately trying to understand the forces during the McCarthy era that were tearing the United States apart by getting inside the problem and writing my way out of it. That Edmund Cavan commits suicide at the opening of the book has a dramatic effect on his friends and colleagues throughout the story. Years after the suicide, those most affected by this violent act are under investigation by the McCarthy Committee.

"I think I demonstrate another of my writing theories in *Faithful Are the Wounds:* if you create a sufficiently dramatic situation in a novel, you don't have to worry about plot. This book begins with a wallop—a suicide—and its effect on other people creates the plot. Something happens to everyone who is close to a suicide and that is what this novel is about."

Sarton feels the first scene in a novel establishes the rhythm of the book. It should also suggest the theme, tell what the book is going to be about, introduce the major characters, and place them in their particular way of life. To Sarton, the first scene is a spell that pulls the reader into the book almost like the first line of a poem. The rest of the novel is a series of scenes, each rising to a climax; then the climax is resolved, which opens the door to the next scene.

Says Sarton in *Writings on Writing:* "At the end of each chapter or section, some precipitation must take place between the characters, something must have changed. Of course some of this shaping is done when one has roughed out the whole thing and can revise for the dynamics of each scene in relation to the dynamics of the whole. I find myself cutting ruthlessly to keep the rising curve clean. It often happens that whole chunks can come out because what they convey is absorbed in the total drive of the book."

Still, Sarton feels that creating the design of a novel is an organic process and there is a danger in mapping it out too meticulously. That would destroy the pleasure of exploration and discovery in writing the story, of constructing a novel while letting it construct itself. There must be a delicate balance in maintaining a creative fluidity while hanging on to the theme and not losing your way in the writing.

As for the worlds Sarton writes about in her novels, she says: "They very much reflect the world I live in. They are peopled by characters I am very familiar with—well educated, cultivated men and women. Sometimes I've been sorry that my world has been so middle-class, so intellectual—in a way, so rarefied. But I think the proof is that writing about my world, I've been able to communicate with people way outside it, who feel strongly about what I do. I admire the style of Carolyn Chute, who wrote *The Beans of Egypt, Maine,* but my trying to do something like that would be grotesque. I couldn't."

What Sarton could do is reveal an innermost secret in one of her novels. *Mrs. Stevens Hears the Mermaids Singing,* written in the 1950s, is the novel in which Sarton told of being a lesbian long before it was acceptable to do so. "I wrote the book to understand myself," she says, "but I lost friends, even some jobs as a result. However, as the women's movement came into its own, much of my work was swept up in a crest of popularity. *Mrs. Stevens* and many of my other books are now taught in women's studies programs in colleges throughout the United States.

"I wrote about homosexuality as a way of life, a kind of sensitivity. No one else had written about it in that fashion before I did though I have never written graphic sexual scenes and think most of them are vulgar. I don't like graphic descriptions of bodily functions of any kind.

"Imagine someone eating an ice cream cone. Her tongue comes out of her mouth, laps up the ice cream, then swallows it. It's disgusting. It's much better to eat ice cream than watch someone eat it. The same is true of sex. The physical act is so mixed up with feelings, I think it's hard to separate the two.

"Many of my novels deal with the subject of friendship between women; women who stand up for their individuality is a recurring theme. *Self-actualization* is the term I like best to describe what my novels are about, and I think this element is most important to me in my own life, as well."

These same strong themes are woven through all of Sarton's journals, which ironically she considers the most minor of the mediums in which she writes, but the genre that has earned her such a large following.

"The journals are not at all directed to lesbian women," says Sarton. "They appeal to all kinds of women because they explore what women's lives are like. I get so many letters from people all over the world who tell me that I've taught them how to look at everyday things in a different way, how to enjoy them.

"Someone recently wrote a master's thesis comparing my writing and Vermeer, the famous Flemish painter, and I wondered what she saw to put us together. She wrote that there were three things: the woman alone—Vermeer's paintings often have a single woman as their subject, the treatment of light which is so important in all of my books and especially my journals—light in a room at different times of the day, light through flowers; and the sacramentalization of everyday life."

This passage—the entry for one entire day in *Journal of a Solitude*—is an excellent example of the way May Sarton looks at life:

> A gray day . . . but strangely enough, a gray day makes the bunches of daffodils in the house have a particular radiance, a kind of white light. From my bed this morning I could look through at a bunch in the big room, in that old Dutch blue-and-white drug jar, and they glowed. I went out before seven in my pajamas, because it looked like rain, and picked a sampler of twenty-five different varieties. It was worth getting up early, because the first thing I saw was a scarlet tanager a few feet away on a lilac bush—stupendous sight! There is no scarlet so vivid, no black so black.

The mystical quality of Sarton gives to what she sees around her moves readers of her journals to deluge her with letters telling her how much they identify with her feelings. As Sarton stops to revel in the beauty of a sunrise, as she is comforted by the warmth of a cat nestled next to her in bed during a worrisome night, she is able to propel these feelings straight to the heart of people who read her work. Then readers see their worlds as May Sarton sees hers— as poetry.

"Keeping a journal is much harder than it looks. I know that I have underrated its form compared to the novel and poetry and even the memoir, which is distilled, but there's no doubt it does have a discipline of its own. For any writer who wants to keep a journal, remember to be alive to everything, not just to what you're feeling, but also to your pets, to flowers, to what you are reading.

"Remember to write about what you are seeing every day, and if you are going to hold the readers's interest, you must write very well. And what does writing well mean? It means seeing very well, seeing in a totally original way.

"Look at the bowl of irises on the table in front of me. Five different people who are asked to draw them would produce five totally different works of art, which is good. In the same way, journal writers must be just as honest in what they see because it's the freshness that matters. Keeping a journal is exciting because it gives a certain edge to the ordinary things in life.

"Let's use another example. Say you've burned something in a pot and you're standing at the sink scrubbing it. What comes to your mind as you are doing this? What does it mean to you in a funny way? Are you angry because you burn pots all too often? You can rage against the fact that it seems to be women who are mostly having to scrub pots, or you can ask yourself why you are bothering about this pot anyway. Why not throw it away if you can afford to get another? Is there something wrong with you that you are so compulsive you must try to clean something that is really beyond repair?

"Keeping a journal helps you get in touch with your own feelings. I think that's why I started the first one. I was in a depression when I began *Journal of a Solitude;* I was in the middle of a very unhappy love affair, and writing was my way of handling things.

"But a writer must always be perfectly honest. That's the key to people wanting to read a journal and that ingredient always astonishes me. When I've written things I felt were awfully weird and that no one would agree with, those are the very things that have made people say, 'You know, that's just how I feel.'

"My advice to any writer is never think of the effect of what you are doing while you are doing it. Don't project to a possible audience while you are writing. Hold on to your idea and get it down, and then maybe there'll be an audience, and maybe there won't. But have the courage to write whatever your dream is for yourself."

Sarton has lived these words, though she feels she has suffered because of it. Even though her audience is wide, even though W. W.

Norton, her publisher, announces each of her new books with a full-page ad in the *New York Times Book Review,* the ingredient she misses is validation by the critics.

"Until about 20 year ago, when my audience was getting bigger and bigger, I was getting less and less critical attention," says Sarton. "I've never had a single important critic in back of me since the years in England when I received so much critical attention before I was thirty.

"In America, I think I'm pushed aside as that awful thing called a sensitive feminine writer. The very ingredient that makes me universal has kept me from being interesting to the critics. You can't say that I'm a Maine writer, or a New England writer. I'm not regional. I can't be labeled as a lesbian writer because only one of my books deals with that subject.

"Poets consider me a novelist. Novelists consider me a poet. It sounds so dull, but I feel that what I write about is the human condition. I hope I'm a good writer, but the critics have no handle on what I am because not many distinguished writers work in as many forms as I do. That's why I feel I'm brushed aside by the most important reviewers, not taken as seriously as I'd like.

"I never went to college. Anne Sexton and Sylvia Plath did. Both of these women were enormously talented, so I'm not saying the people who get the prizes don't deserve them. I'm just saying that sometimes people who do deserve them don't get them, which is my case, I think.

"I've had a lot of blows and I feel I've been badly treated. Anyone but me would have stopped trying because these setbacks are hard to take. Still, I've never stopped writing and my advice to young writers is that you must always keep trying. If you can't take the criticism, then you're not a writer. You've got to be able to take it. Hold on, trust your talent, and work hard."

Living by her own advice, Sarton writes prolifically, has continued to gather an even larger audience, and has accumulated more than a dozen honorary college doctorates. Though her advances from Norton are modest compared to the megabuck deals many authors of less reputation are able to negotiate, she says she is satisfied with her life. "Though I wasn't able to live from my writing alone until I was sixty-five years old, money isn't everything. I lectured, taught; in the early days, I even wrote 200 letters to schools offering to read my poetry for $25. Now I'm as comfortable as I need to be. I even have money to help other writers, to give to charities I care about such as Amnesty International.

"Fame to me is not writing a bestseller, but knowing someone, somewhere in the United States is reading one of my books. Norton keeps twelve to fourteen of my books in print at any one time. They've told me they've made a million dollars selling my work. As an example, *Journal of a Solitude* has sold 2,000 books a year for twenty years. I receive so many letters from people who tell me my books have changed their lives. I feel loved by so many people. Let's face it, that's better than money."

Writing in the Upward Years: May Sarton
Stephen Robitaille/1990

This transcript was edited by Stephen Robitaille, English instructor and documentary filmmaker from an audiotape interview which he conducted in conjunction with the March 1990 conference "Writing in the Upward Years" held at Santa Fe Community College, Gainesville, Florida. The conference also featured Pulitzer Prize winning poet Richard Eberhart and poet-psychologist Molly Harrower, both 86. The focus of the conference was themes of aging in poetry and the role of creative expression in the upward years. A series of films on the three authors, also entitled "Writing in the Upward Years," will be available from Terra Nova, Chicago, Illinois.

Robitaille: I wonder if you might respond to the phrase "writing in the upward years" which is the focus of this conference?

Sarton: Well, of course, I have to laugh a little bit because I'm afraid I think of them a little bit as Leonard Woolf does in his autobiography, *Downhill All the Way.* But I did write a big novel when I was 75, which I'm very proud of. I don't think I could do it again. The problem is a lack of psychic energy to do a sustained thing.

I was asked to read from *As We Are Now,* which I have done for audiences in the past. I did it at Notre Dame. But I couldn't do it now, because I don't have the sustained energy. But this is very good for poetry. You can write a poem in two or three days, whereas a novel, you have to work for two or three years and have to sustain it.

But I don't know since I'm always waiting for a miracle. My friends at this wonderful place called "H.O.M.E." in Maine who build houses for the very poor—their motto is "Expect a miracle." And this is, more or less, my motto now. I expect to feel better. It may take six months to get back to a new journal—that is the one thing I still have the energy to do because it's only a paragraph a day, something like that, a page a day.

I love it—I love to see what's been important in the day. Sometimes it's something very small, like seeing a pheasant out on the lawn. It may not be a great event, but then you think, what a great thing to be alive and see it!

But it's maddening not to have the energy. The big word for old age is *frustration,* there's no doubt. You're frustrated all the time. You can't do this; you can't do that. I wanted to mail a postcard today; I couldn't walk that far. Well, things like that are very irritating.

Robitaille: You're noted for carving out a routine or a ritual for charting out your day in a specific way. How has this routine or ritual been modified by older age?

Sarton: I've said it in the journals: routine is your freedom. I get up quite early, partly to put out my Himalayan cat and to put the bird feeder out. I mean about six. I have some breakfast and look at the news. But I'm always at my desk by half past eight or nine. Those are the good hours for me. I'm a lark, not an owl. Some people can only work at night; I can only work in the morning. So three hours in the morning is it for me. Then I go get the mail. It takes me two hours to read the mail everyday. That's a tremendous burden in itself. It's fascinating! I would miss it if nobody said, "You're a wonderful writer." I would say, "What's wrong? Nobody's written me today." I shouldn't complain about it, but it's quite a weight. And that doesn't mean answering! Then I have a nap in the afternoon. Then at about four I'm at my desk or doing something in the garden. But now after my illness and my heart and so on, I can't garden anymore. That's very sad. I have a wonderful woman who does it for me and who I can talk it over with. But I notice that when I was not planting the seeds and I was not watching them grow—I didn't go down there and keep looking and say, "Oh, the nasturtiums are up this much!" It was no longer my garden. Somebody else was doing it, you see. That's a big difference.

Robitaille: Many people of all ages drawn to this conference not only know about your work, but also about the great persistence you've brought to continuing your writing, oftentimes in spite of considerable health problems as well as the silence of critics and reviewers. I wonder if you could comment on this notion of persistence on your part, as well as on the part of younger writers who may be just beginning their work?

Sarton: I think if you are a poet nothing can stop you, because the poetry comes from, I like to say, from something much greater than I am. And if a poem comes, I brush everything aside for that. Even if I'm finishing a novel, I still finish the poem. And so, with the poem there is no choice. You're going to do it if you're a poet. The three great gifts which are composing music, mathematics and poetry all begin very early. They're all sort of sown into a character so that Mozart at eight is writing symphonies. It's hilarious to compare it to Mozart. I was writing a poem when I was nine about a pigeon. I was *very* proud of it . . . the pink toes. It was a descriptive poem, not about my feelings. And that's one thing I'm proud of: that I started out wanting to recreate something that was there, not by saying, "Oh, how I love pigeons," or, "Damn this pigeon who is making that noise!" So that was the beginning for me and I never stopped.

It's been hard not getting the critical attention. Naturally, you have to believe in yourself. If you didn't then you'd stop. And what's helped me to believe in myself has been, of course, the people who write, and the people who tell me what the work has meant to them. Many people, of course, don't get the poems. The journals are the easy access, then the novels. The poems are the last thing. But when they come to the poems they realize this is the essence and what I care about the most.

Robitaille: There is a phenomenon in your poetry that fascinates me. I keep coming to phrases that have something to do with "flow" and "streams." I think of Heraclitus, for example. I wonder if you could talk about this notion of flow and the endless stream of change that permeates your work and also about this sense of flow as it relates to aging and the upward years?

Sarton: It's all part of a great rhythm, of course. This is, I suppose, what one has to learn to deal with—that to shut it out, to try to be young, say, at 80, to pretend that there's no old age, then you miss something. You miss a quality that if you don't have it, you haven't lived a complete life. My problem now is health, I'm not well enough. If I were better, and I'm hoping to be better in a month or so, then I would be feeling very young. I mean young for my age; not young, but happy in age.

As for the flow, I'm trying to place that. I'm certainly more aware of time—so was my father. My father was producing this incredible, this heroic history of science, so that he was always driven. He worked until midnight every single night. He was driven, absolutely driven and to some extent so am I. Though, perhaps, with less sense that it's very important what I do. I mean, he was doing something radically important and all you can say about an artist's work is: I hope it will last. I hope there's something here that will last.

This all comes down to Thoreau's statement, "I've never known someone who was fully awake." And one thing you *can* be awake to is this moment, this flow of time. And one thing that makes growing old lovely is that you have more time to look at it. I mean, I have a chaise lounge where I read and it looks out on the bird feeder and part of the sky and, if I turn around, on the sea. And I spend a great deal more time just looking than I've ever been able to because I was always pushed to work—finish a novel, whatever it might be. So this is an emancipation in a way. And I'm enjoying it.

Robitaille: Does the romantic notion of "emotion recollected in tranquility" have a certain significance to a writer in their upward years?

Sarton: Well, it would for a novel; it doesn't for poetry. Not for a journal either. The journal is taken on the pulse. You see, this is something I'd like to say about the difference between the journal and the memoir. In the memoir you might have the advantage of looking back at something that took place five years ago, whereas with the journal, it's on the pulse; it's the moment. And that's what makes it fascinating. I made it a thing of pride in the journal; I never go back and finish what I began the day before because I didn't have the time to finish it. It has to be *then*—what happened today. Where was I in my life?

Robitaille: You have commented extensively on the writing process and on the importance of revision in the composition of your work. How has this revision process been affected as you've grown older?

Sarton: I certainly revise poetry a great deal and it's fascinating because Dick Eberhart doesn't, you know? He comes with a suitcase full of poems—it's so wonderful! I mean I envy him—he's never going to revise at all. For me a poem may go through sixty drafts until I believe its absolutely down to the essence and that's that!

Robitaille: You read several poems that were related to your parents. I wonder if you could comment on the experience of writing those poems?

Sarton: I wrote "A Celebration for George Sarton" five days after my father died. I'd written one other poem which was perhaps a month or two after he died—the sense of being suddenly liberated in a way. And I discovered I loved both my parents very much, especially my mother. But I've come to love my father more since he died because I've come to understand him better, I think it's really that. But I haven't written more about him.

One thing about my family, just the three of us, was that we all wrote letters. I wrote twice a week to my parents when I was in France, and when I had the theater, all those years—and they wrote to me. This record is incredible. It's almost an autobiography. I'm amazed people are reading the letters now. I don't go back and read them, but they send me pieces and ask if I remember saying this or that. There will no doubt be a flood of books written after I die in which letters will become the fifth mode of my writing.

Robitaille: You make a number of references to the phoenix in your work and suggestions that your life has been a series of birthings, so to speak.

Sarton: I feel that very much. I feel that I've died several times, not physically, and had to remake myself after a disastrous love affair, say, or deaths of people who were very important to me. Or failure . . . you see my theater failed when I was 26 years old, from 19 to 26 I was in the theater and I had my own company during the Depression. Well, that failure was extremely hard to overcome . . . it was a real failure, a curtain coming down, and then I started writing seriously. I'd always written poems and even published in magazines, but I hadn't said I was a writer primarily—at that point, at 25, I said, "I'm a writer," and never looked back. Interesting in that today I never go to the theater. It was like a fever—over at a certain point. I think the phoenix is a rather good image for me, actually.

Robitaille: There is also a certain mystical element to your work . . . mystical without being religious in a sectarian sense. I wonder if you could talk about your relationship to the mystical and, more specifically, how this notion of the spiritual may have developed in your upward years.

Sarton: It certainly has, and there have been rebirths. There have

been writers who have had considerable influence on me. Simone
Weil is one, the great Tillich is another. I spent a whole year reading
Tillich. So there have been periods where I was very immersed in
theological writing of a certain kind. I mean, my poems are easy to
understand, but they have come from quite deep and often I'm
saying something quite complex and that I'm proud of but it's not
fashionable. It's fashionable to be mystifying and people have to
explain you. But I think I'm certainly a mystic, if being a mystic is
being very aware of something that's back of ordinary life all the
time. And it's even in the journals.

Someone did a thesis on Vermeer and Sarton in which the point
was really the sacramentalization of the ordinary, as you get with the
light in the Vermeer paintings. And it's quite true. I mean, the
journals, it gives people back a sense of their real lives—that making
a loaf of bread in the kitchen is not to be sneered at as nothing, but
that you can sacramentalize it by the way you live it—and this is
really what my journals are all about. They are about a way of life—
they're not about giving a reading, or even what I've read. And I've
been recognized more by the churches than by the literary critics.
The Carmelites invited me to stay with them in Indianapolis, and they
knew my work intimately. They used *Journal of a Solitude* in their
meditations. The Unitarians gave me their "Ministry To Women"
Award which really touched me very much. It's what's pleased me
most of any honor I've ever had. So there is a connection between
me and the mystical side of life.

Robitaille: There's an interesting tension in your poems that
seems to grow out of an effort to balance the quietude of those "still
waters" to which you refer, and the energy that is derived from that
constant "flow" of the stream in motion. I'm wondering how this
balance has tended to work itself out in recent years?

Sarton: Well, there's less tension, I must say, because I've had to
give up so much. I can't push myself as I used to and the tension
came about almost entirely because of the war between art and life
which I've fought since I was very young. Because every single
day going up to my desk I would have a fight with myself saying,
"There is that old lady from Oregon who has been waiting for a letter
from you for three weeks and is ill, and are you going to write to her,
Sarton, or are you going to go on with your novel?" You see, there

was this terrible fight between art and life, and it went on, it exhausted me. Sometimes I write to that old lady. But then in the middle of the afternoon I'd say, "You didn't do that chapter of the novel." I think that the work came out of the tension. I don't think the tension was bad; it was painful. I was never without guilt. And I'd go to the psychiatrist and he'd say, "May, you don't have to answer all the letters."

Robitaille: You've spoken in the past of the importance of self-actualization in your creative life and since we've been dealing specifically with writing in the upward years, I wonder if you could talk about self-actualization as it might relate to those who might be turning to creative self-expression in later life?

Sarton: That's what life is all about—actualizing yourself. Jung would say it. Maslow was given to me. I was very struck by it. I understood something I hadn't understood before. It has to do with becoming whole. And you can become whole when you do actualize yourself and when you don't leave out things that are driving you crazy but which are very important. So I think maybe in the end I will be seen as someone who was able to do it through a lot of work. I don't know. We'll hope for the best.

A Conversation with May Sarton
David Bradt/1990

From the *New Hampshire College Journal* 8.1 (Spring 1991):
4–15. Reprinted by permission of the interviewer, David Bradt,
who conducted the interview with May Sarton 20 July 1990.

*Suppose that the muse came down to writers who work in various
genres, and said, "You can be only one thing. Choose." Maxine
Kumin has said she would choose to be a poet. Would you make the
same choice?*

Absolutely. But I believe that poets are already chosen, like mathematicians and composers of music. Mathematics and music and
poetry are closely related, in their use of space and time—between
notes, between words, and in cadences. Most great mathematicians
do their best work when young, like Mozart and Wordsworth.

*You have often said that you get more satisfaction from poetry
than from prose. What is it that gives you that satisfaction?*

In the first place, you know you're going to finish. You work so
intensely, and then you have this wonderful moment, when it's *there*.
It's like a war to get it right, and you're struggling to dig out what you
really mean. It's an experience, a real experience, which is what
poems are about. That's what takes the digging. At a certain time
everything is in place and no word can be changed, and at that
moment you know it's done. In prose, you could rewrite a page
forever. You can never have that finality—which is so exciting about
poetry.

Have you ever gone back and rewritten any of your poems?

No, I haven't. For one thing, I work so hard. My poems go through
fifty to a hundred drafts, so they have been very much worked over.
Of course, occasionally you kill a poem by working it too hard. You
lose it, and that's a horrible thing. It has happened to me more than
once. But if all goes well, you can keep that intensity. The thing
about poetry is that you have to be emotionally intense, but your pen
must be as cold as ice, able to analyze, to criticize yourself and your

200

words. This is why there are so few good poets. Few people can combine the intensity of both things, feeling and thought. So you get poets who are thinkers rather than feelers, and poets who are the opposite. You can't learn to write poems by heart. It's a mysterious thing, very mysterious.

When does the intensity come for you? Are you a morning writer?

Yes, I'm definitely morning, a lark not an owl. In fact, what isn't done before eleven in the morning doesn't get done. When I'm well I get to my desk about half past eight and work for two to three hours. They're very intense.

Then there's the correspondence. I used to answer the ten or so letters a day that come in here, but I don't have the energy. People want so much from me. They write and send poems. Nobody would go up to Horowitz and say, "You're such a marvelous pianist. I love watching you play. Would you give me lessons?" But they think nothing of writing me and saying, "I love your poetry. I feel very connected. You think the way I do, and so I'm sending you some of my poems, and I hope you'll write a criticism."

It's different from being asked to give an interview, because I have the opportunity to say yes or no. Asking people to talk about themselves is different from asking them to talk about you. If you had said, "I'm bringing you some poems to analyze," I would have said, "Sorry. I can't see you."

Why is it so difficult in America for a poet to make a decent living?

Well, of course, it's easier than it is in England and easier than it used to be in America. One thing that pays well is readings. I used to read for twenty-five dollars, and then a hundred dollars, and when I went out on this last trip, they paid me four thousand dollars for each reading. But of course readings take time away from writing, and the market for poetry is limited.

What amazes me is that some people, like Maxine Kumin, are able to bring up a family and also write—and write as much and as well as she does. I've always felt it was not possible. You had to make a choice. If you look at the most distinguished women poets, certainly many of them, in the last thirty years anyway, have been single: Marianne Moore, Elizabeth Bishop. . . .

May Sarton.
May Sarton.

Are there circumstances that make it more difficult for women?
There's quite a lot of misogyny. I'll give you a good example of one of the ways I learned this. After my theater days, I was living in Cambridge, and John Ciardi and Richard Wilbur and John Holmes and Dick Eberhart and I met about four times a year and read each other our new poems to criticize. It was thrilling, but I used to cry all night after the sessions, because I was probably less mature as a poet than the rest of them, and I got very severe criticism. But very useful.

Years later, Ciardi did a preface for a book of his on writing poetry, in which he talked about this group, and omitted that I was there. I liked Ciardi; there was something about him, very male, virile, with a good sense of humor. He was a wonderful man in a way, and I think probably a very good teacher, and a superb translator of Dante. But that's cruel, it seems to me, to leave out one name.

How important is critical recognition?
Well, we are talking about what will last. I think it's very important. When we realized that atomic energy can destroy the earth and that nothing will remain, not Sarton's poems, nothing, I realized then how much I'd counted on time. There would be time to work; there *would* be time. And suddenly I realized that there is no time. My hope is that people will come along, in the next thirty years, like the woman who wrote a thesis on Vermeer and Sarton. A lot will happen as soon as I die. A lot of things will come out, and then we'll just hope.

When I went out to give readings, which I can't do any more, I realized how many people found my poems moving. I got a last hurrah this past spring in Seattle and Portland, Oregon. My voice was not very good, and I had to be helped onto the stage in a wheelchair. The audiences were enormous, and sold out three months in advance. When I got on stage, I felt this tremendous love pour out. It made me feel that there must be something in my work, or people would not be so moved by the reading.

What advice would you give to young people who wish to be writers?
My advice is never to read what you think is fashionable or you

ought to read. Read what you love. If you discover a poet—like Gerard Manley Hopkins, say—in an anthology, then go and read all his work, devour it, and build your poetry on influences, deep influences, not just superficial influences. But read. So few young poets read anymore. I ask them who are their favorite poets, and they don't really *know* any poets, especially from the past.

Read. Then get criticism. Try to find a friend who will be brutal enough to say, "This just doesn't work." Such a person could be a teacher. Once in a while you can find a generous teacher, but it can also be a contemporary.

Were there other poets you read and admired as a young poet?
It was the time of the great fame of Edna St. Vincent Millay and Elinor Wylie and other women lyric poets. But I soon realized their faults, and found what I must do was to go back, to Donne and Herbert. And Yeats was a great influence. Yeats because he grew so much. He began in this rather sentimental vein, like Sara Teasdale; but he stripped it down, he dug closer and closer to the rock, and that's what's exciting about his development. I was also tremendously influenced by his passion, a hard passion, very deep and full of anger.

In As We Are Now, *Caro Spencer talks about serenity as a mask old people are expected to wear, and she finds this impossible. Like Yeats, her passion is deep and full of anger. Do you have anything in common with her?*
Oh, yes. That novel is based on a true story, you know. The nursing home was in New Hampshire, and I first went there to visit a friend. The day I walked in it was pouring rain, and by each bed there was an old man sitting, and there was no light. It was like some sort of prison. Then these women came out, and greeted me, and told me that my friend had a private room. Caro appeared the second time I went. She was crying and wandering around. When I asked about her, the women answered: "Oh, she thinks she's some sort of an aristocrat and above everybody. We had to put her in a room without windows, she cried so much and made such a fuss." I went home and couldn't stop thinking about her. *As We Are Now* has been dramatized several times, and Joanne Woodward is interested in making it into a movie for television. Several of my other novels

have options on them for movies. My latest novel, *The Education of Harriet Hatfield*, has been bought.

People like to make hard distinctions between fiction and non-fiction. Wright Morris has said that "everything processed by the memory is fiction." Do you think that non-fiction is really fiction masquerading as truth?

Well, that's probably true. The point is that one's past changes so much. I think of it in my relation to my father, how it's changed in the thirty years since he died. At one point I felt one way; now I feel differently. What's the truth? And I think all autobiographies are full of delusions, and what a lot of people hope was true perhaps wasn't. But insights also change with time.

Are the new insights better than the old?

Tremendously. They're richer and they're probably also more generous. I'm thinking of my father, again, as he really wasn't a very good father, but he was a very great man. It's as a historian I treasure his values now, and I miss him terribly because if he were alive, he would be suffering so over the Near East. He knew so much about Arabic science. He was adored by Arabs, and he also was very much a Jewish scholar.

Your father opposed you early in your life, when you wanted to seek a career in the theater.

Yes. At seventeen I left home to join Eva Le Gallienne's Civic Repertory Theater in New York. I fell in love with that marvelous theater, which did great plays in repertory. I went there instead of going to college at Vassar, where I had been given a scholarship. As you can imagine, I had a big fight with my father, who was a university professor. But finally, bless his heart, he let me go. He gave me a hundred dollars a month to live on, and my mother found a women's hostel there where I could live. I was there three years; the third year I was put in charge of the student group, the apprentices, and I had a chance to direct several plays. But you see this was just the beginning of the Depression, nineteen twenty-nine, and Le Gallienne's theater closed. She needed only a hundred thousand dollars a year to support eighty people and a repertory of twenty-six plays, but you couldn't get any money then. There has been no repertory since—I mean real repertory, a different play every night.

How did you move from theater to writing as a profession?
When the Civic Repertory closed, I founded and held together a
small company of the apprentices from the Civic. We had a glorious
first year producing in rehearsal performance ten modern European
plays that had never been produced in the United States. But after
the three difficult years it was not possible to raise enough money to
keep going—although it would have required only five thousand
dollars! But this was at the height of the Depression. We closed after
three disastrous weeks at the Charles Street Playhouse in Boston.

What did you do then?
I had a kind of breakdown for a year, but I had always written
poetry. *Poetry* magazine had accepted poems of mine while I was an
apprentice at the Civic Repertory. I soon found that writing was *it*
for me, and I never looked back. I have an idea that those six years
were a more meaningful education than college might have been.
Amongst other things it taught me how to use my voice, to project
poetry to large audiences, and, more importantly, it took me right out
of the academic world I had been brought up in and into a more
human world where talent was all that counted.

How have political events affected your writing?
In the journals especially I often talk about political things. One
reason I found it hard to begin the new journal is all these political
upheavals that were taking place, in Eastern Europe, the Mideast,
Africa. I'm not saying much about political matters in the new journal,
but I will talk about Mandela, because for the first time in years I
cried good tears. When they came out of the jail, he and Winnie
holding hands and walking down that dirt road to a car, that was a
great moment. It was so moving, just to be in the presence of such a
person. And of course he was in jail for twenty-seven years. I wonder
what will happen now.

Do you see writers as having an obligation to take political stand?
Yes, I think so. What your question brings to mind is the case of
Ezra Pound. I feel that poets should not be asked to be less than
human. What we ask of them should be what we ask of our best
people, not of the worst people. To say that his poetry made up for
his war-time attacks on his own country and his violent anti-Semitism

at a time when Jews were being burned alive is hard for me to accept. Most poets at that time felt that he was wrong, though they tried to get him out of the asylum.

I feel that poets should be responsible. Once, at a reading during the war, I said that I felt ashamed of being only a poet and not doing more, and after the reading a woman from Oslo came up in a fury and said, "You must *never* say that. You don't know what poetry has done for people in solitary confinement." She had been in solitary confinement for six months, and she lived on Goethe and the classic German poets, and without that she would have gone mad. But she would never have said she spent all that time reading Pound.

The South Americans have a tradition of making ambassadors out of poets and writers.

We are more likely to reward businessmen who gave money to political candidates. One nice thing about Kennedy was that he did at least try to make Robert Frost a real symbol. Now there's an example of an extraordinary fellow who will last—and also of how reputations change. When I was growing up Frost was *the* poet. Nobody could imagine that he was such a wicked old man. He was mean to his son, who committed suicide, and he was not good to his wife, who wouldn't see him when she was dying.

I remember a party on Christmas Eve, when World War II was still on. It was fairly clear we were going to win, and Frost said, "It doesn't interest me any more now; it's just a bore. We know who's going to win." Meanwhile thousands of people were dying. I was furious and I attacked Frost. I thought that was cheap, awful. But he was a great poet.

You've expressed a fondness for Dutch painters. Your work is often admired for similar reasons. Both succeed in portraying the inner and, one might even say, spiritual lives of the characters.

Yes. It's the sacramentalization of the ordinary that you get so much of in Vermeer. A woman pouring water out of a jug becomes a sacramental thing. I think that's what I've done in the journals, made people realize that doing the day to day things can be made sacred or not, depending on how you look at them and how you do them. There was an MA thesis written on Vermeer and Sarton, and I thought, "What is she going to say?" She talked about this sacra-mentalizing of your own life.

Many people write and tell me how much the journals have helped them, that they take one of my journals wherever they go and find so much comfort in it. Perhaps it's because the journals are so ordinary. They do something about the ordinary that suddenly makes it seem worth living with.

What do you hope your life as a writer will add up to?

I've always felt that if they all work together—the poems, the journals, the novels, the memoirs—it would all eventually be of a piece, a vision of life. They all belong together, and that's what will come through, I think, as finally people do write about my work. It has to do with living alone; partly it has to do with a homosexual life, which is rather special in some ways. I mean in dignity and the ability to give, to give to many, many people. That's come through, I think.

The poems are there, and the novels and journals. That's the great satisfaction. As you know, if you believe in your talent, as I do of course believe in mine, you also believe it's going to be discovered. All my papers are in the Berg Collection in the New York Public Library, along with Auden's and Virginia Woolf's. There are all the letters from people I've known, and my own letters to all these people. And I am certain those old correspondences and manuscripts will, like those of so many others, bear fruit after I'm dead.

Other than perhaps more valid insights, has growing old had any other rewards for you?

Yes, except I never thought I'd be ill. I was counting on a serene old age, a lot of work behind me, enough to live on, and writing poems. I don't think it is old age that I'm confronting. It's illness really. That's why I am having trouble with my journal, because I find old age interesting. It's certainly true that you give up readily things that you wouldn't have thought you'd be willing to give up, simply because your whole *gestalt* has changed. I thought I would love my old age. But I'm not able to do the things I thought I would do. One of them is traveling. I really can't travel any more. And I'm terribly alone. I have nobody here, no family; and while I have good friends, I don't have very good friends in York or nearby.

One wonderful thing is I earn money. I never earned much until I was over sixty. I earned quite a lot last year. That means I can give money away, to a place like Christ House in Washington, which is a hospital that takes in street people, especially those with AIDS. It's like a family, with a young doctor who gave up his private practice to go there. They are doing extraordinary things. You see, in a funny way I'm in their lives, like having them around me at a distance. Of course I can't give them thousands, but I can do much more than most old poets can, and that is a great satisfaction.

Someone who has heard you read several times over many years said you had the most commanding voice he's ever heard.
That's interesting. It certainly isn't true now.

But the voice is also on the page.
Yes, that's true.

And it will always be on the page; that's a consolation.
Yes, that is the consolation.

Index

209